ECONOMIC POLICY in POSTWAR JAPAN

Published under the auspices of
THE CENTER FOR JAPANESE AND KOREAN STUDIES
University of California, Berkeley

THE CENTER FOR JAPANESE AND KOREAN STUDIES of the University of California is a unit of the Institute of International Studies. It is the unifying organization for faculty members and students interested in Japan and Korea, bringing together scholars from many disciplines. The Center's major aims are the development and support of research and language study. As part of this program the Center sponsors a publication series of books concerned with Japan and Korea. Manuscripts are considered from all campuses of the University of California as well as from any other individuals and institutions doing research in these areas.

PUBLICATIONS OF THE CENTER FOR JAPANESE
AND KOREAN STUDIES

Chong-Sik Lee
The Politics of Korean Nationalism. 1963

Sadako N. Ogata
*Defiance in Manchuria: The Making of Japanese
Foreign Policy, 1931–1932.* 1964.

R. P. Dore
Education in Tokugawa Japan. 1964.

James T. Araki
The Ballad-Drama of Medieval Japan. 1964.

Masakazu Iwata
Ōkubo Toshimichi: The Bismarck of Japan. 1964.

Frank O. Miller
Minobe Tatsukichi: Interpreter of Constitutionalism in Japan. 1965.

Michael Cooper, S.J.
*They Came to Japan: An Anthology of European Reports on Japan,
1543–1640.* 1965.

George Devos and Hiroshi Wagatsuma
Japan's Invisible Race. 1966

Postwar Economic Growth in Japan. 1966
Edited by Ryutaro Komiya
Translated from the Japanese by Robert S. Ozaki

Robert A. Scalapino
The Japanese Communist Movement, 1920–1966. 1967

Soon Sung Cho
Korea in World Politics, 1940–1950. 1967

C. I. Eugene Kim and Han-Kyo Kim
Korea and the Politics of Imperialism, 1876–1910. 1967

Economic Policy in Postwar Japan

GROWTH VERSUS ECONOMIC DEMOCRACY

Kozo Yamamura

UNIVERSITY OF CALIFORNIA PRESS

BERKELEY AND LOS ANGELES

1967

University of California Press
Berkeley and Los Angeles, California

Cambridge University Press
London, England

Library of Congress Catalog Card Number: 67–29726
ISBN 978-0-520-30718-6

TO   *Professor Richard B. Heflebower*

PREFACE

The purpose of this book is to examine a few important aspects of postwar economic policies of Japan. Broadly speaking, there were two policies: the economic democratization policy of the Supreme Command of Allied Powers (SCAP) and the policy of the Japanese government. The two central questions examined here are: What were the nature, rationale, and result of the respective policies? and why and how was one set of policies superseded by the other?

The first five chapters examine the ambitious rise and rapid fall of the economic democratization policy and the emergence of the Japanese policy and its continued pursuit of economic goals. The major areas of our concern in these chapters are market structure (technological efficiency *vs.* competitive structure issues), the Anti-Monopoly Act (its idealistic beginning and rapid erosion), concentration of economic power in general (Zaibatsu dissolution and the pro-monopoly policy), and other related issues. The two policies are examined for their respective goals, the impacts of the respective policy measures, and the transformation in the nature of the respective policies.

Chapters 6 to 9 deal with specific questions which amplify and add dimension to our examination of postwar economic policies. Chapter 6 examines the rationale of the Japanese policy and presents its effects on the market structure and the size distribution of firms. (This is the only chapter that noneconomists might find abstract and that demands a basic knowledge of some economic and statistical concepts; however, noneconomists could skip this chapter with no material loss to the understanding of the main thesis of the book.) Chapter 7 discusses the so-called Zaibatsu question, which is widely debated among Japanese economists, and offers a comparison of prewar Zaibatsu and postwar "Zaibatsu." Chapter 8 is a review and analysis of postwar tax policies.

As in chapter 7, contrasts between the two policies observed in this chapter are most revealing of the fundamental differences between American and Japanese policies. Chapter 9 evaluates the impact of these two policies—especially the Japanese policy—on labor and wages.

The final chapter is an attempt to assess the success or failure of the two policies. I fear that my reflections and assessments so expressed would find few friends in Japan. Many Japanese economists of the so-called Marxist line, whose views and empirical findings were very useful to the author, would undoubtedly question most of this book rather fundamentally. The author hopes that the Japanese government officials, whose kind assistance in the early stages of this book was extremely valuable, view the author's increasing doubts and criticisms of the post-1959 policy as a reflection of the author's sincere interest in the course of the policy and the future of the Japanese economy. In a highly policy-oriented subject such as this, each reader, however, is the final assessor and evaluator of the postwar Japanese economic policy.

The author wishes to add an explicit disclaimer. This small volume is far from a comprehensive examination of the postwar Japanese economic policy; rather, it is merely an attempt to fill a gap in the discussion of postwar policy. Recent works contributed by Professors H. Patrick, S. Levine, M. Shinohara, R. P. Dore, G. C. Allen, and others (see the bibliography) in the areas of their expertise already form a core of valuable literature. I should also add that I have tried—given the nature of the subject—to present the contents and the main thesis in such a way that this book is not addressed only to those who are either economists or specialists on Japanese economic problems. I fear that I have not been entirely successful in this attempt, but I hope that many noneconomists will find this book readable and that few economists will be offended by the lack of technical rigor.

Here I can acknowledge my debt to only a few of the many who, on both sides of the Pacific, made this study possible. To Professors Richard B. Heflebower, Harold F. Williamson, and Karl de Schweinitz, all of Northwestern University, no word is sufficient to express my gratitude. Their patience and generosity in training me and in commenting on earlier drafts of this manuscript far exceeded that which any former student could expect. My present and former colleagues Robert Barckley, Adam Gifford, William Leasure, and Marjorie Turner provided friendly criticism and useful comments on the manuscript at different stages of its formation. To Denis Flagg, the understanding chairman of the Department of Economics, I am very grateful. Although I cannot name them all, my colleagues in Japanese economy across the nation were also very kind and instructive in corresponding with me and providing me with their counsel. I thank the editors of the *Journal of Asian Studies, Industrial Relations and Labor Review, Journal of Political Economy, National Tax Journal, Southern Economic Journal,* and *Journal of Indian Economics* for their permission to present in this book some material that was published in their respective journals. They, along with their referees, contributed significantly in improving several points in this book.

The financial aid given by Northwestern University made my stay in Japan (1961–62) possible, and the San Diego State College Foundation provided small grants to defray the cost of calculations. A summer library fellowship from the Graduate School of Business, Harvard University, enabled me to use materials necessary in the late stages of the manuscript. For all these financial aids, I am very grateful.

My debt in Japan is even greater. To the kind officials of the Ministry of International Trade and Industry, the Ministry of Labor, the Economic Planning Agency, and the Fair Trade Commission, I express my appreciation for their valuable time and information. The Economic Research Institute of Hitotsubashi University and the Economic Society of Aoyama Gakuin University kindly granted me the privilege of frequent discussions with their members and the use of their library facilities and office space. The numerous discussions I had with Professor Hitoshi Misonou played an important part at the formative stage of this manuscript. As is made clear, the value of his continued friendship has been immeasurable. Many others of Tokyo, Hitotsubashi, Kobe, and Aoyama universities generously aided my research by responding to queries, sending their reprints, and commenting on parts of manuscripts.

My appreciation is due to Mrs. Boris Wolkonsky who defended the correct usage of the English language against my constant abuse of its grammar and syntax. Through numerous drafts, she performed the roles of editor, typist, and advisor. My thanks is also due to Miss Anita Pearson who, with accuracy and a smile, typed and corrected the typescript.

CONTENTS

LIST OF TABLES

1
THE AMERICAN POLICY OF
ECONOMIC DEMOCRATIZATION

When hostilities ended in August 1945, it was the foregone conclusion of the Supreme Commander of the Allied Powers (SCAP) that Japan would be subjected to a series of "economic democratization" policies. The initial policy aim was stern and unequivocal, and reflected the attitude of the Allied governments toward the country that had been their enemy only a short time before. In *Reports on Japanese Reparations to the President of the United States*, Edwin Pauley has written:

> [The Allied Powers] should take no action to assist Japan in maintaining a standard of living higher than that of neighboring Asiatic countries injured by Japanese aggression, insofar as such assistance will divert food or other material aid from these other countries, or will require the retention in Japan of industrial capacity, the removal of which is required on grounds of security. Under this principle, a broad view should be taken of the economy, and especially of the varying degree of industrialization of Eastern Asia as a whole. The over-all aim should be both to raise and to even up the level of industrialization. This aim can be served by considered allocation, to different countries, of industrial equipment exacted from Japan as reparations. Reconstruction is an urgent need of all the countries against which Japan committed aggression. Reconstruction is also needed in Japan. In the over-all comparison of needs Japan should have the last priority.[1]

This was the climate in which the Allied policy was formulated. The policy goal of SCAP was to "reform," and the supreme commander was specifically ordered to assume "no obligation to maintain particular standards of living in Japan." The intent was clear. Stern actions were demanded against Japan and especially against Zaibatsu,[2] the giant

[1] E. W. Pauley, *Reports on Japanese Reparations to the President of the United States* (Washington, November 1945), pp. 6–7.
[2] Readers who are not familiar with Zaibatsu and their economic dominance in prewar Japan, see chap. 7.

financial cliques of prewar Japan, which worked "for and with" the
military machines of Japan. Given the central objective of reforming
the Japanese economy, the question of economic recovery was not the
concern of the occupying forces.

As the initial phase of this economic democratization, SCAP cen-
tered its attention in three major areas: the deconcentration of economic power, labor reform, and land reform. To better understand the
nature of the SCAP policy and to be able to appraise the policy of the
Japanese government, we must observe the outlines of these three major
policy areas. With regard to the first, the deconcentration of economic
power, the basic philosophy was given as follows: "It shall be the policy
of the Supreme Commander to favour a program for the dissolution of
the large industrial and banking combinations which have exercised
control over a great part of Japan's trade and industry as well as to
permit a wide distribution of income and of the ownership of the means
of production and trade." [3]

With this as the foundation, SCAP began to "democratize" Zaibatsu
which, SCAP considered, "made possible all Japan's militarism as much
as the militarists themselves." This basic philosophy was then put into a
more definite language by Professor Corwin Edwards, who headed the
so-called Zaibatsu Mission. He recommended that:

> The controlling power exercised by Zaibatsu over the Japanese eco-
> nomy is beyond comparison with any other capitalistic industrial
> nation.
> The responsibility of the Zaibatsu for the aggressive actions of
> Japan is essentially in its structure. It is not of importance if the
> leaders of Zaibatsu were, as individuals, war-merchants or not. The
> important point is that the Zaibatsu structure offered a setting suit-
> able for military aggression.
> A few large Zaibatsu, controlling the industry and international
> trade of Japan, were supported by the Japanese government. Con-
> centration of economic control enabled them to continue a semi-
> feudal relationship between themselves and their employees, to
> continue to suppress wages and to hinder the development of inde-
> pendent political ideologies. Thus the formation of the middle class,
> which was useful in opposing the militarist group in other demo-
> cratic countries, was retarded.
> The main purpose of the American policy is, by destroying the
> structure which invites such consequences, to develop a group of
> people who are capable of preventing the militarists who try to
> control the policy of the government in a democratic country. [4]

[3] The Statement of Post-Surrender U.S. Policy (September 22, 1945), as quoted
in the Fair Trade Commission, *Annual Report of 1949* (Tokyo, 1950), p. 4.
[4] Beginning in January 1946, Edwards, at that time a professor of economics at
Northwestern University and representative of the Army Department and the State

Professor Edwards focused attention on the concentrated structure of the Japanese economy and called for the formation of a middle class. This was to be reform for the purpose of developing economic democracy, based upon a middle class who would be "capable of preventing the militarists" from controlling the policy of the government.

Following these lines, SCAP began to implement its policy on four major fronts—restriction of designated Zaibatsu-connected firms, dissolution of holding companies, elimination of excessive economic power, and the introduction of an anti-monopoly act. As each program was announced in detail, the implication of the reform for the Japanese economy and the whole society became evident.

The reform was to be thoroughgoing. The Japanese economy was to have a competitive economic structure, free of any vestige of Zaibatsu power, and this was to be accomplished as quickly as possible. If we recall the predominance of Zaibatsu in the prewar economic structure of Japan and the fact that the highly concentrated monopolistic structure was partly a product of the government encouragement, the economic structure visualized in the recommendations of the Zaibatsu Mission was totally alien. Throughout her industrial history, Japan had never had a competitive economic system.

The program was drastic by any standard. Formerly, the government had fostered the power of Zaibatsu monopolies, helped to organize and to enforce cartels, and encouraged mergers of larger market-leading firms. It was not the Japanese way to enforce competition, to disallow all types of cartels, or to encourage a wide dispersion of stockholding.

A large segment of Japan welcomed these reform measures. The Social Democrats and the Communist party hailed the program as the best alternative to the complete nationalization measures they advocated. The labor unions, newly legalized and their membership increasing daily, supported the program. The Zaibatsu interests and the Conservative party, on the other hand, expressed their views opposing the policy, but there was little they could do under the circumstances. They chose to cooperate with the occupation authority hoping for milder actions.[5]

Department, spent three months investigating the basic problems involved in the Zaibatsu dissolution. This special investigation committee is often referred to as the "Zaibatsu Mission." Cf. Fair Trade Commission, Showa 23-nendo Kōsei Torihiki Iinkai Hōkoku (Annual Report of 1948) (Tokyo, 1949), p. 3.
[5] Early in 1946, the Yasuda Zaibatsu submitted what is now known as the "Yasuda Plan." This plan was drafted by Yasuda Zaibatsu in the hope that it would be adopted by SCAP. It generally agreed with the Zaibatsu Mission recommendations

This was the measure initiated for the purpose of freezing the assets of those firms which SCAP considered as requiring dissolution or reorganization on the grounds that they were either Zaibatsu-controlled firms (affiliated and subsidiaries) or Zaibatsu-owned firms. The measure was initiated by the "Decree on Restriction of Designated Companies" issued on December 8, 1945. Immediately the decree was applied to 18 holding companies, consisting of 10 Zaibatsu and other large firms that had the characteristics of holding companies and possessed assets of more than five million yen.

Subsidiaries were defined as those firms in which 10 percent or more of the stock was held by the designated Zaibatsu. The affiliated firms were defined as those firms in which more than 10 percent of the stock was held by subsidiaries of Zaibatsu or by those firms in which 10 percent or more of the stock was held by more than two of the firms of the same holding company group as designated by SCAP. By the end of 1946, when designations were completed, 1,204 firms were designated as falling in one of the three categories specified above.

Under the terms of the decree, these firms were ordered not to dispose of any types of assets, including land, buildings, and machines. Restrictions were placed on the issuance of new stock, dividend payments, and payments of salaries to higher echelon executives. In fact, the quantity of assets held by the designated firms in any firm were frozen, except with specific SCAP approval, which almost never came. Therefore, no easy evasion was possible.

There was, however, one exception to SCAP's consistency. It allowed the trading of securities of the designated firms by those who owned less than 1 percent of the total share of each designated firm. This policy was to protect the "little people" so that they would not suffer merely because their holdings happened to be in the designated firms.

In July 1946, this freezing operation was strengthened by another decree, the "Limitation on Stockholdings and Other Matters." This prohibited the designated firms from possessing stock in other firms, from having interlocking directorships, and from making any other type of exclusive dealing arrangement with any other firm. The decree also prohibited any capital or personnel relationship among designated firms, their subsidiaries, or their affiliated firms. The intent of these decrees was, in short, to freeze the 1,204 firms in readiness for the complex operations which had begun.

---

except that the Yasuda Plan anxiously tried to keep the assets held by each Zaibatsu family intact, though they were willing to liquidate their holding company assets. Although endorsed by other Zaibatsu families, the plan was rejected by SCAP in favor of the recommendations made by the Zaibatsu Mission.

DISSOLUTION OF HOLDING COMPANIES AND
DEMOCRATIZATION OF STOCKHOLDING

Dissolution of Holding Companies. On the basis of the decree
issued on the "Dissolution of Holding Companies" on November 6,
1945, the Holding Companies Liquidation Committee (HCLC) was
formed to carry out the intent of the declared policy. The duty of the
committee, though composed of Japanese, was to dissolve or reorganize
numerous holding companies existing at the close of the war. The action
was performed under the direction of SCAP representatives. The committee designated 83 firms as holding companies which were composed
of ten Zaibatsu head companies (*Honsha*), their related holding companies, and "local" holding companies. These firms were then classified
into two categories—for dissolution and for reorganization—based upon
the following criteria:

1. Dissolution Group—The head offices of the Zaibatsu and those
firms which were considered bona fide holding companies.

2. Reorganization Group—Those firms which possessed important
means of production and which were not considered bona fide holding
companies were ordered to be reorganized.

Although according to the above classification they should have been
in the reorganization group, Mitsui Bussan and Mitsubishi Shoji (both
general trading companies in a third designation group) were ordered to
be dissolved. Clearly, these two firms were considered deserving of
disolution by SCAP for their "ruthless activities" [6] before 1945. Two
communications firms were dissolved to clear the way for nationalization.[7]

Forty-two companies were dissolved by the end of 1947: 16 went out
of existence and 26 were dissolved after forming their non-
holding-company second firm, or "heir" company. Forty-one companies
remained after reorganization, that is after eliminating their holding-
company characteristics. But, as of the end of 1947, these 41 firms were

[6] As of January 1946, the Mitsui Bussan had paid-in capital of 100 million yen
and controlled 58 firms. In 24 of these firms it owned over 50 percent of the total
shares of respective firms and in no case did Mitsui Bussan hold less than 10 percent.
The Mitsubishi Shōji, also as of January 1946, controlled 49 firms. It owned on the
average 25 percent of the shares of these controlled firms. The holding was in most
cases between 15 and 33 percent. It was estimated that these firms handled nearly 40
percent of Japan's export-import business in the years preceding the Manchurian
invasion. The above is based on data submitted to SCAP by Mitsui and Mitsubishi
Honsha (February 1946), SCAP-GHQ, papers 48 and 49.

[7] For details of this aspect of the dissolution policy, see Holding Company
Liquidation Committee, *The Japanese Zaibatsu and Their Dissolution* (Tokyo,
1950), pp. 400–445.

still the "designated" firms whose activities were severely restricted as mentioned earlier.

Stock Liquidation. The stocks of these holding companies were handed over to the HCLC, which in turn liquidated them on the basis of the five criteria specified below, in order to make the stockholding "democratic"; that is, the shareholding was to be diffused in the hands of the public.

1. The employees of the company of which stocks were sold had priority in purchasing.
2. No stock was sold to the holding companies or to the Zaibatsu families.
3. Subsidiaries and affiliates of the holding companies were ineligible for these stocks, except when there existed a proper reason for obtaining the stocks.
4. No sale of stocks was made when the additional purchase would make the total possession of the stock of a company over 1 percent or when the purchaser already owned over 1 percent of the stock of the company.
5. Even in cases where the ratio was less than 1 percent as stated above, if the committee felt that there existed a case of excessive investment concentration, the limiting ratio could be reduced.[8]

The number of securities, stocks, and bonds received by the HCLC from the holding companies and Zaibatsu amounted to 165,673,117 shares and was valued at 7,751,655,876 yen.[9] Also, under the provisions of the same decree, the Zaibatsu family members who owned shares of these designated holding companies handed to the HCLC nearly 500,-000,000 yen in shares.[10] To evaluate the magnitude and the nature of the measure, the data in Table 1 show the process of stock liquidation.

According to the stringent stock liquidation principles stated above, about 26 percent of the liquidated stocks were sold to the employees of the firms. However, to show more clearly the degree of democratization of the stockholding accomplished, see Table 2. The statistics involve 631 companies in the 1946 figures and 677 in the 1950 figures, and not all of their stock was liquidated by the HCLC. But, as Table 2 shows, a gradual "democratization of stockholding" took place. During this period, the number of stock owners increased from 1.7 million to 4.3

---

[8] *Ibid.*, pp. 432–433.

[9] Since 1947, the exchange rate is 360 yen per dollar.

[10] In addition, the Ministry of Finance received the value of 2.1 billion yen in securities through a capital levy, and the FTC liquidated 3.3 billion yen in stocks under the intercorporate stock divestiture provisions of the Anti-Monopoly Law. Both of these will be described shortly.

TABLE 1
The Stock Liquidation, 1947–1950

PERIOD	SOLD TO EMPLOYEES [a]		OPEN-BID SALE [b]		ACCEPTANCE SALE [c]		TOTAL	
	STOCKS (NO. OF SHARES)	LIQUIDATION VALUE (¥1000)	STOCKS (NO. OF SHARES)	LIQUIDATION VALUE (¥1000)	STOCKS (NO. OF SHARES)	LIQUIDATION VALUE (¥1000)	STOCKS (NO. OF SHARES)	LIQUIDATION VALUE (¥1000)
1947.6–1948.2	689,043	32,791	290,399	24,644	406,000	13,964	1,385,442	71,399
1948.3–1948.10	7,324,026	358,296	4,909,734	681,321	844,522	61,141	13,078,282	1,100,758
1948.11–1949.3	10,607,321	548,312	9,226,008	909,313	7,406,280	691,916	27,239,609	2,149,541
1949.4–1949.9	12,258,116	636,506	5,867,737	872,639	15,390,987	1,547,122	33,516,840	3,056,267
1949.10–1950.3	3,883,426	204,394	1,633,679	52,932	688,325	111,083	6,205,430	368,409
Total	34,761,932	1,780,299	21,927,557	2,540,849	24,736,114	2,425,226	81,425,603	6,746,374
Percentage	42.69	26.39	26.92	37.66	30.38	35.95	100	100

[a] "Sold to employees" means that either the stocks were sold preferentially to the employees of the company whose stocks were being liquidated or, in case the employees were unable to buy all stocks available, to private individuals who were residing in the city or the village where the company was located.

[b] "Open-Bid sale" refers to the method of sale in which security dealers placed these stocks on open bid to the public and sold to those who bid the highest price.

[c] "Acceptance sale" refers to the method in which the stocks were sold to security dealers by the HCLC. *Ibid.*, p. 433.

SOURCE: Figures are computed from HCLC, *Japanese Zaibatsu and Their Dissolution*, pp. 450–455.

TABLE 2

Stock Redistribution, March 1946 and March 1949

SHARES HELD	1946				1949			
	NUMBER OF PEOPLE	PERCENT	NUMBER OF SHARES (MILLIONS)	PERCENT	NUMBER OF PEOPLE	PERCENT	NUMBER OF SHARES (MILLIONS)	PERCENT
Less than 100	1,150,417	67.17	39	8.93	1,428,923	33.32	52	2.61
100–499	471,366	27.52	77	17.41	2,162,157	50.41	424	21.23
500–999	46,642	2.72	27	6.31	368,723	8.60	232	11.63
1,000–4,999	36,908	2.16	59	13.51	294,563	6.87	484	24.22
5,000–9,999	3,555	0.21	22	5.10	17,177	0.40	109	5.49
Over 10,000	3,762	0.22	216	48.74	16,980	0.40	696	38.82

SOURCE: Computed from Tokyo Security Exchange, *Showa 34-nen Toshō Tōkei Geppō* (Tokyo Stock Exchange Annual Statistics, 1959), pp. 84–85.

million, and the healthiest gains in percentage increase in holdings were shown by the people of the medium range holders, that is, those who owned between 100 and 5,000 shares.

War Indemnity Special Law, Capital Levy, and Purge. To achieve the goal of the occupation authority, other major steps were taken in the War Indemnity Special Measure Law and the Capital Levy Law issued respectively in October and November 1946.[11] The former levied a tax on individuals and corporations in the identical amount to offset claims they had against the government. These claims arose from contract termination, war damage, insurance, indemnity for plant expansion ordered by the government, depreciation and obsolescence guarantees, and so forth, which were, under a law passed during the war, to be paid by the government. The latter imposed a graduated tax on individuals who owned real and tangible assets exceeding 100,000 yen. The total yield of these taxes is estimated to be in the neighborhood of 135 million yen,[12] which was paid by the top 5 percent of the population.

Another decree was issued in January 1947 which purged about 2,200 persons, mostly the officials of 250 designated companies, along with the political purgees. They were purged from "any position in public service" and from directorship in any formerly Zaibatsu-connected companies which held "the lives and destinies of the majority of Japan's people in virtual slavery." [13] All of the executives of formerly large corporations, especially those of the Zaibatsu subsidiaries and affiliates, were placed in this category. All the Zaibatsu family members were also placed in this category, thus effectively barring them from all the above-specified positions.

The Anti-Monopoly Act. As the above measures were being carried out, the first Anti-Monopoly Act in the history of Japan was being prepared "to safeguard the fruit of these accomplishments," based on a draft presented by the Anti-Trust Division of the Justice Department of the United States. A bill was presented to the Diet on March 22, 1947, after consulting ministries, academicians, and the interested groups.[14]

---

[11] War Indemnity Special Measure Law, Law No. 38, October 18, 1946; Capital Levy Law, Law No. 52, November 11, 1946, *Official Gazette (Kompō) of the Japanese Government.*

[12] Due to the rapid inflation then taking place in Japan and the lapse of time between assessment and payment, precise real value of the levy is practically impossible to ascertain.

[13] J. B. Cohen, *Japan's Economy in War and Reconstruction* (New York, 1949), p. 432.

[14] Records of that period indicate that little public interest was aroused by the content of the law, except for the opinions expressed by the business leaders. Their opinions were guarded criticisms against the law, though they unfailingly paid lip

The bill was enacted on April 14, 1947, and the exact title of this "Economic Constitution" reads "Act Relating to Prohibition of Private Monopoly and Methods of Preserving Fair Trade" (*Shiteki Dokusen no Kinshi oyobi Kōsei Torihiki no Kabuho ni kansuru Hōritsu*) (see Appendix IV). The act consists of ten parts with 114 articles and is patterned after the Federal Trade Commission Act and the Clayton Act. In some aspects it is more ambitious and includes a few unique articles. The spirit of the act can be found in its first article which reads:

> This law, by prohibiting private monopolization, unreasonable restraint of trade and unfair methods of competition; by preventing excessive concentration of power over enterprises; and by excluding undue restrictions of production, sale, price, technology, etc., through combinations and agreements, etc., and all other unreasonable restraints of business activities, aims to promote free and fair competition, to stimulate the initiative of entrepreneurs, to encourage business activities of enterprises, to heighten the levels of employment and national income and, thereby, to promote the democratic and wholesome development of the national economy as well as to assure the interest of the general consumer.[15]

The main points of the act could be summarized as follows: [16] Cartels and collusions of all types were prohibited in Article 4. That is, any concerted action to fix prices; to restrict output, new technology, and expansion of capacities; or to control purchases and sales on exclusive contract bases, when the competition could be hindered significantly, was prohibited. In Article 5 any monopolistic and monopsonistic organization was made illegal, and Article 6 prohibited any cartel agreement or any restrictive contract with foreign firms.

Article 8 prohibited "undue substantial disparities in bargaining power," which were defined as "those not based upon technological grounds." When such a power was found, the article stated, such power would be eliminated by means of transferring "a part of his business facilities" or by "any necessary measure."

Article 9 prohibited holding companies, defined as those firms which were established for the purpose of "controlling the business activities of another company." Article 10 made it illegal for nonfinancial firms to acquire the voting stock of another company, except where integration was justified on technical grounds.

Article 11 prohibited financial firms from buying more than 5 percent of the stock of another firm, be it industrial or financial. The financial

---

service to the necessity of competition. *Jiji Press*, December 15, 1946, and January 6, 1947.

[15] FTC, *Fair Trade*, Vol. 1, No. 2 (Tokyo, 1958), p. 6.

[16] See Appendix IV.

firms also were prohibited from buying the stock of any competing firm. Article 13 prohibited interlocking directorship. A prohibition was made also against one-fourth or more of the officers of either of two firms holding positions concurrently in a third company.

Article 14 prohibited an officer of a firm from acquiring stock of competing firms. No one was allowed to own stock in two or more firms if it would substantially restrain competition. If a person wished to buy stock exceeding 10 percent of a competing firm, an FTC approval was required. Article 15 prohibited mergers in those cases where it did not help to rationalize production (increase efficiency) and where it gave rise to substantial disparities of bargaining power or restraint of trade. The act established the Fair Trade Commission (FTC) as the agency to enforce the act.

IMPACT OF THESE MEASURES ON ZAIBATSU FAMILIES

These measures had a visible impact on the economic power of the Zaibatsu combines in general and the Zaibatsu families in particular. The losses the Zaibatsu families suffered were great. By the end of 1947, the Zaibatsu families (comprising 56 individuals) handed over to HCLC stock valued at 1,865,000,000 yen as of December 1945. Under the provisions of holding-company dissolution, this action was required by the Ministry of Finance, under the Capital Levy Tax, and by the FTC in compliance with the intercorporate stock divestiture provisions of the Anti-Monopoly Act. The data released by HCLC in 1950 (the last year for such figures) show that these members of the Zaibatsu families had received, as of March 1950, 1,830,000,000 yen in nonnegotiable, noninterest-bearing government bonds of ten-year maturity. But it must be noted that due to the rapid inflation then taking place, the real value of the bonds reimbursed them was no more than 5 percent of the real value of these liquidated stocks as of 1945.[17]

The stockholdings that the Zaibatsu families had in numerous firms were now completely gone and their names disappeared even from the lists of stockholders of the Zaibatsu banks, once the central nerve of their empire. These individuals were, as noted earlier, also purged from all public and corporate positions of any consequence. The lives of the former Zaibatsu families changed, in short, as Japan itself had changed.

---

[17] The price level continued to climb a steep hill between 1945 and 1950. The consumer price index of 1950 was nearly 500 times as large as that of 1945. The reimbursement was made over six years of inflationary period, thus a precise estimation of the amount reimbursed in real terms is impossible, but devaluation of the Zaibatsu asset by 95 percent seems to be a widely accepted assessment. From what the Zaibatsu families received, 10 percent was exacted by HCLC as "service charges."

These individuals did not usually possess managerial skills or business acumen and were merely the titular heads of their empires. They were powerful only in the long tradition of their "houses," which controlled immense fortunes. Consequently, these former noblemen [18] were totally unprepared to carve their niche in a new way of life. A few of them retired into a secluded life of their chosen academic pursuit, while most of them became inactive rentiers. Observing in 1953, a Japanese writer commented, "The former Zaibatsu has been dissolved. Mitsui, Sumitomo, and other Zaibatsu families sold their stockholdings and then they had to liquidate their real estate and even their art collections to survive in the [postwar] inflation. Several years ago they became *Shayō-zoku* [the tribe of the setting sun]." [19]

ELIMINATION OF EXCESSIVE CONCENTRATION
OF ECONOMIC POWER

The measures so far mentioned effectively abolished holding companies. The ties that held the Zaibatsu combines were now cut. The problem still remaining was the size of the firm per se. The subsidiaries or affiliates of the former Zaibatsu group were often still extremely large firms, relative to the size of the other firms in Japan. Following the guidelines provided by the Zaibatsu Mission, the Occupation Authority proceeded to tackle this problem at the close of 1947. The Japanese Diet, acting under the order of the Authority, enacted Law 207 (Elimination of Excessive Concentration of Economic Power Law) in December 1947.

Article 6 of the law gives its essence quite clearly:

> The HCLC shall decide and make public the specific standards for determining what shall constitute excessive concentrations of economic power upon consideration of the following factors:
> 1. Percentage of amount of production or other economic activity of any enterprise in Japan (exclusive of colonies) to the total amount of production or other economic activity of Japan in the respective field of activity.
> 2. Comparison of present production capacity of any enterprise in Japan with maximum production capacity in Japan on or prior to June 30, 1937.
> 3. Comparison of percentage of present production capacity or amount of other economic activity in Japan of any enterprise based on the total production capacity or total amount of other

[18] The members of the Zaibatsu families (Mitsui, Mitsubishi, Sumitomo, and Yasuda) were noblemen at the time of the surrender. Their title could be considered the equivalent of knighthood in England.

[19] H. Higuchi, *Zaibatsu no Fukkatsu* (The Revival of Zaibatsu) (Tokyo, 1953), p. 227.

economic activity of Japan in the respective field of activity, with such maximum percentage on or prior to June 30, 1937.
4. Relationship of control over other enterprises.
5. The number, location and other geographic conditions of plants operated by any enterprise.
6. Whether plants are interrelated in productive processes and extent of such interrelation in use of raw materials, products produced or in markets for products.
7. Control of raw materials by any enterprise.
8. History of expansion of business activity by means of merger of independent enterprise or other means.
9. Comparison of the efficiency of production of any enterprise with the efficiency of its separated parts or combinations of separate parts.
10. Participation of any enterprise in or the existence of any arrangement or relationship including exclusive sales or purchasing or other similar arrangements of a monopolistic or restrictive character, or which provides for special privileges in the purchase or sale of materials, restrictions upon business or sales areas, or the exclusive exchange of patents or technical information.
11. Control over substantial business activity operated by individuals or members of family.
In determining "efficiency of production" of Clause 9 of the preceding paragraph, consideration shall be given whether quantity of output or unit costs will be affected by changing the organizational structure of the enterprise.[20]

The specific Standards which HCLC was to specify were issued immediately following the enactment of the law and stated:

Excessive Concentration

Any private enterprise conducted for profit, or combination of such enterprises, will be considered an excessive concentration if it meets any of the following criteria:
1. Produce or have the capacity to produce a sufficient portion of the total supply of a commodity or service that a substantial price increase or hardship to potential buyers or to the general public would result if such supply were withdrawn from an uncontrolled market.
2. Distribute sufficient supply of commodity or commodities that a substantial price increase or hardship to potential buyers or to the general public would result if it withheld such supply from the market.
3. Have sufficient influence and power in its field of operations that it could take action which would make it very difficult for another entrepreneur to enter the same field of activity with reasonable opportunity to compete successfully.
4. Acquired other organizations, operating units or concerns or any part thereof and enjoyed special monopolistic privileges and

[20] Law No. 207, *Official Gazette* (December 18, 1947).

dominating controls as a result of war mobilization policy since
1937.

5. Have sufficient cumulative influence and power through its
activities in unrelated fields of operations to restrict competition
or impair opportunity for others to engage in business independently.[21]

An examination of Article 6 of Law 207 and the Standards issued by
the HCLC indicates that the reduction in the firm size was not to
hamper "efficiency of production," and quantity of output or unit cost
was not to be "affected by changing the organizational structure of the
enterprise." These criteria are far from quantifiable standards. Other
examples of such phrases are: "a sufficient portion of total supply" and
"sufficient influence and power in its field of operation." The latter were
to be criteria for deconcentration measures. At one point, the Japanese
government's Economic Stabilization Committee suggested as the
standard of "largeness" capital assets of over ten million yen and a
market share of at least 20 percent of the total output.[22] But decisions
on the standard of deconcentration had not been made as of the end of
1947.

LABOR REFORM

As is well documented, Japanese workers before the end of
World War II enjoyed virtually none of the advantages of trade union-
ism. Their wages were low by any Western standard, and the numerous
controls legislated during the war introduced many provisions for forced
labor. Since the beginning of the Meiji industrialization and through
the quasi-war and war periods following the invasion of Manchuria in
1931, the status of labor in Japan has been an internationally condemned black mark on Japan's phenomenal record of industrialization.[23]
SCAP stated the pre-1945 condition eloquently:

> Thus at the conclusion of hostilities, employment conditions of
> Japanese workers were deplorable. Not only did there exist a complex
> wage structure but earnings for the vast majority of workers were far
> below subsistence level. Hours of work were long and unregulated;
> child labor was rampant; safety and sanitation conditions were such
> as to present a constant menace to health and welfare; and little
> protection was provided against occupational injury or disease.
> Japanese workers were subject to various feudalistic practices, such as
> money-in-advance contracts, compulsory savings and other forms of

[21] HCLC, *Public Notice*, No. 2 (Tokyo, February 2, 1948).
[22] S. Giga, *Gendai Nippon no Dokusen Kigyō* (Monopolistic Enterprise of
Contemporary Japan) (Tokyo, 1962), p. 133.
[23] In prewar Japan, no mechanism to solve economic issues between employers
and employees existed. For discussion of prewar union activities and movements, see
the source cited in footnote 29, this chapter.

involuntary servitude. This was particularly true with regard to women and minors who formed an especially docile segment of the labor force. The situation with regard to women workers living in dormitories was particularly bad. For these women life in the dormitory was completely regulated by the employer so that dormitories were aptly described as "high class penal institutions."

Not only were the working conditions deplorable but no adequate administrative organization or staff existed to correct this situation. In 1945, labor administration was decentralized among various ministries. There were only sixty-eight labor administration officials dispersed among the prefectures who were responsible for varied labor functions and whose salaries were paid from the national budget. On the local level, organization and staff of the sections responsible for carrying out labor functions were even more inadequate.[24]

Facing this condition, the economic democratization measures taken by SCAP in the labor area were no less thorough and dramatic than those carried out in relation to the Zaibatsu dissolution. Here, SCAP's five major goals were:

1. Creation of conditions under which a free and democratic movement could develop
2. Encouragement of sound collective bargaining and labor relations
3. Creation or extension of democratic labor legislation and administrative agencies
4. Education of workers, employers, and government officials in proper practices inherent in democratic labor movements and administration
5. Effective use of Japan's manpower for purposes of economic rehabilitation [25]

To achieve these goals, numerous laws were enacted immediately following the occupation. In some cases, where possible, existing laws were amended to redirect their intent in line with the basic principles of the occupation. Otherwise completely new laws were drafted. The best way, perhaps, to appreciate the nature and scope of the laws enacted is to describe five of the more important laws among the fourteen which were put into effect during this period:

1. The Trade Union Law promulgated in December 1945 sets forth the basic right of workers in private industry to organize, to bargain collectively, and to strike; provides for democratic proce-

[24] SCAP, *Missions and Accomplishments of the Supreme Commander for the Allied Powers in the Economic and Scientific Fields* (Tokyo, 1952), p. 51.
[25] *Ibid.*, p. 41.

dures in all union activities; establishes the labor relations commission; prohibits unfair labor practices on the part of employers.

2. The Labor Relations Adjustment Law, promulgated in October, 1946, sets forth procedures for conciliation, mediation and arbitration in private industry, and for cooling-off periods but no prohibition against the right to strike in certain industries of public utility nature [was set forth].

3. The Employment Security Law, the fundamental piece of legislation in the field of manpower, became effective in November, 1947. It contains authority for the government to operate a system of free public employment exchanges on a broader and more democratic basis than under the former Employment Exchange Law. It also provides for public services to the handicapped in securing employment. Further, it outlaws labor bosses and other undemocratic forms of labor recruitment.

4. The Unemployment Insurance Law became effective in November, 1947, and provides for a system of benefits to industrial workers who become unemployed and are in the labor market seeking work. It covers the majority of employers of five or more employees. An amendment of May, 1949, provides a supplementary system for day laborers, extends coverage to construction workers and liberalizes benefits. Employer, employee, and the government assume responsibility for administrative costs.

5. The Labor Standards Law, promulgated in April, 1947, prohibits all forms of involuntary servitude; establishes standards relating to wages, hours of work, rest days, overtime, vacations, safety and sanitation, employment of women and minors, apprenticeship, workmen's accident compensation, and dormitories; provides for an inspection organization; and contains penalty provisions for violations.[26]

These laws, in turn, established new bureaus to enforce the letter and spirit, under the newly created Ministry of Labor. They were the Labor Policy Bureau, Labor Standards Bureau, Women's and Minors' Bureau, and Employment Security Bureau. Also, the central Labor Relations Commission and 46 prefectural Labor Relations Commissions were established by the Trade Union Law to provide services of conciliation, mediation, and arbitration specified in the Labor Relations Adjustment Law. None of these services existed before 1945.

The effects of these laws, bureaus, and the atmosphere of democracy were instantaneous. The union movement mushroomed as a SCAP

[26] *Ibid.*, 43.

source documented: "By January 1946 the number had grown to 1,179 unions with almost 900,000 members; by the end of 1946 the number stood at 17,000 unions and 4,800,000 members; by June 1948, 33,900 unions and 6,668,000 members; by June 1949, 34,688 unions and 6,655,483 members."[27] In fact, two-fifths of the unions existing in 1948 were founded in the first six months of 1946. In the same year, three major labor federations were organized, namely, the General Federation of Japanese Labor Unions, All Japan Congress of Industrial Unions, and Japanese Congress of Japanese Unions.

Collective bargaining became the byword of the day. Employers and employees alike were caught by the enthusiasm generated by the intensive educational campaigns and public directives of SCAP. The pent-up desires and needs of the Japanese workers appeared to focus their energy on the new "democratic movement." The enthusiasm was such that SCAP found: Both sides [employers and employees] zealously accepted the principles of the new management-labor relationship although they did not thoroughly understand its practical application and the proper balance between union and managerial functions and powers. In some cases collective bargaining agreements were entered into granting to unions power in excess of those which are normally considered to be sound either from a labor or a management viewpoint.[28]

These were products of the American policy which hoped to create a strong middle class as the Zaibatsu Dissolution intended. A leading student of Japanese labor, Professor Kazuo Ōkochi summed up the views of many in the early years of the occupation of the labor reforms: After the end of the war the Japanese working class was freed from the semi-slavery to which it had been condemned for eighty years, and was given the right to organize independent unions, and the Labor Standards Law of 1947 for the first time prohibited "primitive working conditions" sanctioned by long tradition. For these boons the Japanese working class had to pay the heavy price of unconditional surrender.[29]

LAND REFORM

Although this book will not be concerned with the land reform undertaken by the occupation, a brief description of the reform is given below to complete our outline of the economic democratization.[30]

[27] *Ibid.*, p. 45.
[28] *Ibid.*, p. 46.
[29] Kazuo Ōkochi, *Labor in Modern Japan*, Science Council of Japan Series, No. 18 (Tokyo, 1958), p. 73.
[30] For a detailed discussion of the land reform, see R. P. Dore, *Land Reform in Japan* (New York: Oxford University Press, 1959).

The Japanese farmers in 1945 suffered, to a greater extent, the lot of their fathers and grandfathers who bore the main burden of the post-Meiji industrialization with the factory workers in the cities. When the occupation arrived, two-thirds of all Japanese farmers rented all or part of the land they cultivated, and the tenure system was in many ways feudalistic, requiring payment of exorbitant rents in money and kind often amounting to more than 50 percent of the gross product.

The democratization policy of SCAP had two major objectives, (1) to transfer land ownership to farmers who actually tilled the soil, and (2) to improve farm tenancy practices for those who continued as tenants. These objectives were carried out, breaking down the centuries-old institutions of Japanese agriculture. Before the beginning of the program, only 54 percent of the cultivated land was owner-operated, but by the beginning of 1950 this figure reached 90 percent. Tenancy provisions now included "written farm leases, rent ceilings, cash rentals, restrictions of transfer, and safeguards against arbitrary changes in rental contracts." [31]

The effect of such a program was literally revolutionary. The dreams of a large number of small tenant farmers were realized overnight at a cost far below the market value of the land they now acquired. Many large absentee landlords, who literally ruled the lives of their tenants, joined the "tribe of the setting sun," following the Zaibatsu families in the cities.

TAX REFORM

Although not a major reform in the same sense as the areas discussed above, the tax reform undertaken by SCAP was no less significant.[32] SCAP's purpose was "to bring about the existence of a tax system consistent with democratic concepts of equity and justice." In the words of Harvey Shavell, taxation adviser to SCAP, the aim was to overhaul "archaic, inefficient, and complicated assessment machinery which contributed in large measure to the unproductiveness and inequality of the personal income tax." [33] Specifically,

> There was no single progressive personal income tax, but rather a series of taxes on various forms of income. Some forms of income completely escaped taxation, such as capital gains. Postwar inflation had, in effect, changed income taxes in some cases into taxation on

[31] SCAP, *Missions and Accomplishments*, p. 64.
[32] The capital levy described above was also a part of the tax reform. For further discussions and references, see chapter 8.
[33] H. Shavell, "Taxation Reform in Occupied Japan," *National Tax Journal*, Vol. 1, June, 1948, p. 129.

capital because of the unrealistically low depreciation charges allow-able in computing taxable income. The tax system as a whole was highly regressive, with the greater burden falling inequitably upon those least able to pay. Indirect taxes, which were particularly burdensome upon the lower income groups, made up a major portion of total tax revenues. Local governments had few productive sources of tax revenue and consequently were completely dependent upon the national government for assistance in maintaining a minimum level of necessary local services. A reallocation of revenue sources was long overdue. Numerous regressive, nuisance and minor-revenue-producing taxes, which occupied a large portion of the tax adminis-trators' time, were incorporated in the tax structure. Information as to the provisions of the tax law, in general, was not available to the tax-paying public—or even to the tax officials, to a large extent—be-cause most of the information was buried in thousands of Cabinet Orders, unpublished ordinances, and unpublished ministerial regu-lations, many extending back to a date beyond the turn of the cen-tury.[34]

The primary goals of the SCAP tax policy were (1) to levy a wealth tax on concentrated wealth, and (2) to reform the entire tax system, especially personal income tax, to distribute the burden of tax more equally.

Along with the capital levy, which was "pointed at the topmost strata of Japanese society, a segment of 2 to 3 per cent, consisting almost exclusively of Zaibatsu," SCAP adopted completely new personal in-come tax laws. Capital gains from all sources and labor compensation in kind, previously tax free, were made taxable. A single, sharply progres-sive income tax scale was prescribed for all forms of income, replacing "a plethora of differentiated normal and surtax rate scales." [35] The new personal income tax rates began at 20 percent and reached 85 percent for those earning over one million yen.

It should be noted that the personal income tax introduced by SCAP was wide based. This meant that the lower income class, which had escaped direct personal income taxation before 1945, was now required to pay personal income taxes. Independent of SCAP's "punish-the-rich" measures, high expenditures, which were required in those years, and rapid inflation and occupation costs imposed a heavy tax burden on all Japanese. For example, the total tax revenues, which never exceeded 11.4 percent of GNP during World War II, reached 24.2 percent of GNP during the 1947–48 fiscal year.

The corporate sector shared the burden of increasing expenditure. The corporate income tax rate was 35 percent of net income, which was

[34] SCAP, *Missions and Accomplishments, op. cit.*, p. 6.
[35] H. Shavell, "Postwar Taxation in Japan," *Journal of Political Economy*, LVI (1948), p. 135.

defined as gross profits during any accounting period minus gross losses. No component of the corporate tax might be included in losses or expenses in computing taxable net income. An excess profits tax was levied on earnings exceeding 20 percent of capital employed. The rate rose to 30 percent. In addition, capital stock and surplus reserves were taxed at 0.5 percent, and depreciation allowances in effect bore no relation to steadily climbing price levels.

CONCLUSIONS

Leaving a tentative evaluation of SCAP policies for the end of Chapter 2,[36] we need to emphasize that these programs were motivated to punish a specific group of Japanese and to institute measures that had been designed to democratize the Japanese economy. Disavowing an "obligation to maintain particular standards of living in Japan," SCAP was able to concentrate on democratization without fear of possible conflicts of these measures as contrasted with the economic recovery and growth of the defeated nation.

[36] An evaluation of the SCAP measures will be made in the final chapter with a perspective of time vis-à-vis the Japanese policy that followed.

2   *FROM REFORM TO RECOVERY*

THE AMERICAN POLICY QUESTIONED

As the economic democratization measures were carried out into 1948, the war-torn Japanese economy continued to linger on the line of semistarvation: "By the war's end Japan's food supplies had fallen so low as to support a basic staple food ration of only 297 grams, or 1,042 calories per capita per day for the normal urban consumer. In actuality the planned basic ratio allowances were cut by delays in delivery in 1946 and during a part of 1947." [1] Gross National Product in 1947 was only slightly over 50 percent of the 1937 level. The index of real income per head stood at 54.9 in 1947, as against 100 in 1934–1936. All raw materials were in extremely short supply, and by October 1947 the total production of coal and electricity fell below the level considered the critical minimum. Labor unrest and mounting inflation further aggravated the situation.

From the spring of 1948, a period of reevaluation of the economic policy of the occupation forces began. Washington was receiving a series of news items informing it of the critical condition in Japan. The political mood of the administration was also changing as the public hostility toward Japan began to dwindle rapidly after V-J Day. The punish-and-reform policy, so clearly enunciated only a short time before, began to face questions such as, How long do the American taxpayers have to support the Japanese by providing the necessities of life? and How quickly can Japan stand on its own feet?

While the administration was taking a hard second look at SCAP's economic policies, Senator Knowland of California, who learned the details of the economic democratization policy and especially of the

[1] SCAP, *Missions and Accomplishments of the Supreme Commander for the Allied Powers in the Economic and Scientific Fields* (Tokyo, 1952), p. 11.

content of Law 207 (Elimination of Excessive Concentration of Economic Power Law) charged, on the Senate floor, that the measures were "socialization" [2] and contrary to the spirit of free enterprise. General Draper, then Undersecretary of the Army, expressed his views on Law 207 publicly, and stated that it must be applied with common sense unless the United States was prepared to make Japan "a permanent ward of the United States." [3]

Then, in April of the same year, the Johnstone Committee Report [4] was issued after the committee had toured Japan and investigated economic conditions. It recommended, in essence, "a new lenient recovery program" instead of a "reform-punishment program." The report thus advised the Administration to support, in the national interest, a reasonable program instead of continuing to feed the Japanese, at the cost of $400 million annually to the American taxpayer. With regard to the reparation, the committee further recommended that "Plants which are needed in bringing out the recovery of Japan should be retained and only excess capacity removed. Otherwise, the United States, which is now extending relief to Japan, would in reality be paying the reparation bill. In our opinion, the capacity that can be spared without affecting Japan's peacetime productivity is not great." [5]

At the same time, a question the Japanese began to ask was: How far will this policy be carried out? Up until the end of 1947, no large segment of Japan had expressed openly its doubts about the wisdom of the programs of the economic democratization policy or the general spirit of "reform." But by the time Law 207 was enacted, some responsible Japanese began for the first time to question publicly the direction and depth of the occupation policy.

A leading Social Democrat charged, late in 1947, that if Law 207 was to be instituted, "Japan will not be able to compete against the foreign competition" and this would effectively halt the recovery of Japan. He was joined by a ranking Communist deputy, who argued that a "peace-

[2] *New York Herald Tribune* (February 18, 1948).
[3] *New York Times* (March 27, 1948).
[4] This committee was headed by Mr. Percy H. Johnstone, chairman of the Chemical Bank and Trust Company, and was composed of executives of large firms and bank officials. Bisson said of this committee that the arrival of this Mission, "marked the turning point in the shift of policy that had been in the making since the end of 1947. Charged with investigation of the broad economic problems confronting Japan and Korea, the Mission was necessarily concerned with the working of the Deconcentration Law." T. A. Bisson, *Zaibatsu Dissolution in Japan* (Berkeley and Los Angeles: University of California Press, 1954), p. 142.
[5] These quotations were taken from the United States Department of State, *Reports on the Economic Position and Prospects of Japan and Korea and the Measures Required to Improve Them* (Washington, D.C., April 26, 1948).

ful and democratic Japan would be possible if Japan could promote its productive capacity while rejecting the monopoly." Thus his judgment was that the current Law 207 would not be helpful in bringing about that end.[6]

Representatives of the large firms strenuously objected to those measures, contained in Law 207 as subdivisions, which would cripple the productive capacity of Japanese industries and make normal and smooth operation of the economy impossible. The president of the semipublic Japan Iron and Steel Corporation expressed the view that he preferred "centralized production" (meaning nationalization) to the expected subdivision of his firm.[7]

Questions were also raised in the reform aspects of the SCAP tax policy. Unlike the punishment aspect of the tax policy (capital levy) which was aimed at the most wealthy,[8] the reform programs were beset with serious problems. The administration of the personal income tax became virtually inoperative. As SCAP's high and progressive income tax was grafted on the traditional goal system of collection, local tax offices began to raise assessment of individuals in order to meet their quotas. This arbitrary collection method, when coupled with the high tax rates, became the biggest source of public resentment and collection was resisted. The antitax movement began to spread in 1948, as the real tax burden continued to rise because of the continuing inflation which raised nominal income. Also, business firms severely criticized the taxes on corporate profits. After 1946, business firms found it virtually impossible to replace capital internally, let alone expand it, without evading their tax obligations.

Notwithstanding the glowing reports of accomplishments stated in SCAP's own report of *Missions and Accomplishments*,[9] SCAP's labor policy appeared, in 1947 and 1948, to have yielded results the policymakers had not expected. Instead of growing into the American style, essentially nonpolitical labor unions, the Japanese labor unions emerged under the leaderships of Marxists and Socialists as a strongly politically oriented force.

In October 1946, an extremely left-wing *Sanbetsu* (a Japanese abbreviation of the All-Japan Congress of Industrial Unions) led the so-called October offensive, which developed into a highly political movement. After a series of strikes and so-called production control, in which the

[6] *Kyōdō Press* (October 15, 1947).
[7] *Ibid.* (October 15, 1947).
[8] H. Shavell, "Postwar Taxation in Japan," *Journal of Political Economy*, LVI (1948), p. 131.
[9] See fn. 1, this chapter.

union operated the plant until its demands were met, Sanbetsu called for a general national strike in February 1947. They demanded a basic minimum wage, abolition of the income tax on labor, along with other usual economic demands of unions.

This nationwide strike, which would have paralyzed the exhausted national economy, was banned on its eve by the direct order of General MacArthur. SCAP, which had freed long-imprisoned left-wing labor leaders and gave its blessing to the labor movement, was now forced to invoke its power against the Japanese labor force.

After the ban on the general strike, unions followed a new tactic of scattered strikes, demanding minimum wages geared to the rising cost of living. In March 1948 the Communication Workers' Union led a movement for a nationwide strike for revised wage standards for government workers, but this too was banned by SCAP. By July 1948 it was the policy of SCAP to forbid all strikes by government employees.[10]

In the newspaper accounts of the debate that took place during late 1947 and early 1948, one can fully sense the feelings of the Japanese political leaders, intellectuals, and executives of large firms. They repeatedly asked: Is the basic policy of economic democratization consistent with the economic recovery of Japan which is so desperately needed? But they were in no position to defy the decisions of the occupying authority. The American papers reported their concern over the continued dependence of the Japanese economy on the United States, and more than once editorials urged a need for the reevaluation of the basic policy.[11]

THE VACILLATION OF THE AMERICAN POLICY

Under these circumstances, and undoubtedly influenced by wars in China and Vietnam which were threatening the political balance of the whole of Asia, the economic democratization policies began to show signs of relaxation. In July 1948 SCAP announced that the former Zaibatsu banks would be excluded from Law 207, since, as SCAP stated, these banks had been divorced from the holding companies and were then in the purview of the Anti-Monopoly Act. This announcement was received with surprise by the Japanese public since it had assumed that, along with all the Zaibatsu-connected concerns, these

[10] For a good description of the labor scene following the labor reform of 1946–47, see Kazuo Ōkochi, *Labor in Modern Japan*, Science Council of Japan Series, No. 18 (Tokyo, 1958); and Solomon B. Levine, *Industrial Relations in Postwar Japan* (Urbana, 1958).

[11] See for example *Tokyo Shimbun, Jiji News, Nippon Keizai*, all of May 20, 1948; *Newsweek*, December 1, 1947; and, *New York Times*, December 18, 1948.

banks would also be deconcentrated.[12] Another announcement on the same day stated that Law 207 would not be put into effect until a review board, which was to arrive from the United States, had examined the law and the condition of the Japanese economy. The law originally stipulated that the measures would be completed by the end of 1948.

Following upon the heels of the above announcements, the Trade Association Act (*Jigyōsha Dantai Hō*), which had been in preparation for several months, was enacted at the end of July. Its purpose was to dissolve many private trade associations created before and during World War II, since their dissolution was not complete in spite of the orders of SCAP. Moreover, such associations seemed to desire continuation of their functions in the allocation of critical materials, by making as few modifications as possible in their activities. The occupation authority enactment made it clear that none of them could continue to exercise such a function, except for the public corporations which would be established as government agencies. In short, "the purpose of the law was to supplement the Anti-Monopoly Act and to safeguard vigorously the Japanese economy from returning to old monopolistic practices." [13] The act allowed trade associations to "receive voluntary submission of statistical data and to publish such data in summary form without disclosing business information or conditions of any particular entrepreneur." [14] It allowed cooperation in research, dissemination of technical information, and so forth, while prohibiting—in 18 clauses—all activities that were or could lead to cartel, monopolistic, and unfair trade activities.[15]

During July and August of 1948, decrees were issued to prohibit the use of long familiar trademarks or the names of the Zaibatsu, as well as the names of the former holding companies. This action forced hundreds of firms to change their names and trademarks. The above two measures seemed to follow the spirit of the basic policy, but in both cases the effect of these measures was of minor significance when compared with the measures carried out before the fall of 1947.

Meanwhile, the review board, which arrived in Japan in the beginning of May, was conducting on-site inspections of the Japanese econ-

[12] The decision was a surprise to an English delegate to the Far Eastern Commission who protested, consequently, the decision. See Allied Council for Japan, *Minutes*, 109th Meeting (March 15, 1950), p. 1.

[13] Fair Trade Commission, *Fair Trade* (English version now defunct), Vol. I, No. 2 (1957), p. 22.

[14] The Trade Association Act, Art. 4, Par. 1.

[15] *Ibid.*, Art. 5.

omy and discussions with designated firms. In September, it issued the
following Four Principles to be used in applying Law 207:

1. No order should be issued under the Law unless there is a
prima facie case that the company restricts competition or
impairs opportunity for others to engage in business independently in any important segment of business. In the absence of
such a case, the company should be removed from designation.
2. Mere possession of non-related lines of business is not in itself
sufficient, in any case, to establish that a company is an excessive
concentration under the Law.
3. Submission of a voluntary plan of reorganization is not in itself
sufficient to confer upon the Holding Company Liquidation
Committee (HCLC) authority to issue an order under the Law.
4. The action a company is ordered to take by the HCLC, under
Law 207, should be directly related to the facts upon which that
company was determined to be an excessive concentration.[16]

A careful comparison of Article 6 of Law 207 and the Standards
issued by HCLC with the above Four Principles clearly reveals that the
burden of proof shifted from the designated firms to the law. The size
per se, which was to be judged on the basis of "a sufficient portion of the
total supply" and "sufficient influence and power in its field of operation," was no longer to be a ground for deconcentration. Principles 1, 2,
and 4 clearly limit the scope of the Law from the original statements
made in Law 207 and in the Standards. Principle 3 is significant in
encouraging the voluntary actions of the designated companies, thus
eliminating the scope of uncertainty for the designated firms. Also
eliminated was the reference to the level of production of 1937, clearly
indicating the mood of the board.

Based on the Four Principles of the review board, the law was applied
in 28 cases in the following twelve-month period. The results of the
application of the act could be summarized as follows:

		Number of Companies
1. Reorganization as public utility companies (to be owned by prefectures and cities and in exceptional cases by private financial institutions)		10 firms (all electric companies)
2. Division was ordered		
a. Divided and the parent firm dissolved	6	
b. Divided	5	11 firms

[16] *The Oriental Economist* (September 25, 1948). The board consisted of four
business executives and a Justice Department official.

3. Liquidation of assets was ordered
   a. Some plants liquidated   3
   b. Mining rights liquidated   1
   c. Some stocks liquidated   3   7 firms

To indicate the standard of "largeness," applied in the cases of the six companies that were divided and dissolved, we find that their size, in terms of employment and assets, ranged from the 38,228 employees and assets of 800 million yen of the Japan Steel and Iron Corporation, to the 3,527 employees and assets of 99.7 million yen of the Nippon Beer Corporation.

Besides iron and steel and beer, the industries affected by the above deconcentration measures included heavy machinery, paper and pulp, construction, textile, mining, canning and dairy products, petroleum refining, railway express, and movie industries. The number of firms affected by the law was much smaller than Japanese businessmen feared. The scope of the application was much more limited that would have been the case if the criterion once suggested of 20 percent of the market share had been used. While the deconcentration measures were being carried out, SCAP issued orders removing the designations from nearly 600 firms during the period between the summer of 1948 and the spring of 1949.[17]

The thaw in the policy was also visible in an increased willingness of SCAP to consent to measures designed to supply funds for resumption of industrial production. The Reconstruction Bank (*Fukkō Kinyū Kōkō*) was established with the consent of SCAP at the beginning of 1947 for the purpose of supplying operating funds for firms and for paying out, as a subsidy, the difference between the cost of production and the decreed maximum price. But by 1947, the bank began to make loans for the purpose of capital investment, and late in 1948 it had become by far the largest supplier of capital for the coal, iron and steel, fertilizer, electric, shipping, and textile industries. These industries were chosen on the basis of the weighted production policy (*Keisha Seisan Hōshiki*), then adopted for the purpose of concentrating the recovery efforts (capital) on these basic industries. As of March 1949 the loans made to these sectors amounted to a large proportion of the total investment made by each of these selected industries (see Table 3).[18]

[17] The exact number was 598; see S. Usami, *Nippon no Dokusen Shihon* (The Monopolistic Capital of Japan) (Tokyo, 1953), pp. 283–285.
[18] For other related data and discussions, see Seiji Kaneko, *Nippon Keizai no Seicho to Kōzō* (Japan's Economic Growth and Structure) (Tokyo, 1965), especially chap. 6, "Postwar Growth and the Government Funds," pp. 63–79.

TABLE 3

Proportion of Capital Supplied by the Reconstruction Bank
as a Percentage of Total Investment Made by Various Industries
Between September 1947 and March 1949

INDUSTRIES	COAL	IRON, STEEL	FERTILIZER	ELECTRIC	SHIP-BUILDING	TEXTILE
Proportion of total by the bank	98.1	73.4	64.0	92.9	84.0	44.9

SOURCE: Computed from the Ministry of International Trade and Industry, *White Paper*, 1958, p. 53; and T. Miyashita, "Reconstruction of Zaibatsu," *Nippon Shihon Shugi Taikei* (The System of Japanese Capitalism) (Tokyo, 1957), p. 91.

The total loans made by the bank amounted to 74.1 percent of the total investment of all industries, and 84 percent of the bank loans were concentrated in the coal, iron and steel, fertilizer, electric, shipbuilding, and textile industries. A striking fact is revealed when we examine how these loans were made. Sixty percent of the Reconstruction Bank loans involved sums of one billion yen each to 97 large firms. Smaller firms received only 9.9 percent of the total, and the maximum loaned was one million yen. The largest firms receiving loans included those second or "heir" firms which were formed in the place of dissolved firms, indicating the reliance of the weighted production policy on the largest firms and the degree SCAP had retreated from the previous policy.

Another encouragement given to business was the 1948 enactment of new relaxed schedules of the excess profit tax. The new schedules set the rate at 10 percent for profits exceeding 30 percent of capital employed, 15 percent for profits exceeding 50 percent of capital employed, and 20 percent for profits exceeding 100 percent of capital employed. In an economy that was experiencing a rampant inflation, this was a significant boost to the firms.

These large-scale loans and the relaxed schedule for excess profit taxes, however, were not congruent with the policy of curbing inflation, especially when the securities issued by the Reconstruction Bank were being bought by the Bank of Japan, which literally was printing money for the Bank of Reconstruction. The price level continued to climb,[19]

[19] The price index rose from 14,956 (1926 = 100) in 1948 to 24,336 in 1949. For an excellent description of the postwar Japanese inflation, see T. Yamane, "Postwar Inflation in Japan," unpubl. doctoral diss. (University of Wisconsin, 1955).

and black markets flourished in all parts of the economy, while the index of production failed to respond.[20]

THE DODGE LINE

In July 1949 the government, under these circumstances and upon direction of the allied powers, adopted the so-called Dodge Line [21] to alleviate the mounting difficulties. The Dodge Line was to implement the nine-point program, earlier issued by SCAP for the purpose of reviving the Japanese economy. The major aims of the Dodge Line were twofold. First, it sought to curb what was then called the Reconstruction Bank inflation by means of curtailing loans for the purpose of reconstruction.[22] Secondly, it sought to attract foreign investment, which was critically needed to alleviate the capital shortage then manifest in Japan, by establishing an official exchange rate.

The first objective of "dis-inflation" was to be achieved by balancing the national budget and, if possible, by creating an excess of revenue over expenditure. One of the planks of the Liberal-Democratic party's platform, which had just won the election, was a reduction in corporate profit tax rates and a revaluation of capital assets. But this promise was buried under the Dodge Line, which demanded that all types of tax collections be maintained and enforced for the sake of curbing inflation. To facilitate the second objective, an official exchange rate of 360 yen to the dollar was established and parts of the Anti-Monopoly Act were amended. SCAP's authorization to amend was "for the purpose of quickly increasing a smooth inflow of foreign capital in Japan." [23]

The purpose, according to the Annual Report of the FTC, was to correct the points which the FTC considered to be the result of "overshooting the aim of the occupation authority." The amendments were to make the desperately needed flow of foreign capital to Japan possible.[24] In fact, the Japanese capital market after the war had been extremely

[20] The growth of GNP for 1949 was only 3.9 percent above 1948 in real terms. This must be considered vis-à-vis the fact that the base GNP of 1948 was still extremely small.

[21] Named after Detroit banker Joseph M. Dodge, who came to Japan as financial adviser for the GHQ-SCAP in February 1949. The essential points of this policy were based upon his recommendation. Also see S. Tsuru, "Toward Economic Stability in Japan," *Pacific Affairs* (December 1949), for contemporary observation.

[22] Mr. Dodge has written that the Japanese suffered from the delusion that "granting progressively larger amounts of commercial bank credits for capital purposes can be substituted for the normal process of capital accumulation without creating current credit shortages and possibility of later difficulties." J. B. Cohen, *Japan's Postwar Economy* (Bloomington: Indiana University Press, 1958), p. 90.

[23] *The Oriental Economist* (October 30, 1948).

[24] FTC, *Fair Trade*, Vol. I, No. 3 (1957), p. 37.

meager and overdrawn. It was incapable of digesting the stock being marketed, by the HCLC and by other normal channels, for the purpose of forming new firms as the result of the Zaibatsu dissolution. The international balance of payments showed deficits, and in 1949 imports were nearly twice exports.[25] The *Annual Report* of the FTC stated in 1949:

> In order to establish companies' accounting orders, which became extremely unwholesome during the war, a tremendous amount of additional capital and sales of stock for the second companies [formed after the dissolution of former Zaibatsu-connected firms] was needed. On the other hand . . . huge amounts of stock formerly held by holding companies, Zaibatsu firms, designated firms and other companies came under the Elimination of Excessive Concentration of Economic Power [Law 207] Law . . . and stock paid in as in-kind payment of Estate Tax had to be digested. This was, however, extremely difficult for the Japanese capital market which was exhausted.[26]

The Amendment of 1949 relaxed the provisions concerning international agreements, stockholding, interlocking directorships, and mergers. But the most significant change was made in Article 6 which originally prohibited any entrepreneur from entering into "an agreement or contract relating to restriction on exchange of scientific or technological knowledge or information necessary for business activities." This clause was deleted in order to enable any capital inflow which would be more likely to come on the basis of patent, or exclusive dealing arrangements between a Japanese firm and a foreign firm. Also, the original validation requirements of international agreements were replaced with the mere necessity of *post facto* notification to the FTC. In other parts of the act, all discriminatory clauses against foreign firms were eliminated to place them on an equal footing with any Japanese firm.

Article 10, which originally prohibited buying of voting stock of a firm by a nonfinancial firm, was changed to read that "any company whose business is other than financial shall not acquire or own stock of another company . . . in case such acquisition or ownership may result in a substantial loosening of competition between any such firms." This meant that a firm could possess stock in its subsidiaries up to 100 percent if the acquisition did not violate the clause specified.

From Article 13 of the original act on interlocking directorship, two restrictions were eliminated. One was the restriction in the case where one-fourth or more of the officers of either of the two companies

[25] Tōyōkeizai Shimpō-sha, *Keizai Tōkei Nenkan* (Year Book of Economic Statistics) (Tokyo, 1962), p. 63.
[26] FTC, *Annual Report of 1949*, pp. 6–7.

involved were concurrently holding positions in a third company. The other was the restriction stating that "no officer of a company shall in any case hold a position of officer in four or more companies." The only prohibition retained applied to cases where "both of the companies were in competition with one another" (Article 13, Clause 1). Article 15 on mergers was amended from validation requirements to pre-merger notification. The *Annual Report* of the FTC observed these amendments as "improvements," since the change in Article 6 would "enhance the chance of inviting inflow of foreign capital" and the changes in Articles 10 through 15 had "relaxed mechanical prohibitions" which were "unnecessarily severe." [27]

From the end of 1949 to the spring of 1950, however, the stock market became more sluggish,[28] and the Dow-Jones average declined from 150 to 101 in the four-month period.[29] The condition of the Japanese capital market seemed to be quickly reaching the point of exhaustion. Following the Dodge Line, the Reconstruction Bank had discontinued its liberal loaning; the government was now practicing "surplus budget" policy; investment achieved via stock sales fell in 1950 to 22,587 million yen from 40,367 million yen in 1949; and the economy was gradually showing the signs of a deepening recession.[30]

SHOUP TAX MISSION

By 1949 the whole tax system was in critical need of a formal reevaluation. The tax burden in the fiscal year 1949 reached 24.1 percent of the GNP, and the "super-balanced" budget under the Dodge Line demanded vigorous enforcement of tax laws. The antitax sentiment of the public was strong, as inflation and unemployment plagued the economy. The corporate sector also pleaded for "realistic depreciation and revaluation" provisions, for the sake of "adjusting accounting orders." Pleas were made more and more vocally for tax laws that would help the reestablishment of the Japanese industry.[31]

In May 1949 a group of tax specialists, headed by Professor Carl Shoup of Columbia University, arrived in Japan by request of SCAP to recommend a course for the Japanese taxation policy. The purpose of the mission, it was reported, was to recommend a tax system that would

---

[27] FTC, *Annual Report of 1952*, p. 16.
[28] M. Maruyama, "The Amendment of Limitation on Stockholding," *Kōsei Torihiki* (November 1949), p. 7.
[29] *Year Book of Economic Statistics*, p. 64.
[30] M.I.T.I., *Industry Rationalization White Paper* (Tokyo, 1957), p. 57.
[31] Numerous articles and editorials published during January, February, and March of 1948, in the conservative *Nihon Keizai*, a daily, reflect the views of the corporate sector.

contribute to the economic stability of Japan and that would require no changes for several years to come.

The 65,000-word report of the Shoup mission was made public in September 1949. The major points of recommendation were:

1. Given the public's antitax sentiment in 1949, to effect a tax cut for every Japanese in the balanced budget framework.

2. To maintain the progressive and broad-based personal income tax as a mainstay of the Japanese tax system. But a relaxation in progressivity of personal income tax and an increase in the allowance for dependents and exemptions were recommended.

3. To revaluate capital and land, in order to adjust the value of these assets to the existing price level, and to abolish all excess profit taxes.

4. To emphasize direct taxes and only those indirect and excise taxes which were not levied on daily necessities. Emphasis was to be placed on personal income tax, corporate profits, and taxes on alcoholic beverages and tobacco. Repeal of numerous excise taxes on a long list of commodities was recommended.

5. To stress the importance of the fiscal autonomy of local administrative units, the tax jurisdiction of respective levels of government was specified.

6. To replace revenue lost by the relaxed progressivity in personal income tax, the net worth tax, the accessions tax, and the value added tax were added.

The report was detailed and thorough. It was an ambitious document by capable American tax specialists.[32] Its recognition of needs for a general tax, for the elimination of the excess profits tax, and for revaluation was hailed by a large number of Japanese in late 1949.

READJUSTMENT ON THE LABOR FRONT

The labor front in 1949 saw an important change. In the economy which failed to gain momentum, with the deflationary policy of the Dodge Line and the continued rapid increase in population, unemployment began to increase sharply. Hastily organized unions and many who joined merely following the "tide of democracy" managed, in the preceding few years, to lose public support. This was due mainly to the excesses in the demands (often political) and tactics under the politically ambitious leadership.

It was time for a management offensive. With the consent of SCAP,

[32] Two familiar names for economists in the Shoup Mission were professors William Vickery of Columbia and J. B. Cohen of City College of New York.

the Trade Union Law was amended in 1949 so that the union officials could no longer receive salaries and be provided with offices by the company. The stated reason for the amendment was to insure the independence of the unions, but the immediate effect was unmistakable. Given the fact that nearly half of the unions were then nonfederated company unions, the revision often struck hard at the existence of small unions, on which the financial burden of such a change was heavy. Eloquently attesting to the effect of the 1949 management offensive was the sharp drop in union membership beginning in 1949. The figure which stood at 6.7 million in 1948 dwindled to 3.3 million by the end of 1949.[33]

A REVIEW OF THE SCAP POLICY

In this chapter we have just seen vacillation and the gradual relaxation of the SCAP policy after 1947. Observing as we did in chapter 1, many would agree that the initial aims of the economic democratization policy were carried out effectively in the first two years of the occupation.

The tightly knit Zaibatsu empires of holding companies were dissolved and shareholding had become diffused.[34] The first Anti-Monopoly Act in the history of Japan had been enacted. On the labor front, as in land reform, the success of the SCAP policy was visible. The number of unions mushroomed and membership increased rapidly. The labor laws enacted appeared to solidify the place of the Japanese labor movement and to insure that the traditionally oppressed Japanese labor force would have a strong voice in determining the future of their own welfare. The capital levy and the sharply progressive personal income tax appeared to work toward a more equal distribution of the tax burden and income.

Then the ground began to shift. Reappraisal of the U.S. policy was in effect forced upon SCAP. First, we should recall that the world political balance was quickly changing. The prospect of China falling into the hands of Communists forced the administration to reexamine its disavowal of any obligation of rebuilding an economically strong Japan. Secondly, Republicans and the U.S. business sector began to express serious doubts about many aspects of the administration's policy to the point of condemning it as socialistic. Thirdly, there was the problem of

---

[33] Ōkochi, pp. 76–78.
[34] For example, the former Mitsubishi Bank which had been owned by the Iwasaki family was in 1948 owned by approximately 30,000 shareholders. See H. Higuchi, *Zaibatsu no Fukkatsu* (The Revival of Zaibatsu), p. 45. The ownership pattern of the former Zaibatsu banks will be discussed in detail in chapter 7.

literally supporting the Japanese and further taxing the already heavily committed U.S. dollars, unless Japan could stand on her own two feet.

Japanese reactions to the SCAP measures during the initial years of the occupation changed from blind obedience, out of fear and of total admiration of all that was called democratic, to polite expressions of doubt and gradually to open criticism of SCAP measures. In late 1947 the Japanese criticisms appeared to have been directed to the immediate consequences of the SCAP punish-and-reform policy. It was argued that the initial designation of nearly 1,200 of the largest firms for restriction was a considerable threat to the minimum flow of industrial production. The majority of these designated firms, exclusive of the large financial holding companies, were the largest manufacturing firms in Japan. When they were frozen, it in effect prevented them from making transitional arrangements to peacetime production. They were forced to wait idly; thus the actions which might have been taken against them by SCAP—either dissolution or reorganization—in the midst of mounting inflation were not taken. These firms were, therefore, unable to make adjustments to minimize their losses resulting from it. At the end of 1947, more than half of these 1,200 large firms (by definition each having assets exceeding five million yen) lay shackled by legal restrictions.

Another, though less tangible, consequence of the SCAP policy, it was said, stemmed from the uncertainty of the enforcement criteria in both the provisions in the decree on dissolution of holding companies and some of the provisions in the Anti-Monopoly Act. These laws specifically stated that, in those cases where the efficiency of production warranted, exclusive dealing arrangements and vertical integrations were allowed, provided they did not substantially lessen the competition in the field of operation. In spite of this fact, the Japanese business leaders, totally unfamiliar with the spirit of the law and unprovided with the precedents of enforcement and the working definitions of the concept used in the laws, inclined to do nothing that might offend the occupation authority and bring yet harsher measures upon them. This they preferred rather than take a chance on the unfamiliar concepts and risk the attention of SCAP.

The disruption of the capital market by SCAP policy was also serious, according to some. Huge amounts of formerly Zaibatsu-held stock were liquidated with ensuing scandals and speculation. Noteworthy was the fact that many large firms, whose former executives were purged, were left in the hands of former section chiefs and bureau chiefs. The latter were often less than competent to deal with the immense tasks facing the large firms in the stormy weather of the postsurrender economy.[35]

These short-run effects of the SCAP policy on the state of the Japanese economy in 1947 could, however, be considered as the minor, transitory cost of transforming a Zaibatsu-controlled economic structure of prewar Japan into a "democratic and competitive" structure. The freezing of 1,200 large firms certainly was necessary to prevent a large-scale evasion of the deconcentration measure. The negative attitude of the Japanese businessmen vis-à-vis the provisions of the Anti-Monopoly Act, it could be argued, was a matter of experience and gradual education. This attitude could be eliminated by application of the act, from which would evolve working definitions of the concepts used in it, as has been done in the United States since 1900.

We cannot, of course, seek a facile cause-effect relationship between the reform policy of SCAP and the economic conditions of Japan existing in 1947. The Japanese economy then was plagued with rampant inflation and a critical shortage of capital, raw material, and power (coal and electricity). The nation's industry in fact had been reduced to a state of near-total devastation as the result of the long, destructive war. The labor force was, to compound the difficulties, restive and demoralized in the days of the postwar disruption of the economic and social order. Realizing these difficulties in the economy, we can, however, venture to examine the possible impact of the postwar SCAP reform policy on the immediate postwar economic condition of Japan, at least as far as it contributed to the prevailing economic difficulties.

In this atmosphere, in late 1947 and the early months of 1948, the basic SCAP policy, as enunciated in the Pauley report, Zaibatsu mission, and other official pronouncements, began to undergo a series of de facto revisions. It would be futile to search for a specific event or date that could be designated as the turning point of the basic policy. It eroded gradually in step-by-step concessions to reality. As our examination of the unfolding events in 1498 and 1949 makes clear, the policy of SCAP had to drift away from the basic policy in searching for ways to deal with particular problems.

Although as late as New Year's Day 1948 General MacArthur was reiterating the original policy in firm language to the public,[36] it was known that SCAP had already consented to the weighted production

[35] In large firms, only minor officials were left after the purge. Journalists popularized a phrase Santō Jūyaku (The Third Rate Executives) as they often reported serious, as well as amusing, problems caused by the sudden assumption of responsibilities by former minor officials.
[36] Contemporary Japan, Vol. XVII, Nos. 1–3 (Tokyo, 1948), p. 97.

policy which would try to revitalize the large firms in the basic industries by means of large loans by the Reconstruction Bank. In the summer of 1949 the Trade Association Act was enacted and the use of trademarks and names of the former holding companies and Zaibatsu was prohibited. But these measures were at best weak continuations of the original policy.

The exclusion of the former Zaibatsu banks from Law 207 alone was more than sufficient to indicate that the ground was shifting. It is true that the new ownership of the banks had then been widely distributed and the Ministry of Finance had been cautious so that no stockholder acquired more than 2 percent of the total shares of the respective banks, but they were still large in relative size. Although of much smaller significance, considering the reduced size of the capital market of Japan at that time, nearly 30 percent of the total loans made by private banks were still made by "the largest six"—four former Zaibatsu banks, plus two that were formerly closely connected with the Zaibatsu families.[37]

Not only the exclusion of the former Zaibatsu banks, but also the manner in which Law 207 was applied, revealed the degree of change in the policy. Law 207 was carried out under the guidelines provided by the Four Principles of the review board, as we have seen earlier in 28 cases. If we closely examine those six cases in which division of firms was executed, we find the following: The six firms were the largest in their respective industries.[38] Their market shares, in terms of percentage of the total output contributed by each firm as of 1937, ranged from 84 percent of the pig-iron market by the Nippon Iron and Steel Corporation, to 13 percent of the cotton weaving market by Teikoku Textile.[39] Four of these six firms, heavy machine, steel and iron, paper, and beer had market shares that were in excess of twice that of the second largest firm in their respective markets.

All of these firms had been dominantly or exclusively Zaibatsu con-

[37] *The Oriental Economist* (October 30, 1948); also see Table 25, chapter 7, for a comparison of the market share of the four largest banks.

[38] All of these firms were the largest in their respective *industry*, but they also were largest in the important markets of their industry, such as Japan Iron and Steel Corporation in pig-iron, steel products, and scrap iron markets. The concentration ratios used here are the ratios of the product in which they held the highest ratios among many products they produced. These firms were dominant producers in several markets of their respective industry in the sense that they were the largest producers.

[39] The six firms involved and their respective market shares, shown in parentheses with the specific market, as of 1937 are as follows: 1. Mitsui Heavy Industry (shipbuilding, 35 percent); 2. Nippon Iron and Steel Corporation (pig iron, 84 percent); 3. Oji Papers (paper, 49.3 percent); 4. Nippon Beer Corporation (beer, 63.5 percent); 5. Teikoku Textile (cotton-weaving, 13 percent); 6. Daiken Construction (unavailable). See FTC, *Nippon Sangyō Shūchū no Jittai* (The Reality of Industrial Structure) (Tokyo, 1957), Appendix, p. 285.

trolled either as subsidiaries or as affiliates. Before 1945, one-half of the Japan Iron and Steel Corporation had been owned by the government, making a classic case of government-Zaibatsu joint venture. In short, these were the cases which, SCAP apparently reasoned, offended the first of the Four Principles of the review board. Each of these firms was "a *prima facie* case where the company restricts competition or impairs the opportunity for others to engage in business independently in any important segment of business." Considering the government policy before World War II, the power enjoyed by the Zaibatsu, and the relative dominance of these firms in their respective industries, SCAP's judgment as to the existence of a prima facie case, in the sense quoted above, could not be questioned for the period prior to 1945.

At this point one is puzzled to find what could be considered an inconsistency in SCAP's attitude vis-à-vis the former Zaibatsu banks and these six firms. These firms had been democratized in terms of ownership, as the banks were, and they also were in the purview of the Anti-Monopoly Act. Did SCAP use "the present condition" as the criterion when it excluded these banks from Law 207, while "the past [circa 1937] condition" was considered in the case of these six firms?

If the criteria used in selecting firms were common denominators which we could delineate by examining these six firms (that is, being formerly Zaibatsu connected, violating Principle 1 of the review board, interested in more than one market, and dominant in more than one market in terms of market share), then why were only these six firms dissolved? Why, for example, were not the Nissan Automobile and scores of other firms which met these criteria dissolved?

SCAP's attitude toward the supply of capital is another puzzle. In spite of the weighted production policy and the liberal loan policy of the Reconstruction Bank, which it had consented to previously, the limited amendment of 1949 was made only as a consolation to the deflationary policy of the Dodge Line. The Limitation was partially relaxed after the increasing war demand had become a heavy burden to the already exhausted capital market of Japan. It should also be recalled that SCAP's authority was invoked to suppress the corporate tax reduction program, which was promised by the victorious Liberal-Democratic Party.

Did the qualified relaxation of the Limitation and the promised corporate tax reduction appear more threatening to the intent of the basic policy than the large loans, of one billion yen each, which were made to 97 of the largest firms in Japan by the Reconstruction Bank before the Korean War?

These are the puzzles partially arising out of the fact that some measures were ad hoc, in the sense that they were forced on SCAP by the swiftly changing objective conditions. The notable divergence between the basic policy and the policy after 1949 could be interpreted as a result of a series of revisions made to deal with the problems at hand. As such, some of the complex operations might not have kept pace with others, in the degree of transition from one policy to the other.

3 THE EMERGENCE OF
THE JAPANESE POLICY

KOREAN WAR

In June 1950, when the index of manufacturing production was barely one-third that of the 1931 level, the Korean War started. This rude shock of another war so close to Japan immediately began to affect the Japanese economy in many ways. The policy of SCAP underwent a dramatic change in the few months following the start of the war. The first sign of change came in August, when those who were purged on the grounds of prewar economic activities were depurged.

The economy began to expand rapidly with the *Tokujyu* boom (Special Demand of War boom), stimulated by the war demand of 149 million dollars in 1950.[1] This amount was approximately five times the volume of the stock sales made in 1950. The Dow-Jones average bounced back to over 200 from nearly 100 in 1950.[2] Hoping to increase the supply of funds for investment needs, the occupation authority took another significant step in reversing the measures carried out earlier. In November, it announced an amendment to the decree on Stockholding Limitation and Other Matters issued in 1947 in order to bring it into line with the amended Anti-Monopoly Act and to meet the need of capital expansion. The changes could be summarized as follows.

The original Limitation decreed that no financial institution could buy the stock of companies that were formerly connected with itself

---

[1] The special procurement connected with the Korean War began at 149 million dollars in 1950 and rose to 592 (1951), 824 (1952), and 806 (1953). In 1954, however, it fell to 596. As we shall discuss shortly, these special procurement expenditures played an important role in the Japanese economy during this period. These data are based on the Bank of Japan's "Foreign Exchange Statistics."

[2] M. Maruyama, "The Amendment of Limitation on Stockholding," *Kōsei Torihiki* (November, 1949), p. 7.

financially. This meant that former Zaibatsu banks were not allowed to deal in stock of former Zaibatsu or Zaibatsu-connected firms. The amendment now provided for two exceptions to this rule: (1) any financial institution could "accept and digest [resell]" stock of any firm, providing the amount did not exceed 19 percent of the total issued by the firm;[3] and (2) financial intermediaries could not acquire stock for collateral, following Article 11–4 of the amended Anti-Monopoly Act.[4]

Secondly, the original categorical prohibition of buying stock of manufacturing firms by financial intermediaries and designated firms was relaxed. After this amendment, they could buy stock of manufacturing firms when the following five conditions were met:

1. The stock-issuing firms were not "General Merchant" (*Shoji*) firms.[5]
2. The stock-issuing company could not be one which in the past had been connected financially; that is, stock of a former Zaibatsu subsidiary could not be bought by a former Zaibatsu bank.
3. The stock-issuing company had a common interest with the financial intermediary or the designated firm in the form of patent or innovation.
4. After reasonable efforts had been made, the stock-issuing company found it difficult to sell stock unless the financial intermediary or the designated firms acquired them.
5. Permission to obtain stock of manufacturing firms must be obtained in each case from the HCLC.

The third aspect of relaxation was seen in interlocking directorships. Formerly the interlocking of directors or officers was permitted only when a company had been declared bankrupt or dissolved; for example, a creditor firm could send its representative to protect its interest in such bankrupt firms. This was amended so that the interlocking of officers was permitted to protect substantial interests of stockholders or creditors.[6] At the same time, by governmental decree No. 567, the ceiling on the quantity of the sale of stock of designated companies and financial intermediaries without permission of the Minister of Finance was raised to 10 percent of designated firms' stock and 25 percent of that of financial intermediaries. Formerly, the ceiling was 1 percent and 10 percent respectively.

---

[3] This amendment, for example, enabled the Chiyoda Bank, which was formerly a part of the Mitsubishi Heavy Industries, to accept and digest the stocks of the "heir" companies formed by the Mitsubishi Heavy Industries.

[4] See Appendix IV.

[5] This, also, is a reflection of consistent punitive measures taken against these firms in the economic democratization policy.

[6] Maruyama, p. 8.

The FTC expressed alarm over what it considered the sudden overre-laxation of the anti-monopoly policy in the midst of the first postsurren-der boom, which tripled pretax corporate profits and brought the index of the manufacturing output over the prewar level for the first time. The Socialist and Communist parties, along with the labor unions, protested these moves which they considered as "undermining the Economic Constitution."

As the war continued in Korea the production index continued to rise, but the increase in production was in most cases achieved by extensive use of the overdepreciated productive capacity then available. Much of the investment made during this period was for the purpose of stop-gap measures, lest no industry miss the tide of the *Tokujyu* boom which came suddenly and unannounced.

In the iron and steel industry, the increase in output was obtained by operating the existing plants at their fullest capacity. These plants, overused and having deteriorated during the war, were technically out-dated and inefficient by Western standards. The cost of some steel products was as much as 50 percent higher than that of the equivalent products produced in the United States.[7] In the textile industry the capacity of cotton weaving machines increased rapidly after the restric-tion was lifted by SCAP in June 1950. This increase in capacity had to be made rapidly in order to enjoy the *Tokujyu* boom. As the Ministry of International Trade and Industry noted, the textile industry, "unable to increase its capacity quickly enough, began to duplicate the existing models and techniques of production which were then known to be inefficient, and in most cases the increased capacity was achieved by those machines which were considered outdated by the English mills before the beginning of World War II."[8]

Other industries followed the pattern of these two industries. A frenzy of investment to increase capacity continued in the wake of the Korean War, as if the boom was to continue for a long time. The *Tokujyu* boom was a shot in the arm for the Japanese economy, and the injection of the large amount of dollars began to show its effects by the end of 1950.

TAX LAWS OF 1950

Meanwhile, the essential parts of the Shoup recommendation had been enacted and became effective in April 1950. The modifica-tions, made by the Japanese government, relaxed some Shoup recom-mendations and lowered the tax rates. Personal income tax began at 20

[7] M.I.T.I., *Sangyō Gōrika Hakusho* (Industry Rationalization White Paper) (Tokyo, 1957) pp. 338–339.
    [8] *Ibid.*, p. 439.

percent for incomes below 50,000 yen, and rose in eight gradations to 55 percent for income exceeding 500,000 yen. This was considerably less progressive, when compared with the tax rate of 55 percent for income exceeding 300,000 yen recommended by the Shoup Mission. From the income tax schedule of 20 to 85 percent then in effect, the 1951 income tax schedule thus achieved a considerable decrease in progressiveness. Following the recommendation, 25 percent of dividend income was exempted from personal income tax to avoid a double taxation at corporate and personal sources.

The value-added tax was not adopted by the Japanese government on the grounds that it was too complex to administer,[9] but the recommended net-worth tax was adopted at 1.6 percent with an exemption of 10,000 yen for each type of asset (land, house, depreciable assets, and so forth), the recommended 3 percent without exemptions having failed to pass the Diet. The accessions tax was carried out as recommended and became payable cumulatively by heir or donee at rates ranging from 25 to 90 percent.

The corporate tax law was revised to allow for revaluation within the limits set by an authorized price index. Though revaluation was made optional, contrary to the recommendation, a recommended 6 percent tax on revaluation was adopted. This measure was especially significant when many firms were attempting to expand their capacity in the face of a rising price index.[10]

This is far from a complete summary of the tax laws of 1950. There were many other changes, including the recommended repeal of numerous indirect taxes,[11] and an extensive change in tax laws governing local taxes and changes in jurisdiction between local and national governments. However, it was clear that the impact of the tax laws of 1950 was extensive. Although the following comparison must be made with the knowledge that the economy in 1949 and in the war boom of 1950 were subject to different sets of variables, a decrease in the tax burden from 28.5 percent of GNP in 1949 to 22.4 percent in 1950 is an indication of the impact of the changes in tax laws.

The Shoup Mission returned in July 1950, and after two months of on-site reexamination recommended that:

[9] For an excellent discussion of the "disadvantages" of the value-added tax, see Hanya Ito, *Essays in Public Finance*, The Science Council of Japan, English series, No. 3 (Tokyo, 1954), pp. 26–47.

[10] For a detailed discussion of the revaluation tax and its effect on capital accumulation, see H. Hayashi, "Capital Accumulation and Taxation in Japan," *National Tax Journal*, XVI (June, 1963), 174–192.

[11] These included sugar and textile products taxes. See chapter 8 for discussions of direct taxes.

1. The basic exemptions (for the head of the household) be raised to 30,000 yen from the current 25,000 yen.
2. Exemptions for dependents be increased within the constraints imposed by revenue needs.
3. Reduction of the personal income tax, especially for those groups earning over 50,000 but less than 150,000 yen. No further reduction was to be made for those earning over 300,000 yen.
4. A further cut on commodities tax in addition to those adopted in April 1950 following the initial recommendation of 1949.[12]

A PHASE OF TRANSITION

The index of manufacturing output had been climbing steadily in the twelve months after the beginning of the Korean War, and the *Tokujyu* boom, it appeared, would continue for years to come. In view of the drastically changed political condition of Asia, the Supreme Commander of the Allied Powers was hastening the clock to terminate the occupied status of Japan. SCAP had just issued a directive authorizing the Japanese government to review all the laws and orders promulgated since the beginning of the occupation. The Liberal-Democratic party, then in power, established an Occupation Legislation Screening Committee for the purpose, and the public began to anticipate an early arrival of independence.

With the swiftness with which it came, however, the *Tokujyu* boom suddenly slackened for some industries in the middle of May 1951, when the United States began to reappraise its initial purchasing policy of war material. As a consequence, the price of leather and rubber fell sharply and textile producers suffered a large number of canceled orders.[13] The change caused the bankruptcy of many textile and export-import firms, including the larger ones. In June, nearly three hundred cotton weaving firms suffered bankruptcy in a matter of a few days. In July, when the initial "peace talks" started, several industries—textile, rubber, artificial fibers, and leather among them—knew that the *Tokujyu* boom had ended for them; while some others, such as iron and steel, cement, lumber, and machine tool industries, could expect the war demand to continue.

At about this time, in June, the Occupation Legislation Screening Committee recommended among other things a large-scale amendment

[12] H. Matsukuma, ed., *Sengo Nippon no Zeisei* (The Tax Systems of Postwar Japan) (Tōyō Keizai Shimpō-sha, 1959), p. 89.
[13] H. Misonou, *Nippon no Dokusen* (Monopolies in Japan) (Tokyo, 1960), p. 65.

to the Anti-Monopoly Act.[14] The recommendation was promptly hailed by the financial and large corporate sectors, and was denounced by the Socialist and Communist parties, as well as by the Consumer League (*Shōhisha Dantai*). SCAP soon ordered the recommendation suppressed.

Meanwhile, however, a significant step was taken by the Ministry of International Trade and Industry. It recommended restriction of production to less than full capacity operation (*so-tan*) [15] to the three industries most affected by the sudden curtailment of *Tokujyu* orders, the artifical fiber, cotton weaving, and automobile tire industries. However, the "recommendations" were, in fact, administrative orders, since the ministry had control over foreign currencies and could curtail the supply of imported raw materials which were essential to disobedient firms. Also, the Bank of Japan announced that the firms which had complied with the *so-tan* following the M.I.T.I. recommendation would be preferentially considered for loans. Given these conditions, those industries recommended by the Ministry immediately worked out their production quotas, and arrangements were soon extended into price maintenance.

The Fair Trade Commission immediately challenged M.I.T.I.'s action and found that in the case of the artificial fiber and automobile tire industries, their collusive activities were illegal under the Anti-Monopoly Act.[16] On the other hand, for the cotton weaving industry the FTC decided that the recommendation was not illegal since it was "an administrative recommendation which was uniquely in the hands of M.I.T.I." Thus, it consented to the birth of the first de facto cartel since the end of World War II.

The distinction that the FTC drew between the automobile tire and artificial fiber cases and the cotton weaving case was quite delicate.

---

[14] The content of the recommendation of the committee was adopted in the amendment of 1953 which we shall discuss shortly. The fact that the German anti-trust law, *Entwurf eines Gezetses gegen Wettbewerbs des Chränkungen*, was used as a model was revealed to the author by an M.I.T.I. official.

[15] *So-tan* literally means "short operation."

[16] The FTC ruled that they had violated the act by following the recommendation of M.I.T.I. The FTC's judgment on the chemical fiber case read in part: "As there exists a general condition which could be considered responsible for causing the defendants to commit illegal acts, we believe that there is reason to be sympathetic with the industry. The representatives of the association of chemical fibers had to follow the guidance of the Ministry concerned. However, we consider it improper to alter the interpretation of the Act on account of the will of a Ministry which had no authority of interpretation or enforcement of the Act." FTC, *Kōsei Torihiki Iiankai Shinketsu-Shū* (The Annual Report of Adjudged Cases) (Tokyo, 1953), p. 31. Also, for details of the automobile tire and the artificial fiber cases, see the cases Nos. 105 and 106, FTC, *The Annual Report of Adjudged Cases, 1952*.

Those industries that were found to be in violation of the act were much more concentrated, in terms of concentration ratios, than the cotton weaving industry. This fact may have influenced the decision of the FTC, but this thin distinction became the first concession of the FTC to M.I.T.I.[17]

Though the FTC yielded to the policy of M.I.T.I. in the cotton weaving case, it apparently hoped this would be an exception. The activities of the FTC in this crucial year of 1952 testified to their stand. In June 1952, two months after the *so-tan* operation was recommended for the cotton weaving industry, the FTC found that conditions in the industry had improved and expressed the following opinion in an official letter to M.I.T.I.:

> As a result of the recent investigation, we believe that the first series of *so-tan* has had sufficient effect on improving the price of cotton thread and the price is now generally stabilized. If *so-tan* is continued, the general consumer and related industries will suffer, as the evil consequences in those related industries already clearly show. Price manipulation of this type has severely penalized the small and weak weaving specialists to the point of causing numerous cases of bankruptcies.[18]

Finding also that the steel and iron and the ammonium sulphate industries were practicing price maintenance, with the largest producer in each industry as the price leader and without the expressed recommendation by M.I.T.I., the FTC ordered the practice to be discontinued immediately. Both industries accepted the order *nolo contendere.* The Fair Trade Commission at this time also suspected that some type of underground collusions were going on in the silk-yarn, sodium-hydroxide, super-phosphate, and steel rod and sheet industries. However, no action was taken, based on its findings that "the activities were not collusive although they appeared to be collusive." [19]

In August, as a part of what M.I.T.I. then called the "Save the Bankruptcies" policy, the Liberal-Democratic party rushed the Designated Medium-Small Enterprise Stabilization Act through the Diet. The intent of the law was to protect the small-to-medium-sized firms which were most severely affected by the aftermath of the sudden

[17] No question of the constitutionality of the M.I.T.I.'s action was raised, in spite of the fact that the decision was then severely criticized by the purists inside the FTC. *The Annual Report of* 1952 also records a letter sent in protest to the chief of Textile Division, M.I.T.I., stating that the so-called *so-tan* recommendations were against Article 4 of the Anti-Monopoly Act. *Annual Report of* 1952, pp. 38–39.

[18] FTC, *The Annual Report of* 1952, p. 39. However, the operation was continued for 13 months; then the industry came under the Designated Medium-Small Enterprise Stabilization Act and was accorded a recession cartel status in 1953.

[19] FTC, *The Annual Report of* 1952, p. 39.

curtailment of *Tokujyu* orders. The designation included all small-scale textile producers, such as weavers, spinning and dyeing firms, and the china and match industries. The law, in fact, required adjustment (*Chōsei*) of production, investment, and shipment but not price-fixing which would have been impossible in any case. Many of the small firms, which were the subcontractors of the larger firms, now suffered sudden insolvency and large excess capacity.

In September 1951 the Peace Treaty of San Francisco was signed and independence was only six months away. "As soon as this treaty was signed the authority of SCAP was weakened, and the attack on the Anti-Monopoly Act began with the force of water over a dam." [20] In fact, some newspapers began to carry editorials favoring amendments of the Anti-Monopoly Act, and the corporation executives began to express their dislike of the act more openly. In both cases it was indicated that opponents had begun to feel safe in expressing their beliefs, whereas they had been restrained during the pre-peace treaty period. The industries also knew that they had attentive ears in M.I.T.I. and the Ministry of Finance.

Before the end of the 1951 session of the Diet, the Japanese government requested of SCAP that it be allowed to amend the 1948 Export Trade Act, so that cartel activities in the domestic market could be legalized. But permission was denied by SCAP which feared dumping in foreign markets and higher prices in the domestic market. The government also attempted to relax the Trade Association Act, but this, too, met firm refusal by SCAP. Although at this time M.I.T.I. had drafted a bill entitled Important Industries Temporary Stabilization Act to authorize cartels in recessions and to enable M.I.T.I. designated industries to limit production, M.I.T.I. did not submit the bill to SCAP for clearance. Perhaps M.I.T.I. realized that the attitude of SCAP was still firm on the matter of outright admission of legalized cartels as shown in the preceding two attempts and the fact that independence was only a few months away.

Reading the newspaper accounts of what journalists called the "Post-*Tokujyu* boom Recession" and the public pronouncements made by the officials of M.I.T.I. in those days, one infers that the curtailment of the *Tokujyu* orders for some industries really caused a recession of considerable magnitude in Japan. But as we examine the available economic indicators, we find a different story. The index of total investment rose

[20] H. Asano, "Where does the Anti-Monopoly Act go?" *Kōsei Torihiki* (September 1952), p. 12.

to 154 in 1951 from 100 in 1950, and it reached 174 in 1952.[21] The Gross National Product, in real terms, showed a remarkable increase of 13.5 percent in 1951 and 10.5 percent in 1952. The pre-tax corporate profits of the largest 600 firms, according to Mr. Misonou, rose to 1.086 trillion yen in the first two quarters of 1952 from 137 billion yen in the first two quarters of 1951.[22] The index of real wages for manufacturing industries rose steadily from 75.6 in 1950 to 82.3 in 1951 and 91.5 in 1952 (1955 = 100).[23]

A brief discussion with M.I.T.I. officials and an examination of a few trade journals are sufficient to shed light on this apparent contradiction. The wave of bankruptcies, which started in the cotton weaving industry and the export-import firms, was caused by temporary insolvency resulting from the sudden fall in the price of products they had either produced or had bought by that time. Some firms, especially export-import firms that worked on margin, suffered great losses during the months of June and July 1951. The textile, rubber, and leather firms which were filling orders of the *Tokujyu* demand with outdated, costly machines and methods found themselves unable to continue production without the war demand which pegged the price of their products high.[24]

The story of these industries was applicable to other Japanese industries, or to use a phrase of M.I.T.I. officials, the Japanese economy was then extremely "shallow based." This meant that a slight price decline in the international market could topple the whole export outlook of the economy, essentially due to the comparative inefficiency of the Japanese industries.

A few examples serve to illustrate the reasons for the shallow-base effect. For example, the fertilizer industry (chiefly ammonium sulphate), which was one of the major industries of Japan in terms of exported quantity, was then exporting to India, Korea, the Philippines, and other Southeast Asian nations at 66 dollars per ton. But West Germany, which was quickly recovering, was beginning to compete with Japanese ammonium sulphate at prices ranging from 46 to 51 dollars per ton. England also began to appear in the ammonium sulphate market at 45 dollars per ton.

[21] *Year Book of Economic Statistics*, p. 62.
[22] Misonou, p. 66.
[23] *Year Book*, p. 62.
[24] The domestic consumption of these products was strong during 1951 and it continued to rise into 1952. But the firms in these industries were usually separated into two groups. One placed great emphasis on domestic markets and the other on foreign markets, with the latter suffering the most.

The artificial fiber industry (chiefly chemical fabrics) similarly began to face keen competition from Italian firms, which were able to sell at 45 cents per pound against the Japanese price of 60 cents. The iron and steel industry, which was still enjoying the *Tokujyu* demand though in reduced quantity and was also being helped by a steel strike in the United States, was beginning to be threatened by the formation of the European Coal and Steel Community. ECSC seemed ready to return to the markets of Argentina, Brazil, and Pakistan, all importers of Japanese steel. The Marshall Plan had visibly contributed to the cost reduction of West German steel, and mills were beginning to produce steel products below the price of Japanese mills.[25]

Realizing the necessity of quick rationalization [26] (interpreted by the Japanese as "investment to catch up with the Western standards of efficiency"), these industries were anxiously investing in more efficient methods of production. The fertilizer industry, for example, was busily rationalizing its production with the aim of completing the first phase of rationalization by 1953. The steel and iron industry was making a capital outlay to reach the level of Western Europe as quickly as possible, and the move to adopt new equipment had also started in the textile industry. In short, as our indicator of investment informs us, all Japan had begun a race toward rationalization.

This race could continue to an important degree due to the newly authorized Japan Development Bank (*Nippon Kaihatsu Ginkō*), which began to lend for rationalization in large quantities.[27] M.I.T.I. reasoned

[25] Data for these preceding three paragraphs were obtained from M.I.T.I. officials, trade journals such as *Tekko Kai* (Steel World), published by the Japan Federation of Steel, Tokyo; and *Nippon Keizai Nempō* (Annual Economic Report of Japan) (Tōyō Keizai Shimpō-sha, Tokyo, 1953), pp. 129–135.

[26] Throughout this book, the term *rationalization* is used as a translation of the Japanese word *gōrika*, which literally means "to make it logical." We shall use rationalization to mean to adopt a larger unit of production which increases efficiency (a lower unit cost) when produced near or at the optimum level of production of a new unit of production. The common phrase, "catching up with the Western standard of efficiency," is a nontechnical way of saying the same. As done by many Japanese writers, this term will also be used to mean to make any aspect of the operation to yield more than a competitive profit by such means as acquisition of a large market share by whatever means, more effective cartels of various types, etc. If used in this sense the term will be placed in quotation marks. In those rare cases when the word is used to mean neither of the two above meanings, an explanation will be added.

[27] The Japan Development Bank (*Nippon Kaihatsu Ginkō*) was authorized in 1951 for the purpose of aiding rationalization investments. The loans made in 1951 were 20, 592,000,000 yen and it jumped to 64,049,000,000 yen in 1952. When the latter figure is compared with the total loans made by private banks in Japan (175,369,000,000 yen in 1952), we find that the Japan Development Bank made approximately 26 percent of the loans made by all private banks. Computed from *Year Book, op. cit.*, p. 221; and the Economic Planning Agency, *Sengo Nippon no*

that rationalization could continue if the level of profit could be maintained (in spite of excess capacity which was quickly developing) by circumventing the "desperate competition which destroys the hopeful future of the Japanese industrial expansion."

Those firms that were unable to withstand the price decline were eliminated from the rationalization race, but for Japan as a whole the Korean War initiated this rush toward capital investment. If we are to place credence in the economic indicators rather than in the impressions of journalists, the Japanese economy in 1952 was far from a recession in the usual sense of the term.

Meanwhile, the attitude of SCAP was one of apparent inconsistency, as it had given silent consent to the *so-tan* recommendations initiated by M.I.T.I. but refused an amendment to the Trade Association Act. It had sternly rejected the suggestion of an amendment to the Anti-Monopoly Act by the Occupation Legislation Screening Committee, though it was silent when the Designated Medium-Small Enterprise Stabilization Act was rushed through the Diet. To the last moment of its authority, SCAP to all appearances was painfully adjusting to the de facto political necessity and the pressure of Japan's desire to recover and prosper.

RETREAT OF THE SHOUP LINE

Changes in the tax laws were also rapid during the period (1950–1952). Like the de facto revisions of the Anti-Monopoly Act by M.I.T.I., these changes began to reverse the course recommended by the Shoup Mission. When U.S. policy made a sharp turn at the outbreak of the Korean War, the Japanese government was quick to take advantage of the situation. It was argued that rationalization must be aided by the tax laws as well, and the industry made insistent demands "to ease the pain of the American-imposed tax laws." The White Paper on the Tax System published in April 1951 amply suggested the course of the tax policy the Japanese government hoped to follow. The white paper argued in essence that the tax rates were still very high compared with those that prevailed in the postwar years and that efforts should be made to reduce the existing tax rates.[28]

Changes in 1951 began with an increase in the basic exemption (for the head of the household) from 25,000 yen to 30,000 yen and a significant reduction in the personal income tax, shown in Table 4. The gradations in the 1951 tax schedule were increased to 10 smaller steps,

Shihon Chikuseki to Kigyō Keiei (Capital Accumulation and Business Management in Postwar Japan), Tokyo, 1957, pp. 26–27.

[28] Matsukuma, p. 93.

compared with the 1950 schedule of 8 steps of 5 percent. The maximum rate of 55 percent now applied to incomes exceeding two million yen, instead of 500,000 yen as was the case in 1951.

In the corporate sector, two important provisions were introduced in 1951. The first was a special law which granted a depreciation allowance of 50 percent above the rate permitted under the existing law for those firms that were purchasing new equipment. This provision was to apply only to "important machinery," as specified by law for a period of three years.[29] The second was a provision that permitted funds reserved for "losses" due to a fall in the price of products to be treated as a loss. This

TABLE 4

Personal Income Tax Rates (Percentage)
Income in 1,000 Yen, 1950 and 1951

Income Class	Below 50	50–80	80–100	100–120	120–150	150–200	200–500	Over 500
1950	20	25	30	35	40	45	50	55

Income Class	Below 50	50–80	80–100	100–120	120–150	150–200	200–300	300–500	500–1000	1000–2000	Over 2000
1951	20	23	25	28	30	33	38	43	48	53	55

was a measure adopted after a series of bankruptcies had taken place in the textile industry, as described earlier.[30] Professor Shoup, who visited Japan in October 1951, was sharply critical of the general line the Japanese government was then contemplating, especially the third tax cut since the war in the middle of the Korean War when U.S. taxes had just been raised.[31] However, the Liberal-Democratic party then in power was quite certain that by the end of 1951 tax revenue would exceed that calculated before the advent of the Korean War by nearly 153 billion yen (425 million dollars).

The 1952 revision of the personal income tax included an increase in the basic exemption (for the head of the household) from 30,000 yen to 50,000 yen, and the dependents' exemption was raised from 15,000 yen

[29] Fertilizer, pulp, and electric power industries enjoyed the largest benefit under this provision. Y. Hayashi, *Sengo Nippon no Sozei Kōzō* (The Tax Structure of Postwar Japan) (Tokyo, 1958), p. 371.

[30] Firms were allowed to consider the difference between the book value and the current price minus 10 percent as a loss.

[31] Matsukuma, p. 105.

to 20,000 yen per person. This was more than sufficient to compensate for a 26 percent increase in the Consumer Price Index, which had taken place since the beginning of the Korean War and resulted in a significant reduction in taxes. The schedule of the personal income tax was amended again in 1952, as shown below in Table 5. This was a tax reduction for all income classes, except for the class having an income exceeding two million yen.

In addition, the personal income tax was given two significant tax breaks, of which Professor Shoup would have never approved on the grounds that it would be a revival of the prewar type differential treatment of income by its source, thus benefiting the wealthy.[32] One was a provision permitting only 50 percent, minus 150,000 yen, of

TABLE 5

The 1952 Personal Income Tax Schedule (Percent),
Income in 1,000 Yen

Income	Below 80	80– 120	120– 200	200– 300	300– 500	500– 1000	1000– 2000	Over 2000
Tax Rate	20	25	30	35	40	45	50	55

capital gains and transitory incomes, and income generated by the sale of land and forests to be added to other incomes for the purpose of personal income taxation. The other was a provision permitting only 50 percent, minus 150,000 yen, of a lump-sum retirement income to be taxed separately from all other incomes.

In the corporate sector the tax rate was raised from 35 percent to 42 percent, in view of the rapidly rising profits resulting from the Korean War boom, but at the same time a new provision was introduced. This was specifically intended to aid rationalization; for example, firms that bought specified equipment were allowed to depreciate 50 percent of the cost in the first year, in addition to the provisions of the 1951 law that permitted an extra 50 percent depreciation. This new provision covered 32 industries in 1952.[33]

In spite of inflation, the tax burden in 1952 became measurably lighter when compared with that in the years immediately following the occupation. Improving economic conditions, primarily due to the Korean War boom, were responsible to a large degree, but no one can deny the contributions made by the lightened tax burden.

[32] Since 1915, interest income and wage income were taxed at different rates. See Hayashi, pp. 5–6.
[33] Effects of this and other "special deductions" will be discussed in chapter 8.

CONCLUSION

The Korean War played a decisive role in expediting the transition of policy. Following a period of vacillation and relaxation, some of the principal measures of the SCAP policy were negated and the course of reform was reversed. However, this was the course of SCAP's own choosing, since these revisions and amendments could not have been possible without the consent of SCAP. The Japanese government was merely aggressively assertive of the course it wished to follow, taking advantage of U.S. anxiety to build an ally out of Japan, an enemy only a short time before.

Considering the suddenness and extent of the disintegration of the original SCAP policy, many Japanese writers, especially those of the Marxist persuasion, regarded this rapid reversal as a matter of political expediency.[34] This view, however, misses an important point. That is, as indicated strongly in the period of 1948–1950 (the period of reform to recovery), that SCAP's policy to "punish," but with little concern for "recovery," was an idealistically motivated policy that could not have borne the fruit of success without some basic changes in the unique conditions and constraints facing the Japanese economy.

We must recall that the economy being discussed accomplished the feat of industrialization in a matter of a generation, under a principle quite contrary to the one imposed by SCAP reform. What SCAP's punishment had removed by its drastic operation was a cancer in the view of the Zaibatsu mission. But, as Lockwood observed, that portion of the Japanese economy afflicted with the cancer had performed a vital function in the past economic development of Japan:

> Looking back at the broad history of the pre-war era, one cannot fail to be impressed with the constructive role of the Japanese combines in technical progress especially in the earlier decades. The *Zaibatsu* were not merely political wire pullers, or financial manipulators, or even rentier investors. They performed an essential function in large-scale enterprise which could otherwise have been performed only by the state, and not necessarily with greater benefit. If they reaped fabulous gains, as they did, they continued to plough back the larger share in entrepreneurial investment in new and expanding activity. The new is always uncertain, and as Joseph

[34] The Marxist view is that Japan became a full-fledged colony of the U.S., to be exploited by such means as the special procurement. The Korean War, they argue, became the turning point of postwar history, in that the U.S. policy from 1950 was to revive the former monopolists as a base of an imperialist aggression in Asia. See S. Usami, *Nippon no Dokusen Shihon* (The Monopolistic Capital of Japan) (Tokyo, 1953), pp. 105–199; and S. Aihara, *Nippon no Dokusen Shihon: Sengo ni okeru sono Kōzō to Kinō* (The Monopolistic Capital of Japan: Its Postwar Functions and Structure) (Tokyo, 1959), pp. 33–57.

> Schumpeter remarks, some degree of market power to ward off competition is apt to be the condition of successful innovation, especially where large outlays are at stake.[35]

That is, in the prewar economy of Japan, the Zaibatsu monopolies, actively aided by the government, were able to invest their large profits in new adventures in the world of industrialization. They were the financiers of large investments and the risk takers in the application of Western technology and development of world commerce. Their size made it possible to achieve the economies of scale needed in modern industrialization.

If we believe that the desire of an economy to recover and grow is self-evident, some entity must now perform the function once performed by the Zaibatsu. As envisioned in the years immediately following V-J Day, the SCAP policy did not provide for a replacement for the Zaibatsu. This is the reason, given the capitalist framework, the government asserted its power through such measures as *so-tan*, revisions in taxation, and other laws. That is to say, when the relative efficiency of the Japanese industries was made painfully clear during the years of the *Tokujyu* boom and its aftermath, the government chose to nullify some fundamental aspects of the SCAP policy which it considered an impediment to the process of rapid recovery and growth.

The emerging Japanese policy was to sacrifice the "democratic" elements of the SCAP policy, such as a competitive market structure and "just and equal" tax laws, for the sake of rapid recovery and growth. In brief the original SCAP policy was incongruent with the rapid growth the Japanese government desired. To rationalize and to accumulate capital, the Japanese policy now began to follow a course of its own. In the following chapters, we shall examine the path that the Japanese government chose to follow. In doing so, we may be able to show more clearly how and why growth and economic democracy, as envisioned by SCAP, failed to coexist in postwar Japan.

[35] W. W. Lockwood, *The Economic Development of Japan* (Princeton: Princeton University Press, 1954), p. 232.

4 DISINTEGRATION OF THE ANTI-MONOPOLY POLICY, 1953-1957

THE 1953 AMENDMENT

On April 28, 1952, the Peace Treaty of San Francisco went into effect, and SCAP was formally abolished. As if this were a signal, several steps were immediately carried out by the Japanese government to nullify, in fact, the steps that had been introduced by SCAP. The first of these steps was the elimination of the order prohibiting the use of old Zaibatsu trademarks and names. This immediately enabled three splinter firms of the former Mitsubishi Heavy Industry to readopt their familiar three lozenges as their trademark.

Then, the first postindependence amendment, an amendment to the Trade Association Act which had been firmly disallowed until the last days of SCAP, was quickly carried out. Although the journal *Fair Trade* stated that this amendment was merely to mitigate the strictness of the act,[1] it in fact was more than this. The amended act was left with only one significant clause of the original, and even this clause was reduced to no more than a restatement of what could be dealt with by the Anti-Monopoly Act itself.[2] The amendment also excluded cooperative associations from the purview of the act, thus leaving an opportunity for the former trade association to continue its existence under the guise of the cooperative association, though the possibility of evading the application of Article 5 depended on enforcement.

From the end of 1952 to the beginning of 1953, pressure for amending the Anti-Monopoly Act increased. The bill for amendment drafted by M.I.T.I. in 1951 began to be openly discussed by government officials

[1] FTC, *Fair Trade* (this English journal is now defunct), No. 3 (1953), p. 3.
[2] Article 4 of the Anti-Monopoly Act was sufficient to effect what was intended in the clause of the Amended Trade Association Act. See Appendix IV.

and executives of corporations who strongly favored it. However, the ranking Socialist deputies and the leaders of the labor unions opposed any amendment.[3] The medium-small-scale businesses fiercely opposed the bill, arguing that if this bill was passed the amendment would favor large corporations at the cost of small firms. The farmers' associations and the consumer groups also voiced strong protest from the fear that cartels would raise the prices of the products these groups used.[4]

By the time of the general election in April 1953 which returned the Liberal-Democratic party (though now reduced in size), an amendment of the Anti-Monopoly Act had become merely a question of time. The Diet began to debate the bill beginning in April, but each bill among the many introduced in the first independent Diet took considerable time due to the increased power of the Socialist party and to the delicate factional dispute within the Liberal-Democratic party.[5]

In the meantime the economic condition of Japan was becoming one of increasing "overheating" (the condition of increasingly active investment) in the face of lagging exports[6] and domestic demand. The foreign currency reserve in 1953 dropped to 635 million dollars from the 913 million of the year before. Exports in 1953 increased only 7.6 percent, against a 26.4 percent increase in imports, which created an excess of imports over exports of 1,134 billion dollars. The level of inventories of industrial products continued to increase. As an example of over-heating, the investment made in the month of April 1953 was nearly 30 percent higher than that of the annual monthly average in 1952.[7]

There also was no sign that conditions would improve in the near future. The picture appeared to be quite the opposite for the future of the Japanese international market. The Korean War was formally ending and the *Tokujyu* demand visibly subsided, except for lumber and

[3] The newspaper account of these opinions also indicates that the Leftist groups considered these amendments inevitable as long as capitalism continued. In this sense their opposition to the bill was half-hearted.

[4] This disagreement between the large corporate sector and the small-medium sector caused the withdrawal of the medium-to-small firms from the Japanese Association of Manufacturers, and they organized their own Japan Small-Medium Business Association.

[5] The Liberal Democratic party was reduced from 222 to 199 while the two factions of the Socialist party together (which may not always vote together) gained 12 seats. Thirty-five members of the faction of the Conservative party now established a split party, making the Diet procedure for the Conservative party extremely delicate. *Asahi Shimbun* (April 27, 1953).

[6] "Over-heating" (*kanetsu*) is a phrase often used by economists and government officials to mean that the country is investing too quickly and too much at once.

[7] These data are computed from the M.I.T.I. publications and the *Year Book. op. cit., passim.*

cement.[8] The Commonwealth nations announced that the quota for Japanese exports of cotton weaving products would be cut to 20 percent of the low level of 1952. As of May 1953, industries such as ammonium sulphate, steel rod, cotton weaving, and artificial fibers were practicing dumping in foreign markets. Following the end of the Korean War and the death of Stalin, the Western nations were expected to concentrate on peacetime production, meaning that competition for Japanese industries in the international market would be keener.

When we look at the domestic market of this period, the growth of demand considerably lagged behind the increase of output. The real wage level of industrial employees increased nearly five percent in 1953 from the level of 1952, but even that did not help the index of consumption as saving went up by five percent during the same period. Consequently, department store sales were off 10 percent from the peak period of the *Tokujyu* boom.[9]

Finally, in September 1953, the Diet passed a law amending the Anti-Monopoly Act to an extensive degree and also abolishing the Trade Association Act. This large-scale amendment, which was called "a great retreat of economic democracy" and "a qualitative change" of the anti-monopoly policy, could be summarized in the following seven headings.[10]

1. *Admission of Recession and Rationalization Cartels.* Cartels and other collusive activities became legal in those cases where the competent minister deemed it necessary on the grounds of averting a recession or for the purpose of rationalization. Any competent ministry, as well as any industry group, might initiate the action, though when it was initiated by an industrial group, concurrence of the competent ministry was required. In either case the consent of the FTC was also required.[11]

2. *Relaxation of Stockholding Regulations.* According to the amended articles 10 through 16, interlocking directorship, mergers, and

[8] Though the "special procurement" account of *Foreign Exchange Statistics* shows 809 million dollars in 1953 and 596 million dollars in 1954, the special procurement orders began to decrease in 1953.

[9] *The Annual Economic Report of Japan*, p. 153.

[10] See Appendix IV for the contrast of the Anti-Monopoly Act enacted in 1947 and the amended act of 1953.

[11] The amendment eliminated in toto Article 4 which prohibited cartels or cartelizing activities. This article had long been considered as a supplement to Article 3 which read that "no entrepreneur shall effect a private monopolization or shall undertake unreasonable restraint of trade," and which often was invoked in cases involving "cartel-like activities." The well-known *Teikoku* Bank Case of 1947 was prosecuted under the provisions of Articles 3 and 4. (This was a case involving 28 major banks which attempted to set an agreed upon interest rate.) Also, Clause 6 of Article 2 of the original act was superseded by Clause 4, Article 2 of the amended act. The former prohibited cartels or cartelizing activities per se, but the latter prohibited only the consequences of cartels which could be considered "substantial restraint of trade" or "against the public interest." See Appendix IV.

mutual stockholding became legal, except when they conflicted with Article 9 (prohibition of holding companies) or Article 2 (limitation of stockholding by a financial institution), and when the result of these activities did not limit competition in a market substantially.

3. *Redefinition of Unfair Competition.* Unfair competition and the catch-all clause of the original Article 2–7, which read in part lessening of "competition which is contrary to the public interest," were amended to apply only in six specified cases of "unfair business practices," as indicated in the amended Article 2–7 (see Appendix IV).

4. *Admission of Retail Price Maintenance.* Article 24–2 permitted an entrepreneur "who produces or sells a commodity which is designated by the Fair Trade Commission and the identical quality of which can be easily recognized" to maintain retail prices provided that these commodities were "not used daily by the general consumer."

5. *Modification of the Definition of Unreasonable Restraint of Trade.* The original Article 4, which forbade entrepreneurs from entering into agreements with other entrepreneurs on price and output, restraint of technology, and investment, was eliminated. The reason was that Article 3, which states, "no entrepreneur shall effect private monopolization or shall undertake any unreasonable restraint of trade," covered the areas that came under Article 4 previously.

6. *Total Elimination of Two Articles.* Article 5 (prohibiting the establishment of or becoming a party to a monopolistic organization) and Article 8 (prevention of substantial disparities in bargaining power) were deleted in toto from the act.

7. *Abolition of the Trade Association Act.* The Trade Association Act was abolished, and three clauses, which specified illegal activities on the part of trade associations in the amended Trade Association Act of 1952, were incorporated into the Anti-Monopoly Act as Clauses 1 and 2 of Article 8.

The most significant of the above changes was the first, the legalization of recession and rationalization cartels. Recession cartels were authorized by Article 24–3 when the following conditions were satisfied:

1. The supply-and-demand condition of the commodity in question is unbalanced.
2. The price of the commodity is below the average cost.
3. There exists a possibility of endangering the continued existence of the majority of the firms in the industry.
4. The circumstances are such that the above-mentioned difficulties cannot be overcome by means of enterprise rationalization.

This last point includes improvement of techniques in production, improvement in quality of goods produced, economy of expense, and rationalization of production methods. (The term "rationalization here means both rationalization and "rationalization" as defined in footnote 26, chapter 3).

Faced with such criteria which seemed to defy both definition and calculation on any objective basis, the FTC required the following information on each point listed above in its effort to ascertain if the industry in question did in fact meet these conditions.[12]

1. To prove an unbalanced supply-and-demand condition:
   a. Annual production capacity and output produced, number of cartel members, and quantity imported and exported in the preceding three years.
   b. Quantity of the total goods produced in the industry, the quantity produced by the cartel members, nationwide average rate of operation, nationwide quantity of stock of the commodity, quantity of exports and imports for the preceding six months.
   c. Market price of the commodity for the preceding three years.
   d. Other relevant information.
2. To prove that price is below average cost:
   a. Movement of the wholesale price of the commodity for the preceding six months.
   b. Standard *ex factory* cost of production at the time the cartel was requested.
   c. Other relevant information.
3. To prove danger of bankruptcy:
   a. Number of firms producing the commodity at the time the cartel was requested.
   b. Number of exits from and entries into the industry, and the change of production capacity due to the above, for the preceding six months.
   c. Condition of the industry viewed from the accounting data (profit-loss).
   d. Forecast of the market demand and market condition.
   e. Other relevant information.
4. To prove impossibility of rationalization:
   a. Possibilities of reducing the production cost by means of increased productivity, input cost reduction, reorganization of improvement of production facilities.
   b. Possibilities of reducing cost by reducing overhead and/or sales cost.

[12] FTC's by-laws, Article 3–2. See the *Related Laws Concerning Anti-Monopoly Act (Dokusen Kinshi-hō Kankei-hō)*, Tokyo, 1962.

c. International comparison of price and production efficiency and other relevant information.

It becomes immediately clear, in spite of the FTC's checklist above, that several questions remain unanswered. When, for example, does the FTC decide a specific economic condition is a recession? Whose average cost is below whose, and which price is to be calculated for the industry? Can the FTC, though it has the authority to demand to see the books, ascertain the accuracy of the reports made to them by the industries concerned?

On recession cartels, as was proved shortly thereafter, many of these decisions were made for the FTC by M.I.T.I., which notified the FTC of the decision *post facto*. The FTC, facing this drastic change in policy, clearly showed its strained effort to graft the decision of the Diet to the fading "spirit of the Anti-Monopoly Act":

> As has been pointed out, the Japanese economy depends in great part on international trade. Especially after losing its overseas territories and accumulated capital, the economy failed to rationalize its industries while other nations have made rapid progress.
>
> The Japanese economy is unstable and unbalanced today, and under these circumstances, when a recession deepens, the economy does not have sufficient resiliency to recover. It only invites unnecessary depreciation of industries thus causing a great damage to the national economy.
>
> In view of this fact, as well as the fact that many firms are becoming bankrupt, and in order to avoid spreading the recession to other sectors of the economy, recession cartels must be allowed, though it is against the spirit of the Anti-Monopoly Act.[13]

Tortured phrases and strained logic, seen in regard to the admission of recession cartels, were duplicated in the case of rationalization cartels as well.[14] Article 24–4 of the amended act approved rationalization cartels for the purpose of "effecting technical promotion, quality improvement, cost reduction, efficiency increase and other enterprise rationalization" when the following conditions were met:

1. The cartel does not endanger the interest of the consumer.
2. There is no fear of its unduly destroying the interest of the general consumer and of related entrepreneurs.
3. It is not unjustly discriminative.

---

[13] FTC, *Annual Report of 1953*, p. 3.

[14] On August 7, 1953, Mr. Yuasa of the FTC made a nationwide broadcast in which he informed his listeners that "the original Act formalistically oppressed the industries disregarding reality. Therefore, they are now allowed to limit competition to a degree which will not interfere with your interest." See *Kōsei Torihiki* (September 1953).

4. It does not unreasonably restrict the participation in or withdrawal therefrom.
5. It does not concentrate unduly the production of specific kinds
of products in the hands of a particular entrepreneur, in the event
that the substance of limitation on kinds of products is different
between persons participating in concerted activity.

It should be noted that conditions 1 and 3 are extremely vague and
allow for wide interpretation. Number 5 requires an explanation. It
means that firms in an industry should not "rationalize" by specializing
in one particular commodity by agreement, so that no firm will have a
monopoly or a near monopoly in that commodity. For example, Producer A should not specialize in nylon stockings nor should B specialize
in nylon shirts.[15]

In discussing the "rationalization" cartels, an obvious possibility was
that continued practice of this type of cartel, without strong guidance
by M.I.T.I. to control the total industry investment in rationalized
capacity, might pave the way for future recession cartels. But this
obvious possibility was not raised at this time.

By the end of 1953, under the provisions of the amended Anti-
Monopoly Act, the *so-tan* operation, in effect then in the cotton-
weaving industry, was accorded a recession cartel status. "Rationalization" cartels were authorized in the iron and steel industries, so that
they could import scrap for an agreed on price. In the lathe industry, for
the purpose of increased product specialization, price maintenance was
allowed under the provisions of a "rationalization" cartel.

Although the amendment was termed a "death blow" to the spirit of
the Anti-Monopoly Act by a ranking officer of the FTC, industry
executives and M.I.T.I. officials quickly expressed the view that these
amendments allowing for cartels were still insufficient in realizing the
aims of industries.[16] Also, by the end of 1953, the Export Trade Act was
amended[17] and became the Export and Import Trading Act. Thus,
cartel activities were authorized in the field of importation and in
domestic markets. The amendment, which was said to be for the pur-

[15] This need for an explanation is due to the fact that provision 5 tries to deal
with a cartel in an industry with the concept of market. M.I.T.I. specifically stated in
its *White Paper* that Article 24–4 would enable rationalization by allowing "specialized concentration of production" as a part of concerted activity. The latter policy, as
applied in the machine tool industry and recommended for the automobile industry,
amply shows that what M.I.T.I. had in mind by this clause was to allow specialization of *commodity* by firms by agreement. This was contrary to what the law itself
seemed to say and to what many economists thought the clause meant.
[16] M.I.T.I., *White Paper*, p. 252.
[17] SCAP strenuously objected to this amendment before Japan became independent, as we saw in chapter 3, p. 46.

pose of improving the balance of payments condition, now legalized a few types of dumping, and the price of domestic goods and quantity imported began to be cartelized. Also, the Act Concerning the Preservation of Liquor Tax and Liquor Business Association was enacted to authorize cartel activities among wine (sake) dealers and to empower the competent minister to enforce the cartel which was to practice price fixing and output control.

As is clear from the above, immediately following independence, the anti-monopoly policy was visibly altered in the face of the economic condition which was called "shallow based"[18] and "overheated." The industries knew then that they could depend on the government to act sympathetically toward their continued drive for increased investment. The Gross National Product in real terms had risen 6.3 percent in 1953.[19]

CONTINUED RELAXATION, 1954–1957

The economic condition of Japan during the years between 1953 and 1957 continued to overheat, registering an average annual growth rate of nearly 7.5 percent. Investment, output, and export continued to rise.[20]

Behind the scenes of the rapid growth, the de facto amendment of the Anti-Monopoly Act continued. With 1954 came the enactment of the Act Concerning Promotion of Export Marine Product Industry and the Ammonium Sulphate Industry "Rationalization" and Ammonium Export Adjustment Temporary Measure Act. The former authorized agreements among packers of canned goods on price, output, investment (capacity), and methods of sales. The latter legalized agreements among producers of ammonium sulphate with regard to export of their products.[21] In 1955 the Export and Import Trading Act[22] and the Medium-Small Enterprise Stabilization Act were amended to ease the prerequisite for the formation of cartels and to broaden the scope of

[18] This phrase meant that a minor price decline in the world market threatened the stability of the whole Japanese economy.

[19] Year Book, p. 60.

[20] The real growth rate during this period was uneven. In real terms, the growth rates were 6.7 (1953), 3.3 (1954), 10.3 (1955), 9.0 (1956) and 7.9 (1957). The recession of 1953–54 was responsible for the low rate in 1954. The real value of exports, however, rose steadily. The index (1953 = 100) rose from 133.3 (1954) to 174.1 (1955), 207.9 (1956), and to 231.5 (1957). Tōyō Keizai, Year Book of Economic Statistics, 1962, pp. 62–63.

[21] The latter was to be effective until July 1959.

[22] This second amendment of the Export and Import Trade Act legalized cartels among producers of export goods, and/or among importers—international and domestic—as well as in selling and buying. In short, practically no restraint remained after this amendment as long as the firms involved received consent of the M.I.T.I.

agreements. Furthermore, in these two acts, two changes took place in the procedure for validation of cartels.

First, the provisions requiring the validation of a competent minister and the consent of the FTC were changed to the validation of a competent minister and a mere consultation with the FTC. This, of course, meant that the weight of the FTC in admitting cartels was further reduced to the point of being a mere formality. Second, with respect to cartels for export, the validation requirement was replaced by prenotification, thus reducing official control to a minimum.

Although unnoticed by Japanese economists and journalists, a quiet but significant change in the policy of the government took place sometime in 1955. Until this time the government, through M.I.T.I. officials,[23] had taken an aggressive position against what it considered the restrictive clauses in order that industry might have the freedom necessary for economic growth. But in 1955 the Anti-Monopoly Act was no longer a major force, and the government was in a position to start a serious review of its own policy. The Socialist party, the only contending party, was visibly weaker due to an internal factional dispute. Its performance at the polls seemed to have reached its maximum at around one-third of the Diet seats, while the prospering economic condition seemed to secure the position of the Liberal-Democratic party.

The government, therefore, was becoming bolder and perhaps paternalistic. While the economy was in high gear, from the end of 1955 to 1956, the government succeeded in enacting three more laws drafted by M.I.T.I.: the Coal Industry Rationalization Temporary Measure Act, the Textile Facilities (Capacity) Temporary Measure Act, and the Machinery Industry Promotion Temporary Act. The characteristic distinguishing these laws from earlier ones was that it was the government (M.I.T.I.) that took steps to form the various plans. The acts included a fundamental rationalization, promotion or disposition of capacities of these industries, and direction to the industries concerned to establish cartels by suggestion of the competent minister in order to carry out the plans that the government devised.[24]

In spite of the criticisms leveled against M.I.T.I.'s "willingness to foster blind investments resulting from businessmen's belief that the

---

[23] The position of Minister of M.I.T.I. is considered among Japanese politicians to be the choicest in the cabinet as it carries the largest influence and power. Since the end of World War II, except when the Socialists were in power briefly, the Liberal-Democratic party has awarded this post to its top-ranking party officials. Former prime-minister Ikeda once held this post.

[24] For example, in the case of the coal industry, the government took the initiative in gradually eliminating high-cost mines, annually publishing the coal price, and often intervening in investment policy. A more economic discussion of these aspects of the "rationalization" policy will be taken up later.

government would come to help alleviate the consequences by legalizing cartels," [25] more laws authorizing some form or other of collusive arrangements were enacted in 1957. These acts were the Silk Yarn Manufacturing Facilities Temporary Measure Act, the Small Vessels Transportation Association Act, the Licensed Business Proper Sanitation Maintenance Act, the Electric Industry Temporary Measure Act, and the Medium-Small Enterprise Organization Act. All these acts conferred upon the respective industry a wide latitude in organizing price maintenance cartels, investment and output agreements, and other collusive activities in varied degrees.

As seen above, acts exempting industries from the Anti-Monopoly Act came thick and fast. The number of cartels increased with the number of laws and recommendations permitting them. By July 1957, 150 cartels of several types were in effect, in addition to the several *so-tans* recommended by the M.I.T.I. A breakdown of these cartels according to the law and types of cartel is summarized in Table 6.

A few facts are recognizable immediately from Table 6. The first is that the majority of cartels were concerned with international trade. This concern indicates M.I.T.I.'s contention that the export sector must be protected if Japan was "to survive and to grow." These export cartels in fact authorized dumping "to secure foreign markets and to alleviate the pain of over-supply." The exporters were in many cases dumping goods at prices from 20 to 30 percent less than domestic prices.[26] Some of the major export cartels were in paper, vinyl chloride, chemical fertilizers, cement, steel products, china, chemical fibers, and several fishery product industries.

The operation of the cement export cartel is typical of this group. The industry cartel set the domestic price at $17.50 per ton and the export price at $16.98 per ton. Each member of the cartel was required to pay into the "industry export price adjustment fund" according to the amount each member sold in the domestic market, at the rate of 30 yen per ton. This fund was to be distributed according to the loss suffered by each member's export at the rate of 186 yen per ton exported. Each member received quotas for the domestic market and the export market according to the past record and the joint conditions of these two markets.[27]

The FTC, which had the power to supervise the operation of these

[25] Misonou, *Nippon no Dokusen* (Monopolies in Japan) (Tokyo), p. 112.

[26] Domestic and export prices differed approximately 15 percent in steel products to over 30 percent in chemical fibers according to checks with respective trade associations. The quote is a statement by a Japan Steel Federation official.

[27] For these details, see FTC, *Annual Report of 1957*, "Export-Import Cartels," pp. 93–107.

TABLE 6

Cartels in Effect as of July 1957
Under the Laws Authorizing Them

LAW	TYPES OF CARTELS	NUMBER OF CARTELS	TYPES OF AGREEMENT	NUMBER OF AGREEMENTS
Export-Import Trading Act	Cartel of export merchants	17	Quantity	2
			Price	4
			Quality	2
			Trading Method	2
			Exclusive Exportation (region)	8
			Shipping Method	1
	Export producers' cartel	60	Quantity	16
			Price	33
			Quality	15
			Design	17
			Method of negotiation	2
	Importers' cartel	5	Quantity	1
			Price	1
			Buying Method	2
			Selection of imported items	3
	Exporting producers' cartel	7	Market Share of export	4
			Export Price	3
Ammonium Sulphate Industry Rationalization Act and Export Adjustment Act	Producers' cartel	1	Quantity	1
			Price	1
Medium and Small Enterprise Stabilization Act	Recession cartel	41	Prohibition of increasing output:	
			Capacity	30
			Quantity	33
			Price	5
			Quality	3
			Sales Method	7
Fisheries Products Promotion Act	Recession cartel	7	Common marketing	6
			Quantity	1
Act on the Sake Revenue Maintenance	Recession cartel	8	Quantity	6
			Condition of trading	5
	Retailers' cartel	1	Condition of trading	1

(*Continued*)

LAW	TYPES OF CARTELS	NUMBER OF CARTELS	TYPES OF AGREEMENT	NUMBER OF AGREEMENTS
Textile Industry Capacity Adjustment Act (Duration 5 years)	Producers' cartel	2	Reorganization of capacity	2
Coal Industry Rationalization Act	Producers' cartel	1	Reorganization of inefficient mines & establishment of standard price	1

SOURCE: FTC, *Annual Report of 1957*, pp. 47–48. The number of agreements exceeds the number of cartels as some cartels have more than one agreement.

cartels in name only, stated in 1947 that "though there are differences in the domestic price and the export price, it [cartel activity] is carried out for the purpose of maintaining the level of operation, thus these dumpings must be admitted as a matter of little consequence." [28] Import cartels were of much less importance, since they were usually practiced by importers who wished to limit the quantity imported in order to maintain the price level when the imported goods were sold in the Japanese market.[29]

Second, 41 cartels were authorized as of July 1957 under the provisions of the Medium-Small Enterprise Stabilization Act. This also reflected M.I.T.I.'s ostensible belief that if these firms were left alone, they would repeat the "cycle of overinvestment, cut-throat competition and quality degradation and recession." [30] Thus, during the four years from August 1953 to July 1957, M.I.T.I. invoked its authority to enforce cartel arrangements, mainly price-fixing, 11 times. Its purpose was to protect the industries that it believed were incapable of establishing and keeping cartel agreements due to the large number of participants.[31]

On the other hand, M.I.T.I. was not, it appeared, eager to enforce or initiate the control of investment on a cartel basis. There were exceptional cases, however, such as the match and textile industries, in which it supervised partial reduction of specific types of production capacity.

[28] *Ibid.*, p. 104. This statement was made for the paper export cartel.
[29] Usually export firms in Japan are importers. That is, trading firms deal in both export and import. The rationale of these cartels was said to be to limit the import and assure minimization of excess competition of imported goods.
[30] M.I.T.I., *White Paper*, p. 270.
[31] For example, the match industry, where M.I.T.I. enforced cartel activities, included 103 firms which jointly produced 98 percent of the matches consumed in Japan. The agreements included limitations on investment, shipment, price, method of sales, and control of the quality of the product. *Ibid.*, p. 272.

At the same time the nature of cartels began to change as years passed. Their working arrangements were gradually improved, for example, in the fertilizer industry. By 1957 this industry was able to control monthly output based on the figures recommended by M.I.T.I. The original price and quantity arrangements had grown into an elaborate scheme to calculate each member's output and to fix export and domestic price differentials for the purpose of dumping.

In the steel and iron industry the original agreement on scrap price and acceptance of price leadership of the Yawata Steel Corporation was gradually expanded to include calculation of monthly output of each product for each firm (wire, sheet, and so forth by the type of product produced) and designation of wholesalers who were known to observe the sale price set by producers.

Unlike the fertilizer industry, the steel and iron industry was unable to maintain a tight cartel due to a large number of small fringe producers. The M.I.T.I.-enforced joint scrap buying was observed by all, but the price leadership of Yawata was often disregarded by smaller firms. The practical impossibility of enforcement often compelled the larger firms to reconsider their price.[32] Output control, which lacked any kind of legal foundation, was never observed among the smaller producers, and in the meantime total steel capacity rose to 124 (using 1955 = 100 as the base year).[33]

In the textile industry (an example of cartel activities in the small-scale industries), an increasing degree of control of several kinds had been instituted during the same period. The degree of *so-tan* recommended by M.I.T.I. moved between 20 to 40 percent of the total capacity of the cotton-weaving industry as a whole, according to demand conditions, both domestic and foreign. The price maintenance agreement, however, was soon joined by standardization of product quality, limitation of the types of products each firm could produce, enforced observation of monthly and weekly holidays, and joint buying of raw cotton from abroad.

As in many other small-scale industries, these agreements were kept with the greatest difficulty. It was often necessary to seal participants' machines in order to ensure that they were not used against agreements. Some smaller firms found it more profitable to sell at a lower price than that being enforced by the agreements, especially when a 40-percent (of the total weaving capacity of the industry) *so-tan* was in effect. This

[32] In the Kansai area, several small firms originated price revolts against Tokyo-based large firms.
[33] *Year Book of Economic Statistics*, p. 177.

so-called sales leak (*nukeuri*) was a constant problem in all the small-scale industries.

Through the "hard times" (referring to a few years following the Korean War), some marginal cotton-weaving and related firms were either eliminated by bankruptcies or became subcontractors of large artificial fiber industries, such as nylon and rayon. The capacity in terms of weaving machines showed an appreciable increase during the four year period.[34]

These examples of the iron-and-steel industry and the cotton-weaving industry are the rule rather than the exception.[35] Under the protection of cartel arrangements, capacities in these cartel-practicing industries grew over the years,[36] and each cartel showed a tendency to become more elaborate in degree of control (self-imposed or M.I.T.I. sanctioned) and more extensive in scope of agreements.

Closely following the line of the arguments advanced immediately preceding the 1953 amendment of the Anti-Monopoly Act, M.I.T.I. and industry continued into 1957 to press their points. The ever-present excess capacity and the expanding cartel controls were defended as "a transitional phenomenon, and when the current rationalization is completed, the excess capacity representing the older and less efficient methods of production is to be gradually scrapped." [37] M.I.T.I. maintained that the increased number of cartels was a necessity at this turning point of the Japanese economy (*magarikado ni kita Keizai*).[38] The eagerness of entrepreneurs to increase capacity by rationalization would have to be given full cooperation by the government for the sake of the future. This, M.I.T.I. argued, was especially true when the economy suffered a slump as in 1957–58.

This case was eloquently made in a series of publications and state-

[34] The number of cotton-weaving power-driven machines changed as follows:

Year	1953	1954	1955	1956
Machines (1000)	315	334	375	374

(M.I.T.I., *White Paper*, p. 403.)

[35] As an exception to the rule of M.I.T.I.'s hesitancy to "recommend" reduction of capacity, the artificial fiber industry, especially those firms specializing in the weaving of a mixture of cotton and artificial fibers were "recommended" to "discard" (junk) many out-dated machines based upon agreement among the firms concerned.

[36] The fertilizer industry, for example, which in 1957 practiced extensive dumping and constantly suffered from overcapacity, increased its capacity as we see below:

Year	1951	1953	1955	1957
Capacity (1000 tons)	2,290	2,891	3,110	4,282

(M.I.T.I., *White Paper*, p. 403.)

[37] M.I.T.I., *White Paper*, p. 403.
[38] This is a phrase often heard in conversation with M.I.T.I. officials.

ments by M.I.T.I. and the Japan Productivity Center.[39] Evidence was marshaled to show that Japanese industries could cut the cost of production by rationalizing, which inevitably meant adoption of a larger scale of production than that being used in the Western nations. The M.I.T.I. reiterated its constant faith in the market mechanism which would force gradual and orderly elimination of excess capacity provided by the "old," inefficient methods of production. M.I.T.I. felt that as rationalization progressed through rapid investment, the Japanese economy would no longer be on the "shallow base," and increased capacity on a rationalized basis would constantly increase Japan's exports.[40]

CONCLUSION

The changes, de jure and de facto, in the anti-monopoly policy—the reversal of the spirit and letter of SCAP policy—came in rapid succession during the period from 1953 to 1957. Following the 1953 amendment, which altered the Anti-Monopoly Act fundamentally, the government went on to further weaken and circumvent the amended act.

As the commissioner of the FTC is a political appointee of the prime minister, the former's occasional protests of the extralegal "administrative guidance" were in most cases merely inconveniences which could be quickly solved by "reaching an amicable understanding" between M.I.T.I. and FTC. Even this became increasingly unnecessary as more laws were enacted to limit the jurisdiction of the Anti-Monopoly Act. During this period, the policy of capital accumulation-rationalization-export-growth was carried out with vigor. A brief discussion with business executives and a government official made it clear that the term *Karuteru* (cartel) acquired no more opprobrious connotation than *Geisha*, in spite of intense efforts made by SCAP until only a few years before.

[39] The Japan Productivity Center and M.I.T.I. made a joint study of the efficiency of industries. In many cases, such as coal, steel, fertilizer, machine tools, it recommended industry rationalization in terms of importation of new techniques or much larger units of production. For examples, see Japan Productivity Center, *Kigyō no Kibo ni kansuru Kenkyū Chōsa* (Reports on the Scale of Enterprise) (Tokyo, 1956). This is a series of studies on several industries. The reports are for M.I.T.I. use, but copies are obtainable at M.I.T.I.

[40] In this connection, M.I.T.I. argued, there were too many small firms in Japan. "There are more than three times as many firms in Japan as there are in England which indicates that Japanese industries are structurally conducive to excess competition," fostered by "nearsighted small firms which produce at a loss," and to the detriment of Japanese economic growth. "Excessive competition is most harmful," the M.I.T.I. *White Paper* went on to argue, "when it is carried out in international markets among Japanese firms" (p. 401). It inevitably "undermines the reputation of Japanese industry" to the detriment of Japanese exports, and hence the Japanese economy.

What we have examined in this chapter establishes one clear fact: the economic policy of the Japanese government was clearly dedicated to rapid economic growth. To achieve this end the policy was intended to encourage capital accumulation, to aid firms to rationalize, and to protect them from short-run problems of excess capacity. This growth consciousness of the government, expressed as "needs for larger export and rapid rationalization," [41] also resulted in a large number of cartels, extralegal "administrative" production cut-backs and the constant problem of overheating. We shall observe the course and consequences of this economic policy after 1957 in the following chapter. Then we will be in a position to analyze in chapter 6 the rationale and economic consequences of the policies of the postwar Japanese government.

[41] As it is often the case the government statements used the term rationalization in both senses, i.e., rationalization and "rationalization" as we defined in fn. 26, chap. 3.

5 TOWARD THE PRO-MONOPOLY POLICY, 1958–1965

The index of the inventories of finished manufacturing products rose steadily from 100 in the first quarter of 1956 to 160 by the
middle of 1957. Then, the so-called *Nabezoko* (the bottom of the pan)
recession of 1957–58 began. From a statistical point of view, it could be
interpreted as one of stopping an engine momentarily due to overheating which raised the level of inventory uncomfortably high. Lagging
increases in exports and domestic demand were not able to cool the
overheating engine of the Japanese economy.[1]

In late 1957 the government proposed two laws, the Chemical Industry Promotion Act and the Iron and Steel Supply and Demand Stabilization Act, to "alleviate the condition" of large inventories by means of
legal, open cartels.[2] These bills presented to the Diet, however, had to
be withdrawn. They faced the strong criticism of the agricultural groups,
which commanded an appreciable faction of the Liberal-Democratic
party, and the pressure groups formed by the users of the products of
these industries.

Failing to pass these bills, in December 1957 the Cabinet decided to
make a frontal attack on the Anti-Monopoly Act. Perhaps it also realized that the enactment of these numerous piecemeal laws, exempting
industries from the Anti-Monopoly Act, was an unsatisfactory way of
coping with what the Liberal-Democratic party considered a proper
economic policy. Thus, a council to deliberate possible amendment of

---

[1] For excellent analyses of the postwar cycles, see M. Shinohara, *Growth and Cycles
in the Japanese Economy* (Tokyo: Kinokuniya, 1962), pp. 151–202.

[2] These were two major industries which did not have legalized "open" cartels in
effect. Their index of accumulated stock rose from 130 in 1956 to 232 in 1957, in
the Iron and Steel Industry, and 123 in 1956 and 142 in 1957 in the Chemical
Industry (1955 = 100). *The Chemical Industry Promotion Act* was primarily aimed
at the Ammonium Sulphate industry. Computed from *Year Book of Economic
Statistics*, p. 175.

the Anti-Monopoly Act was chosen under the chairmanship of Professor Nakayama, who recommended the amendment of 1953.[3] The committee, consisting of four economists, one lawyer, two bankers, seven industry executives and one editor of a large newspaper—fifteen in all, appointed by the Government—received the following agenda from M.I.T.I.:

1. Is there any need to widen the scope and to relax the conditions in admitting recession and "rationalization" cartels?
2. Is there any need to admit other types of cartels such as structural recession (to be explained shortly) cartels? If so,
3. Is there any adjustment to be made between the provisions for the cartels to be allowed and the law currently exempting several industries from the Anti-Monopoly Act?
4. If regulations for cartels are changed, what are the means to prevent evil effects (sic) arising out of new cartels?

It was evident that the relaxation of the regulations concerning the cartels was to be the prime topic of deliberation. After an FTC representative made a fervent plea for the status quo and objected strongly to any further relaxation of the Anti-Monopoly Act, M.I.T.I. presented a list of cartels which it wished to be allowed in an amended version of the Anti-Monopoly Act. The M.I.T.I. proposal included:

1. Recession cartels to be allowed with more relaxed requirements, and to include structural recession cartels.
2. "Rationalization" cartels to include agreement on types of products and quantity of each cartel member, and to allow joint input buying on a cartel basis, that is, agreed price and quantity.
3. Cartels for investment adjustment were to be allowed to consider the investment factors in industries.
4. Cartels to stabilize the long-range supply-and-demand condition of major products.
5. Cartels to solidify promotion of exports to permit the following:
   a. Complete control of quantity and price, including domestic markets.
   b. Agreement on market sphere and channels of sales, including domestic markets.
   c. Agreement to insure the purchase of materials needed for export goods at "rational prices."

---

[3] The record of deliberation was made available to me by the FTC. The following discussion is taken from the record. The FTC copy of this record is deposited at the Office Administration, FTC. The document is not paged.

From the statements made by M.I.T.I. officials or in the later discussions of the deliberation council, we gain very little information on some of the cartels proposed. We are told that the structural cartels refer to cartels that would be formed to help declining industries. But the coal and the textile industries, two of the major declining industries, were already under M.I.T.I.'s guidance and there was no other major industry at that time which could be properly termed "declining." What M.I.T.I. meant or how it intended to use structural cartels becomes less clear if we also consider the fact that it had proposed relaxation of "rationalization" cartels.

The proposal for investment cartels is noteworthy. Although at the time of the deliberation M.I.T.I. did not make the content clear, we can discern its intention in advancing this proposal from what it practiced after the failure to amend the Anti-Monopoly Act in 1958. The provision was to guide the investment plans of industries so that the total investment plan of each industry would be coordinated. Large steps of rationalization investment, markedly out of pace with the expected foreign and domestic demand, could be supervised by M.I.T.I. in the name of increased efficiency. The ministry could have recommended these steps earlier if it had so wished; and if a provision for investment cartels had been incorporated in the Anti-Monopoly Act, M.I.T.I. would have had formal authority in its guidance. Increased concern by M.I.T.I. that constant overcapacity, caused by uncoordinated investment on a large scale by competing firms in an industry, would result in increased excess capacity became evident in its publications and public statements around the end of 1958.[4]

The fourth proposal, to allow cartels to stabilize the long-range supply-and-demand condition of the major industries, could be interpreted as M.I.T.I.'s effort to revive the proposals that failed in 1957, that is, the Chemical Industry Promotion Act and the Iron and Steel Supply and Demand Stabilization Act.[5] They also sought to strengthen their guidance of investment with formal authority. Although the intent of M.I.T.I. for this type of cartel was never clearly spelled out, an M.I.T.I. official remarked at one point that, if legalized, these cartels

[4] For example, the 1959 issue of M.I.T.I.'s *Nippon Sangyō no Genjyō* (The Reality of Japanese Industries) examines the need for coordinating investments in terms of econometric analyses, and the earlier tone of open praises for rapid rationalization is noticeably underplayed. The terms such as "balanced growth" and "orderly capacity adjustment" are prominently discussed also in M.I.T.I.'s *Shuyō Sangyō no Setsubi Tōshi Keikaku* (The Plans for Capacity Investment in Major Industries) (Tokyo, 1961).

[5] See chap. 4, pp. 65–66, and fn. 2, this chapter.

would alleviate economic fluctuation and excessive competition and solidify the long-run supply-and-demand condition.

The last proposal, cartels "to solidify promotion of exports," could be considered as an attempt on the part of M.I.T.I. to unify the basis of the cartel granting authority into one law, instead of the numerous acts and recommendations which then existed. This was the proposal that drew the most criticism from the economists and the FTC representatives at the committee hearings.

The record reveals that the discussion, which took ten hearings, revolved around the central disagreement between M.I.T.I.'s attitude that "cartels should be allowed to suit the current economic conditions," and the FTC's position that "cartels of necessary types were already admitted and further relaxation of the Anti-Monopoly Act would result in 'cartel capitalism.'" M.I.T.I. officials, in essence, repeated the same argument noted earlier. They emphasized economic growth and the possibility of controlling the undesirable effects of cartels by the Anti-Monopoly Act. The FTC, on the other hand, reiterated the principle of the Anti-Monopoly Act and stressed that the cartels were to be allowed only as exceptions. It argued that the evil consequences of the already existing cartels were manifest.

The representatives of several sectors of the economy also voiced their views on the future of the anti-monopoly policy of Japan. The representatives of the consumers' associations (*Shohisha Dōmei*) argued that the Anti-Monopoly Act must remain as it was, since, in their minds, it already had been relaxed to a degree which endangered the public interest. They asked the committee to revive Article 4 of the pre-1953 amendment and objected to all the *so-tans* being recommended by M.I.T.I. without express legal foundation.[6] Some representatives requested that detailed activities and names of cartels be published, so that consumers would know which industries were practicing which kind of cartels. All the representatives of the consumer groups sharply attacked all aspects of the proposal of M.I.T.I. as being a measure to sacrifice consumers.

Small business groups also joined the consumers. They stated that the cartels among large firms were exposing them to bankruptcy. One of their spokesmen argued that stubborn opposition of small producers to the cartelizing pressure of the big producers, as in the iron-and-steel industry, was protecting consumers.

On the other hand, the large-firm sectors, the banks, and the financial

[6] See fns. 16 and 17, chap. 3.

institutions strongly favored the M.I.T.I. proposal. They advanced an argument similar to the one made by M.I.T.I. The financial sector in addition argued that agreements on interest rates must be admitted, and that interlocking directorships must become free of legal fetters to protect the interest of creditors. As we examine the record, however, for the first time among the reactions of these groups, we find signs of resentment against M.I.T.I.'s increasing intervention in their affairs. At times they clearly stated that cartels were welcome, providing that they did not mean increased governmental control of their respective industries. A banker made it clear that if an agreement on interest rates was to be admitted, it must be of the uncontrolled type which does not call for extended authority of the Minister of Finance or of the Bank of Japan. He was very specific in denouncing governmental encroachment in their affairs. An industry association representative and an export firm executive were anxious to stress that relaxed cartel provisions should not be accompanied by increased authority of M.I.T.I. to dictate their actions, as they had increasingly experienced in the past few years.

In the ten hearings the committee heard sixty-four opinions, but the record reveals that they restated, though in different hues and tones, the positions of the FTC and M.I.T.I. which were expressed at the outset of the first hearing. The chairman's opinion, expressed at the eighth hearing, seems to indicate the consensus of the disinterested group of the committee. He said:

> In short, considering the state of the Japanese economy and its structure, the main question is: "what type of policy is most suitable?" That is, shall we adhere to the principle of competition or should we allow more cartels, or perhaps trusts, in order to have stable economic growth without friction? This is the basic problem. The Anti-Monopoly Act has been very useful in the post-war reconstruction period in promoting competion, but the current state of excessive competition must be taken into consideration in reaching decisions on this basic question.

The quality of discussion and opinions suffered from the members' constant awareness of political practicability and implications.[7]

After ten hearings, the council recommended considerable further amendment. The following lengthy quotation of the complete recommendation may be justified, since it reflects the thinking of the Japanese government then, as well as today.[8]

[7] See K. Yamamura, "A Few Observations on the Japanese Anti-Monopoly Act," *Kōsei Torihiki* (June 1962). I have criticized this attitude of the Japanese academicians in public hearings. The so-called expert opinions in court cases and merger cases suffer from the weakness stated in the text.

[8] To keep the official tone, no attempt was made to make the style more readable.

RECOMMENDATION

The promulgation of the Anti-Monopoly Act contributed much to the democratization and reconstruction of the economy after the end of the War and should be evaluated highly.

But, under the present condition of the economy of our country, with the fact of excessive competition, and if, in the future, a keener international competition is to be faced, and also considering the long-range stable growth of the economy of our country, the regulation of the present Anti-Monopoly Act cannot necessarily be said to be most suitable for the proper operation of the economy of our country.

Especially if we consider that the maintenance of the order of free competition as synonymous with the interest of the public should be judged from the higher standpoint of the producer, the consumer, and the economy as a whole.

This deliberation council, realizing that there are several basic problems which should be solved before it determines its attitudes in regard to the basic problems in the present Anti-Monopoly Act, and after considering several conditions and especially important points which may be impairing the operation of our economy, has come to believe that the following amendments are necessary in the spirit we have stated above.

In the future, the government should continue examination of the basic problems involved and recommend that proper means be taken in the operation of the Anti-Monopoly Act.

1. *On Recession Cartels.* The condition which allows them, under the present Act, is too severe, and requires much time before admittance and also seems to lack real effects as a measure against recession. Thus, the conditions for recession cartels should be relaxed to include those cases where there is a fear of recession. And in those cases, where there are no evil consequences, cartels should be permitted, requiring prior notification alone as sufficient.

   a. Cartel activities on product quality control, setting standards of products, use of transportation and by-products and scrap, have shown no evil consequences. Therefore, they should be permitted on the basis of prior notification alone.

   b. In addition to the above, if it becomes necessary to make an agreement on production sphere for purposes of specialized products, or to buy raw material cooperatively, or in liquidating excess capacity, cartels should be permitted for the purpose of industrial "rationalization."

   c. In order to prevent the evil of parallel or excess investment, and if it is necessary to assure growth of national economy, cartels must be permitted. Cartels whose purpose is to increase investment, or to adjust it, must be permitted with the consent of the Fair Trade Commission.

   d. If there is a special need for promoting exportation, and it cannot be achieved by other means in specific products, cartel permission should be allowed.

2. *Mergers.* As far as mergers are concerned, the present Anti-Monopoly Act prohibits cartels in those cases where they substantially limit the competition, but in special cases where enlarge-

ment of the scale of production is necessary for rationalization, they should be permitted.

3. *Unfair Trading.*
   a. As cartel regulation is relaxed, those who have superior eco-
      nomic power may abuse their controlling power; thus in order
      to prevent improper influence on the small and weak entrepre-
      neurs, and further to prevent the evil effects of excessive
      competition, it is necessary to clarify the content of the regu-
      lations involved in the unfair trading act, and strict operation
      of it should be made easier.
   b. In addition to the above, in order to prevent the confusion
      arising in the trading order due to the excessive competition,
      and to nurture the favorable custom of trading, the entrepre-
      neurs, on their initiative, should refrain from excessive service
      and unfair competition, and in order to normalize the trading
      conditions, other means to establish the proper regulation to
      promote competition should be established.

The recommendation was submitted to the prime minister in February 1958, and a bill incorporating all these recommendations was presented to the Diet during the 1958 session.[9] However, as soon as the
content of the bill became public knowledge, it faced strong opposition
before formal debate began in the Diet. A united front of opposition
was organized by agriculture, medium-small business groups, trade
unions, consumers, and the Socialist party. Facing this opposition, the
Conservative party, though it possessed an absolute majority, decided
not to bring it to a vote.

One of the reasons for this decision was the fact that the economy as
a whole had taken an upturn. This upturn resulted primarily from
sharply increased exports and the gradual fruition of rationalization
measures in several industries. The optimism of the government then
led to an announcement of the Doubling the National Income in Ten
Years Plan. This was to be accomplished by a growth of 9 percent
annually.[10]

In spite of an upturn in economic health, the steel industry was still
unable to produce at capacity, and claiming excessive competition it
gained permission to practice an open price system late in 1960. The
system was, and is, to allow price leadership of the Yawata Iron and
Steel Corporation, the largest producer, by the administrative authorization of M.I.T.I. Also, the Machine Industry Promotion Act was

---

[9] As of December 1958, 21 *so-tans* (output restrictions) were in effect, by the
recommendation of M.I.T.I., under pertinent acts. The degree of *so-tan* ranged from
51 percent in the chemical fiber industry, to 11 percent in the carbide industry.
Analyst (November 11, 1958).

[10] The Economic Planning Agency, *Kokumin Shotoku Baizō Keikaku* (Doubling
the National Income Plan) (Tokyo: The Ministry of Finance Press, 1961).

amended to allow cartel activities to include production and use of processing facilities. The Fishery Product Adjustment Cooperative Act was enacted, allowing collusive activities in output and methods of shipment and giving the government authority to enforce the cartel agreement among noncomplying members. The number of cartels had been growing since 1958 when economic indicators were showing signs of steady growth and a continued increase in investment and export.

Some recession cartels granted by M.I.T.I. in the 1957–58 recession were continued into 1959 and then into 1961. Industries continued to complain about excessive competition, and M.I.T.I. appeared ever ready to foster cartels for the "sake of economic growth." Many types of cartels also multiplied quickly in the small-medium business sector. If we take a census of cartels in operation in 1960 and 1961, we can count 448 and 477 active cartels respectively in these two years. Table 7 is an abbreviated list of these cartels.

However, the overheating continued to plague the Japanese economy. In spite of the steadily increasing exports and domestic demand, the rate of operation of total capacity in machine tool, paper, textile, petroleum derivatives and chemical fertilizer industries remained near the low level of the 1957–58 recession, due to rapidly continuing investment.[11] Facing this persistent overheating, several industries attempted to limit their total investment. But this so-called self-reliance limitation plan (*Jishu Chōsei*) among firms in respective markets nearly always failed to materialize, due to their inability to reach an agreement on the procedure, degree, and allotment of reduction of investment among them.[12] Firms were constantly fearful of being "out-rationalized" by their competitors, primarily because there was a hope that exports would increase and that their respective domestic market share could be increased if the efficiency of production (cost reduction) were increased. All these firms also knew that, when overinvestment (excess capacity) resulted in M.I.T.I.-guided output restrictions, their market shares would be determined by the total of their respective rated capacity. This was another important reason why *Jishu Chōsei* was difficult and overheating was encouraged.

BEGINNING OF PRO-MONOPOLY POLICY

Observing the repeated failures of the *Jishu Chōsei* plans, and now facing certain liberalization of international trade restrictions in the very near future under the pressure of the General Agreement on Tariffs

[11] See fn. 19, this chapter.
[12] This point is further examined in chap. 6.

and Trade, the government began to discuss, from early 1962, a bill
unofficially entitled A *Bill to Promote International Competitive Ability of Specified Industries.*[13] According to the M.I.T.I. officials, "the

TABLE 7

Cartels Existing in March 1960 and March 1961

ITEM	MARCH 1960	MARCH 1961
Cartels exempted from the Anti-Monopoly Act		
Recession	4	3
Rationalization	5	5
Export-import special statutes		
Export cartels	129	144
Exporters domestic agreements	7	8
Producers domestic agreements	34	39
Import cartels	2	2
Fishery products promotion for export		
Associations	11	10
Buying cartel (*Kaiage-Kikan*)	10	10
Ammonium sulphate	1	1
Small Business Association Act (*Chushō Kigyō Dantai-Hō*)		
Manufacturing associations	108	170
Commercial associations	61	43
Association of small vessels (*Kogata-Kaiun*)	10	12
Coal rationalization	1	1
Emergency measure for textile industry	7	4
Sea transportation acts (*Kaijyō Unso-Hō*)	24	0
Sake Association Act	9	9
Agreements on Industrial Machine Act	1	1
Administrative cartels		
Recommended less than full capacity operation (*So-Tan*)	16	8
Inventory freeze (*Zaiko Tōketsu*)	2	0
Buying association	4	5
Open price sales (*Kōhansei*)	2	2
Total	448	477

SOURCE: From H. Misonou's paper at the Economic Policy Association, Meiji
University, Tokyo, May 26, 1962.

basic thinking of the bill is to introduce a mixed economic system, of a
unique kind to meet the Japanese problems, i.e., the government as the
adjuster [*Chōseisha*] guides the working of the economy in the fashion
as practiced in France and Italy"; and more specifically, the bill, if
enacted, would "actively promote concentration of production and

[13] "The Special Industry Promotion Bill and the Future of the Anti-Monopoly
Act," *Kōsei Torihiki* (May 1963), p. 2. This was a round table discussion.

mergers suppressing excessive competition." [14] This, M.I.T.I. argued, was necessary in the face of the liberalization of international trade which would soon begin. As the spokesman of M.I.T.I., Mr. Morozumi outlined the basic policy of the ministry in the following terms:

> Effective competition is the epitome of perfect free competition, and it aims to achieve the effect of free competition without the defeat of excessive competition . . . existence of numerous small-scale enterprises never contributes to the development of new technology. When an excessive number of firms, for a given market size, are reduced by means of mergers and unification, it will lead to economies of scale and ability to expand into a new technological frontier. This will not limit entry of new firms, but it will demand that the entrants possess a high level of technology and productivity. Rising productivity based upon competition among large-scale firms is the best means of increasing international competitiveness of our industries. [15]

The debate on the wisdom of the bill continued through 1962, while a limited liberalization of international trade began in October 1962. Finally, in early 1963 the cabinet decided that the bill would be presented to the Diet under the official title of the Temporary Promotion of Specified Industries Bill, [16] Article 1 of which read:

> In view of the rapidly changing economic circumstance by the liberalization of international trade and other factors, this law aims to contribute to a wholesome development of the national economy by achieving an advanced industrial structure. To achieve this end, for those industries which are in need of promotion of international competitive ability, measures will be taken to effectuate an increase in the efficiency of industrial activities by means of rationalization of the scale of production and/or administration. [17]

The principal aim of the bill was to authorize mergers among the leading firms in an industry, even in those cases that are not permissible under the existing provisions of the Anti-Monopoly Act. Under Article 7 of the bill, the government "must endeavor to assure funds which are needed for rationalization of scale of production and administration," though this would be in exchange for the authority of the government to coordinate and control investment activities. Article 2 of the bill specified the automobile tire and tube, iron and steel, and chemical industries [18] as the initial group which was to be promoted.

[14] *Ibid.*, p. 2.

[15] Y. Morozumi, "A Proposal by M.I.T.I.," in T. Chigusa, ed., *Sangyō Taikei no Sai-hensei* (A Reorganization of Industrial Structure) (Tokyo: Shunjyū Publishing Co., 1963), p. 65. Mr. Morozumi is the chief of the Industry Section of M.I.T.I.

[16] *Kōsei Torihiki* (May 1963), p. 4.

[17] This has been translated from a mimeographed version of the bill made available to me by Mr. Misonou.

[18] Petrochemical by-products and medical products are excluded.

Facing the increasing liberalization of international trade, the large corporations were now anxious to see some basic changes made in the anti-monopoly policy. Also, it was clear that the burden of excess capacity in the major industries was increasingly felt by the large corporations as they planned ambitious investment.[19] But large corporations in all major industries, except the steel industry,[20] were still unwilling to accept the control-and-coordinate provision of the bill. However, they welcomed relaxations on merger restrictions, the possibility of low-cost government loans, and other de facto relaxations of the Anti-Monopoly Act, which would be accomplished by the enactment of the bill. The large firms, ostensibly fearing the revival of the prewar-like government control, argued for the enactment of laws to meet the specific needs of each industry [21] for the sake of promoting international competitive ability of Japanese industries.[22]

However, it was made clear by Mr. Kodo of the *Keidanren* [23] that the

[19] The following data on excess capacity are informative. If we take the index of the capacity of all industry in 1955 to be 100, we find it increased from 127 in 1957 to 205.8 in 1961, while the rate of operation in the respective years was 80.1 and 85.5 percent of the total capacity. The rate of operation of the heavily cartelized chemical fertilizer industry was, for example, 67.5, while capacity index increased from 127.2 in 1957 to 181.2 in 1961. The amount of absolute excess capacity of course has risen quite rapidly. An M.I.T.I. *White Paper* reports that the rate of operation of all industry is approximately 67 percent of total capacity. M.I.T.I., *White Paper* (1963), p. 80.

[20] The steel industry has been one of the industries in which the *Jishu Chōsei* plan was attempted, and that the two largest firms were products of the prewar Nippon Seitetsu, which was divided by the SCAP, and that the products are homogeneous could be considered as the major reasons for this behavior.

[21] *Kōsei Torihiki* (May 1963), p. 2.

[22] One of the consequences of excess capacity is the increasing ratio of capital costs to value added in manufacturing industries, as we see below. (This is due, in part, to relatively high interest costs and a high ratio of borrowed capital to owned capital, *Kariireshihon* over *Jikoshihon*.) The following data are from S. Tsuru, "Formal Planning Divorced from Action: Japan," in E. E. Hagen, *Planning Economic Development* (Irwin, 1963), p. 147. Professor Tsuru's figures are based on those of the Bank of Japan.

Ratio of Capital Costs to Value Added
in Manufacturing Industries

	Depreciation	Interest Charges	Total Capital Costs *
1955: Second half	14.5	13.1	27.5
1956: First half	14.5	11.2	25.7
1957: Second half	13.6	10.2	23.8
1960: First half	16.1	13.3	29.5
1960: Second half	16.5	13.6	30.0
1961: First half	18.3	13.8	32.0
1961: Second half	18.2	14.9	33.1

* Decimal figures may not agree because of rounding.

[23] Though the official title of the organization is known as *Keizai Dantai Rengō-Kai* (The Federation of Economic Associations), *Keidanren* is a commonly

large corporate sector favored a further amendment of the Anti-Monopoly Act, instead of the piecemeal legislation of the pending bill which he was certain could easily be transformed into a policy of bureaucratic control.[24] His argument was based on the following grounds:

> The industries must carry out reorganization of industrial structure by means of merger, especially in those products which will increase the efficiency of production by attaining a large scale. This, however, must be accomplished by the autonomous efforts of the industries themselves. To realize this goal, the prime need is to eliminate all hurdles now hindering the efforts of the industries. That is, the present Anti-Monopoly Act must be amended and all types of necessary cartels for the purpose of achieving rationalization, joint ventures and capital accumulation must be permitted.[25]

Thus, instead of the bill, Mr. Kodo advanced the following seven-point program of the *Keidanren*:[26]

1. Relax conditions pertaining to the admission of recession cartels.
2. Legalize cartels to eliminate excessive competition.
3. Significantly relax conditions pertaining to the admission of rationalization cartels.
4. Legalize cartels for the purpose of permitting a wider scope of domestic price, output, quality, and design cartels.
5. Eliminate all restrictions governing interlocking directorships and shareholding.[27]
6. Relax restrictions pertaining to mergers, to permit mergers for rationalization, even in those cases where the result would bring about a firm or firms with a "decisively large market share."[28]

---

used abbreviation for this powerful politico-economic association of leaders of large corporate and financial sectors of the Japanese economy.

[24] R. Kodo, "Sangyō yori no Ichi-Teian" (A Proposal from the Industry) in Chigusa, T. ed. *Sangyō Taikei no Sai-hensei* (A Reorganization of Industrial Structure) (Shunjyū Publishing Co., 1963), p. 116.

[25] *Ibid.*, p. 134.

[26] *Ibid.*, pp. 131–132.

[27] The Anti-Monopoly Act, as amended, prohibits interlocking directorship and shareholding only when "it substantially lessens the competition"; this, therefore, restricts, for example, a firm buying from a "controlling" share of its competitor.

[28] The term *rationalization* in this paragraph is used loosely to cover both "rationalization" and rationalization, as defined in fn. 26, chap. 3. Mergers which "substantially lessen competition" are still prohibited by the amended Anti-Monopoly Act. In the past there were three major hearings on three cases of mergers involving the largest firms in the dairy products, heavy machinery, and chemical fiber markets, but in all cases the FTC granted permission to merge. However, these required processes of hearings in mergers involving large firms still function as an important deterrent.

7. Abolish all regulations prohibiting holding companies for the purpose of stabilization of management and the financial structure to contribute significantly to the economic future of the nation.[29]

As expected, the Socialist party bitterly attacked the bill as a scheme to revive monopolies and initiated a public campaign against the rising prices which the party claimed were due to monopolists.[30] In this view, Mr. Giga argues that "The monopolistic enterprises of this nation, under the guise of rationalization and improvement of financial structure and in the name of 'New Industrial Order,' aim to achieve a higher economic concentration. Their main interest is to use the functions of the government for their profit in the name of promoting the international competitive ability of Japanese industries." [31] Mr. Misonou expressed in numerous articles his fear that the bill, if enacted, would mark the beginning of an increasing number of regulations and it would inevitably "restrict free entries by legal sanction to create the so-called new industrial order," which he felt would create "a prewar-like economic structure." [32] As these discussions continued, in September 1963 the Arisawa Commission, which was appointed by the M.I.T.I., released its long awaited findings after nearly two years and numerous expert witnesses.[33] The findings and recommendations, however, were disappointing [34] to all concerned. The commission proposed a cooperation policy in lieu of the guidance policy of the M.I.T.I. For example, commenting on investment, it stated:

> This policy emphasizes that decisions on investments be made by representatives of industries, finance, the government and the

[29] Article 9 of the Anti-Monopoly Act as amended reads: "The establishment of holding companies shall be prohibited," and articles 10 and 11 still effectively prohibit de facto holding companies by restricting shareholding of financial institutions.

[30] In the subsequent general election held in November 1963, the Socialist party made the rising prices a major issue. The price level moved as follows in the previous six years:

Year	1958	1959	1960	1961	1962	1963
Consumer Price Index	100.0	101.3	105.1	112.5	115.6	123.0

SOURCE: *Ekonomisuto* (Tokyo, last week of December issues, 1958–1963). (This weekly carries a series on Indexes of Economic Conditions.)

[31] S. Giga, "Recent Industrial Concentration in Japan," *Kōsei Torihiki* (February 1964), p. 14.

[32] H. Misonou, "Han-Dokusen no Tachiba yori" (From the Anti-Monopoly View) A *Reorganization of Industrial Structure, op. cit.*, p. 91.

[33] M.I.T.I., *Sangyō Kōzō Chōsakai, Sangyō-Taisei-Bukai Hōkokusho* (The Arisawa Commission Report) (Tokyo, September 1963) (a mimeographed advance copy).

[34] *Ekonomisuto* (July 9, 1963), p. 14.

neutral groups—all participants of equal weight. Unlike the *Jishu Chosei* plans and the government's "control and coordinate" guidance policy, all participants will set the basic guidelines and establish standards of investment jointly. Once the decision is made under this plan, industry, financial sectors, and government are expected to endeavor to implement the decision made. The government is expected to take measures to aid the realization of the joint decision by tax, fiscal policies and other means at their command.[35]

The commission concluded that: "The central aim of this cooperation policy is for the industry and the government to realize that they share responsibility in the economic activity of today and to move towards formulation of a proper course of the economic policy to be followed in the spirit of cooperation." [36] The policy was severely criticized by industry and the Socialist party for its academic approach, with little chance of practical and political feasibility. M.I.T.I. did little to conceal its disappointment in the failure of the Arisawa Commission to support its guidance policy.

The object of this heated debate—the Temporary Promotion of Specified Industries Bill—was not reported out of the Commerce and Industry Committee of the Diet because, as one member of the committee put it, "no one but the M.I.T.I. officials came to ask for it." [37] It was evident that, as was the case with the 1958 attempt to amend the Anti-Monopoly Act, the leadership of the Conservative party decided not to force the bill since opposition, especially that of the large corporate sector, was strong. Also, as there was then already talk of dissolving the Diet, it was politically unwise, the party leaders must have reasoned, to supply the Socialist party with political ammunition.

In the spring of 1964 the Conservative party, which continued to remain in power after the successful election held in November 1963, still faced a familiar set of problems. But later in 1964 a merger among Mitsubishi Heavy Industry, New Mitsubishi Heavy Industry, and Mitsubishi Shipbuilding was permitted, in spite of the fact that the merged firm had the largest market share in five important heavy industry products, including shipbuilding, and the second largest in the truck and bus markets. The new firm now possessed assets exceeding four times the assets of the nearest competitor in those lines.[38] In 1964 the Ministry of Finance announced that it would continue to find ways to provide loans for the 100 to 150 largest corporations for the sake of "balancing

[35] *The Arisawa Commission Report*, p. 49.
[36] *Ibid.*, p. 50.
[37] "The Special Industry Promotion Bill and the Future of the Anti-Monopoly Act," *Kōsei Torihiki* (May 1963), p. 2.
[38] *Nippon Keizai Shimbun* (April 21, 1964).

future economic growth." [39] Furthermore, a high-ranking M.I.T.I.
officer stated that the cabinet might attempt to amend the Anti-
Monopoly Act in the near future.[40]

In June 1965, with the personal blessing of the Minister of International Trade and Industry, Nissan Automobile and Prince Automobile—second and seventh largest in the industry [41]—merged to create
the largest automobile producer in Japan. Facing the recession of 1965,
the powerful *Keidanren* took the initiative to "remold the basic structure of the economy" which would require "a serious reexamination of
the Anti-Monopoly Act and the elimination of the tendency of government to intervene in the activities of private firms which ought to be
free." [42]

The prospects of the Anti-Monopoly Act, as can be surmised from
the above, are in serious doubt. Mr. Kitajima, the newly appointed
commissioner of the FTC, stated upon assuming his post in September
1965:

> The greatest problem which the Japanese economy today faces is
> the current recession. Cartels, which are called the offspring of re-
> cession, have increased rapidly in number, attesting to the severity
> of the current recession. Active reorganization of firms and the
> formation of cartels are to be expected in a recession as inevitable.
> However, the distinguishing characteristic of the current recession
> is that it is, to a large extent, due to excessive investment. When we
> realize that the results of excessively competitive investment in the
> past are the cause of today's difficulties, we cannot fail to reexamine
> candidly the mechanism of excessive investment activities. A cartel
> is not God, the Almighty, who can suppress recessions. Recession
> cartels, though they can function as modifiers of supply-demand
> conditions temporarily, can neither increase effective demand, nor
> function as a booster of economic conditions. Recession cartels are
> no more than first aid for a recession. *It is hoped that the elimi-
> nation of structural factors contributing to the recession will be
> accomplished by positive measures to revitalize and to rationalize
> industry through the joint efforts of the government and the
> public.*[43]

This is perhaps the best review of the government policy by a government official. Though Mr. Kitajima did not elaborate, the last sentence
of the above quotation indicates that the FTC is ready to continue to

[39] *Ibid.* (May 18, 1964).
[40] H. Tsuchihara, "Views on the Mitsubishi Merger," *Kōsei Torihiki* (February
1965), p. 23.
[41] *Asahi* (June 1, 1965).
[42] *Asahi* (May 31, 1965).
[43] Takeo Kitajima, "Upon Assuming the Commissionership," *Kōsei Torihiki*
(September 1965), pp. 2–3. (Emphasis added.)

accommodate the pro-monopoly policy of the government, as championed by M.I.T.I.

CONCLUSION

In spite of M.I.T.I.'s ostensible belief that the need for cartels is transitory,[44] what we have observed in this chapter shows that cartelization continued at a fast pace in booms and in recessions. As perceptive readers might have noted already in chapter 4, this has in fact been a ubiquitous feature of the postwar Japanese economy. By means of fixed prices and other means, cartels were effective in aiding industries at times of overheating, generally in boom periods. Firms were, one might say, not unwillingly caught in a mechanism built by the growth-minded policy-makers. Once they joined the race for rationalization, aided by cartels and a set of tangible and intangible aids of the government, they continued to overinvest, but again not unwillingly.

In addition to the desires of firms to out-rationalize their competitors, hopefully to increase or at least to maintain their market share and to enjoy a larger share in export markets, there was an assurance that more elaborate and effective cartels would come to rescue their collective and planned overinvestment. M.I.T.I., however, provided more than an assurance. Those who lagged in overinvestment—for reasons of sound financing (not depending on loans too heavily) or conservatism in estimating the future—would be punished. This punishment would come in the form of a reduced relative market share as M.I.T.I. and cartels invariably chose to restrict output by an equal percentage of respective rated capacity. Cartels in effect were used to reward those firms that overinvested and to punish those that failed to do so.[45] As we

---

[44] See fn. 37, chap. 4.

[45] Though other theoretical explanations will be provided in chapters 6 and 10, it is perhaps helpful to add the following at this point. Given the policy goal of rapid growth, one could consider that the sustained overinvestment in Japan was analogous to channeling savings to public works in order to achieve full employment. In the Japanese case the historically high rate of saving and those forced savings (to be seen in chapters 8 and 9) were absorbed for persistent overinvestment to achieve the policy goal.

A simple framework to be visualized here is that of Professor Evsey Domar's well-known discussion in chapter 4 of his *Essay on the Theory of Economic Growth* (New York: Harper, 1957). In his model a is the marginal propensity to save and the Keynesian "multiplier" is $1/a$. Thus $(dI/dt)/a$ yields the "multiplier effect" of increased investment (I = investment, t = time period). Then, what he calls the "output effect" is expressd as $I\sigma$ where σ is the average productivity of investment. To obtain an equilibrium path, the "output effect" and the "multiplier effect" must be balanced, i.e., $I\sigma = (dI/dt)/a$. The solution for this differential equation is $I = I_o e^{a\sigma t}$. Here, if $I > I_o e^{a\sigma t}$, this unequilibrated path further causes I to increase. For a more extended examination on this point, which will be restated in chapter 10 in a more intuitive form, see Kozo Yamamura, *Monopolies and Competi-*

have observed in this chapter, such a course led to the need for various forms of increased insurance and encouragement from the government under real or ostensible pressures facing giant firms, be it the pressure of liberalization of international trade, the burden of absolute amount of excess capacity, or "the need for financial reorganization."

In sum, one could perhaps conclude that the growth-oriented policy has been to encourage overinvestment and to protect the resulting excessive competition by cartels. These cartels encouraged further overinvestment which in turn demanded and received more protection. At the early stage, this cycle was relatively painless and even desirable,[46] but when this cycle began to generate an increased concentration to the point of accommodating monopolies and near-monopolies (and attending effects of concentrating market power), one was faced with the problem of reevaluating the policy that generated such cycles. In the next chapter, we shall examine the "mechanism of excessive overinvestment activities"—in Mr. Kitajima's words quoted earlier—and analyze its functions and consequences to pave the way for our evaluation of the growth-oriented policy.

---

tion in Postwar Japan, unpubl. Ph.D. thesis (Northwestern University, 1964), chap. 7.

[46] This term will be discussed further in chapter 10.

6

THE VISIBLE HAND AND STRUCTURAL CHANGES

INTRODUCTION

In the preceding chapters, we have examined the rapidly chang-ing Japanese anti-monopoly policy since 1953. In slightly more than a decade the original Anti-Monopoly Act underwent fundamental revi-sions. In 1965, the major concern of the government was no longer to relax the anti-monopoly policy, but rather to encourage a more concen-trated market structure. With the hindsight of nearly twenty years, the purpose of this chapter is to ask: How did the structure of the manufac-turing market change and to what extent did the attitude of the govern-ment influence its course? These are large questions which seek to evaluate the role and rationale of the government policy which has come to foster an increasingly concentrated market structure.[1]

The basic data used in this chapter are the concentration ratios of 53 selected markets.[2] With the frequently discussed shortcomings of the ratio as an indicator of the market structure in mind, we can only outline the changes in the market structure. These changes will be observed in two phases. Phase I will encompass the period between 1950 and 1958, and Phase II will cover the period since 1958. The justifica-tion for this division will be provided in the course of these observations. The 53 sample markets are chosen from the publications of the Japanese Fair Trade Commission (JFTC), on the basis of availability of the data required for our analysis.[3]

[1] Professor Robert Barckley's critical comments in the early stage of this chapter are most gratefully acknowledged.

[2] These concentration ratios are in terms of total value shipments in yen by a firm divided by the total value of shipments in a market. The latest concentration ratios available are for 1962.

[3] From a list of 64 markets for which time-series data of concentration ratios are available for the period between 1950 and 1962, these 53 sample markets were

Perhaps any attempt to evaluate the role of the government in the structural change of the market is an attempt to isolate that which cannot be isolated. How much of the observed change is due to economic forces operating in postwar Japan and how much to the policy? However, as we examine repeated public statements of the policy rationale made by government officials and the active means taken to implement it, we can begin to assess the weight of the policy on structural change. This chapter will argue that the hand of the government has been and is becoming increasingly visible. Our task is to see it in the proper perspective of the rapidly growing postwar Japan.

PHASE I (1950–1958)

To acquaint ourselves with the general pattern of concentration in this phase, Table 8 presents the number of markets, classified according to the degree of market concentration for the ten largest firms in 1950 and in 1958. As can be seen, a large number of the sample markets

TABLE 8

Number of Markets in Respective Levels of Concentration Ratios
at Ten-Largest-Firm Level in 1950 and 1958

RATIOS	50 OR BELOW	50–60	60–70	70–80	80–90	90–100 *	TOTAL
Number of markets							
in 1950	8	3	3	5	11	23	53
in 1958	7	8	5	5	8	19	52 †

* Those markets in which the concentration ratio reached 100 before the ten-largest-firm level were included in the 90–100 group.

† Concentration ratios for one market (rayon fabric) are not available for 1958.

SOURCE: FTC, *Nippon Sangyō Shūchū no Jittai* (The Reality of Industrial Structure) (Tokyo, 1957); and *Shuyō Sangyō ni okeru Seisan Shūchū-do* (Degree of Concentration in Major Industries) (Tokyo, 1960).

are highly concentrated. For example, more than half of these markets have ratios exceeding 80 in both 1950 and 1958. Using the Kaysen-Turner classification, which classifies a market as a Type I oligopoly when the first eight firms control 50 percent of the market share, 41 markets in 1950 and 39 in 1958 belonged in this category.[4]

---

chosen on the basis of (a) having sufficient information on the growth (output) to enable the examination required in this chapter and (b) having information on cartel and "rationalization" activities. As seen in Appendix I, the sample covers divergent sectors of the manufacturing market and, in the judgment of the writer, represents the general trend of the manufacturing markets.

[4] Type I oligopoly markets were defined by Kaysen and Turner as those markets in which "recognition of interdependence by the leading firms is extremely likely, and

For example, does the fact that the number of markets having ratios over 80 was reduced from 34 in 1950 to 27 in 1958 indicate that there was a deconcentrating trend in market structure during the period? To ascertain the changes in the market structure of that period, time-trend equations in the form of $C = a + bT$ were calculated, where C is the concentration ratio and T is time at the largest, three-largest-, five-largest-, and ten-largest-firm levels.[5] The result of this calculation is shown in Appendix I with t-values of time-trend coefficients; Table 9 gives a summary of the calculation.

TABLE 9

Signs of Regression Coefficients of
Trend Equations of Concentration Ratios
in 53 Markets (1950–1958)

FIRM LEVEL OF CONCENTRATION	NEGATIVE COEFFICIENTS	t-TEST SIGNIFICANT *	POSITIVE COEFFICIENTS	t-TEST SIGNIFICANT *
Largest †	39	26	14	4
Three largest	37	23	13	3
Five largest	36	20	13	3
Ten largest	27	13	17	8

* At the probability level of .05. The total of negative and positive coefficients do not add up to 53 except at the largest-firm level since some markets reached the concentration ratio of 100 before the 3-, 5-, or 10-largest firm level.

† In 26 markets the largest firm in 1950 was no longer the largest in 1958. Among the ten largest firms, ranking changed frequently and changes were considerably more pronounced among the smaller firms of the ten largest groups. See Table 13.

For the largest firms, the trend coefficients are negative in a large number of markets (26). The coefficients are significant at the probability level of .05 when a t-test is made. This deconcentrating tendency, however, is weaker as we reach the ten-largest-firm level, where we observe 27 that are negative—though still over half of the sample markets—and only 13 of them are significant by the same t-test. When positive regression coefficients are counted, we find that they are found in less than one-third of the sample markets for all four levels; and the

the 75 percent share of the first twenty sellers makes it likely that the response of the smaller sellers will not limit the behavior of the larger firms." C. Kaysen and D. F. Turner, *Anti-Trust Policy* (Harvard University Press, 1959), p. 27.

[5] The JFTC calculated the concentration ratios at these levels. The main reason, the writer conjectures, is that this reflects the common Japanese practice of referring to large objects by saying "Big Three," "Big Five," and "Big Ten." An expression such as *Ote jyutsha* (ten largest firms) is a common expression which has long been in use.

largest number of positive coefficients are observed at the ten-largest-firm level. In other words there has been a visible tendency to equalize the market share among the ten largest firms in these markets during Phase I.

What accounts for these changes in the market structure? Although a comprehensive answer can be obtained only after a thorough examination of each market for relevant variables, it is possible to suggest several factors as possible reasons for the observed changes. The first to be considered—perhaps the most important—is the rapid rate of absorption of new technology which has taken place during Phase I.

As is seen in the data in Appendix I, those industries whose time-trend coefficients were negative for the period for the largest, three-largest, and five-largest firms [6] included such industries as rayon fibers, vinyl chloride, synthetic fibers, sodium hydroxide, ammonium sulphate, synthetic dyes, superphosphate, pulp, cement, ferroalloys, steel vessels, bearings, automobile tires and tubes, pig iron, coal tar, and electric copper.[7] These are the industries, as available studies on technological change in these industries amply document, that underwent the most rapid rate of absorption of new technology.[8]

Before an attempt can be made to explain the observed changes in market structure, it should be stressed that the long-run average cost curves used for the purpose of the following exposition (Diagram 1 on p. 93) are drawn to reflect what the author concluded was the case applicable to most of the postwar Japanese industries. This conclusion is based on a series of intensive queries of industry executives and engineers which the author conducted in major industrial cities in Japan (1961–62), on a massive study conducted under the auspices of the Ministry of International Trade and Industry (M.I.T.I.),[9] and on numerous other published studies.

---

[6] Coefficients are either positive or negative at the ten-largest-firm level.

[7] Markets such as coal and sugar, which are government controlled or nearly entirely dependent on raw material from abroad, are exceptions. Such markets as cotton yarn and *sake* are small scale, low concentration industries. (Cotton yarn, 18.0; *sake*, 7.2 at the ten-largest-firm level in 1958).

[8] Among many available publications on the technological innovation and consequent increase in productivity, the most comprehensive examination is found in *Keizai Seichōka no Rōdō Seisansei* (Labor Productivity in the Growing Economy), published by the Statistical Bureau, the Ministry of Labor (Tokyo, 1961). This study contains detailed statistical examinations of all industries, except electric copper, mentioned in the text. Also M.I.T.I., *Sangyō Gōrika Hakusho* (White Paper on Industrial Rationalization) (Tokyo, 1957) contains detailed examinations of rationalization of the industries mentioned in the text.

[9] M.I.T.I., *Sangyō Kōzō Chōsakai* (The Industrial Structure Commission) (September 1963) (a mimeographed copy). This report is often called *The Arisawa*

The M.I.T.I and other studies presented data and information that confirmed many of the findings made by the author: (1) long-run average cost curves are reverse J-shaped rather than U-shaped; (2) technological "lumpiness" invariably existed, that is, more efficient (cost-reducing) new technological development was exceptionally rapid in postwar Japan as it was imported.[10]

Based on the findings of this available evidence, we can perhaps view the impact of rapid technological change on the structure of the market in the following terms. In a market, firm A adopts new technology, say $f_1(P)$, with a minimum of time lag. Then firm B, or possibly A again, adopts a newer, more efficient technology, $f_2(P)$, which is even more efficient than $f_1(P)$. This again is copied within a brief period by other firms in the market.

During the period under question (1950–1958), very little or no monopoly of technology existed, unlike the prewar years when only the giant Zaibatsu firms enjoyed access to new technology, imported or domestic. In postwar Japan, "adoption of new technology meant copying of existing Western technology which was readily accessible with a large backlog."[11]

Although dating technological changeover is at best a hazardous task

---

Commission Report, since Professor T. Arisawa headed the commission which heard the testimony and opinions of nearly two thousand economists, executives and engineers over a period of two years.

[10] The M.I.T.I. study, *op. cit.*, pp. 10–11, shows the results of its analysis of the long-run average cost curves of eight industries over time. They are all reverse J-shaped and horizontal after respective point of outputs. The sources cited in fn. 8, especially the M.I.T.I. *White Paper*, pp. 297–472, are rich in data. These sources also make it clear that new technology was invariably "lumpy" and more capital intensive. For example, the M.I.T.I. study, cited in the preceding footnote, found that out of 1,036 large firms (with capital assets of over 50 million yen) 841 were found to have enlarged their scale solely to achieve cost reduction by new technology; only 52 firms (5 percent) were found to have expended their capacity without relation to increased efficiency; and others (13.7 percent) enlarged their scale for mixed reasons including the adoption of new cost-saving technology. The rapidity of diffusion of new technology is an interesting story in itself. Along with detailed descriptions in the M.I.T.I. *White Paper*, pp. 297–472, a reading of various trade journals will convince anyone that, as one executive of a machine tool firm put it, "six months is just about the maximum of your advantage before your competitor adopts the new technology, too." An incident that resulted in the arrival of representatives of four large chemical firms in Rome on the same day for the purpose of royalty negotiations with an Italian firm has been widely publicized.

[11] Since the invasion of Manchuria (1931) up until the end of World War II, Japan was isolated from international technological innovation, and there was a backlog of technology to be adopted when the Korean War boom started. By 1953, demand and capital conditions improved sufficiently to undertake a new series of more up-to-date innovations. For the number of cases of "importation of technology agreement" (controlled by the foreign currency restriction law) for 1950–1956, see M.I.T.I.'s *Sangyō Gōrika Hakusho*, p. 132.

of estimating the time when a relatively large amount of technological diffusion has taken place,[12] a careful examination of available data and information leads to observation that, in a large number of industries, the transition from $f_1(P)$ to $f_2(P)$ took place during and immediately following the Korean War and from $f_2(P)$ to $f_3(P)$ in 1954–1956. It goes without saying that the speed of technological diffusion and the peak period of diffusion differed from industry to industry. For example, in the textile industry many firms changed over to the "pattern method," which was considered outdated by English mills before the beginning of World War II, to take advantage of the sudden increase in demand which took place during the Korean War boom. Starting in 1953, however, the larger firms in the industry began to adopt, literally en masse, U.S. technology (the automated rubber-roller method, automatic spooler, and so forth), which was more efficient and more capital intensive, on the strength of the large profits earned during the Korean War boom. Even in those industries such as steel, cement, ammonium sulphate, and others in which technological transition is less marked, an M.I.T.I. white paper stated, "it is easily discernible that up until 1950 a period of modernization of existing capacity existed, and since 1950 strip-mill and other Western methods began to be adopted." [13] This phase of technological adoption ended by 1956.

The preceding serves as an explanation for the deconcentrating trend observed in Table 9 for the ten largest firms, but it begs a critical question. Why did not the firm(s) that adopted $f_2(P)$ before others in the market, and thus that were presumably more efficient (lower cost) producer(s), eliminate or squeeze out the less efficient, that is, the firms still on $f_1(P)$? The answer is that it was essential to introduce cartels which were practiced extensively by manufacturing industries after 1951, at first illegally (but with the tacit approval of the government) and later legally after the large-scale amendment of the Anti-Monopoly Act in 1953, as we have seen in preceding chapters. For the sake of facilitating the following analysis, let us classify firms employing over 1,000 persons as large, from 100 to 999 as medium, and less than 100 as small.[14]

---

[12] Studies available, such as Edwin Mansfield's "Size of Firm, Market Structure, and Innovation," *Journal of Political Economy*, LXXI (December 1963), pp. 556–567, are usually in terms of "domestic" innovation. If new technology is mostly "imported" as in the case of postwar Japan, especially during Phase I, the task of dating technological diffusion is made relatively easier.

[13] M.I.T.I., *White Paper*, pp. 60–61. Also see pages cited in fn. 10.

[14] M.I.T.I. classifies firms employing less than 30 as "small," 30–500 as "medium," and over 1,000 as "large." But for an analysis of market concentration,

Suppose that one of the large firms has just made a transition from $f_2(P)$ to $f_3(P)$ in a market (Diagram 1). It is theoretically possible to set a price at any level between P_6 and just below P_5 in order to squeeze out firms still on $f_2(P)$. However, this practice was not adopted for two reasons. One is that in those cartels operating under government sanction the official policy during this period forbade it as having "monopolistic aspirations." The government, which at this stage (before the 1958 recession) hoped to encourage as many large firms as possible to participate in the race for rationalization, could and did use its power of persuasion, backed by the loan policy (via the Bank of Japan) and its power to withhold allocation of foreign currency (mostly U.S. dollars) needed by disobedient firms to buy raw material from abroad.[15] The other is the fact that scale 6 firms often found themselves operating at

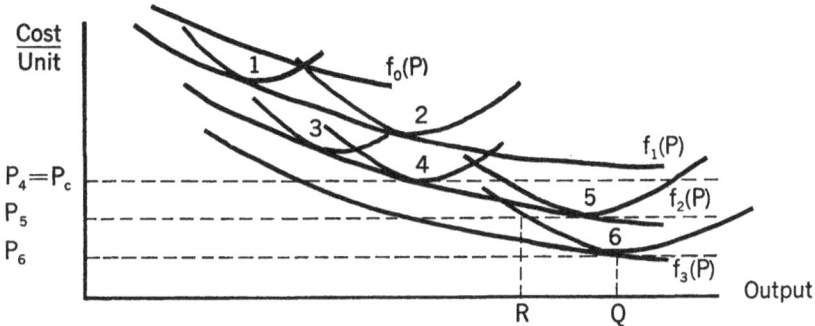

Diagram 1. The Patterns of Rationalization

below the optimum point Q, and at times quite close to R. This was the usual case, especially when the transition to $f_2(P)$ had just been accomplished. This is because the enlargement of scale due to the adoption of new and usually "lumpy" technology was, in postwar Japan, anticipatory; that is, capacity was increased with the hope of increasing exports and domestic demand.[16] In such a case, scale 6 firms were more than

600-odd firms (as of 1958) employing at least 1,000 were the firms which could be considered to be actively in the race for rationalization. (See Table 10.)

[15] Though in different contexts, professors Patrick and Lockwood described these "powers of persuasion" of the government. See William W. Lockwood, "Japan's 'New Capitalism'" and Hugh T. Patrick "Cyclical Instability and Fiscal-Monetary Policy in Postwar Japan," both in W. W. Lockwood, ed., *The State and Economic Enterprise in Japan* (Princeton: Princeton University Press, 1965), pp. 503–516, 601–611.

[16] Though this was true in nearly all cases, the cement industry is a typical case. Its total capacity was 7,686,000 tons and production was 4,992,000 tons in 1950 and the respective figures were 17,690,000 and 13,636,000 in 1956. M.I.T.I., *Sangyō Gōrika Hakusho*, p. 422.

anxious to maintain the relatively high rate of profit prevailing in postwar Japan and were not inclined to cut prices. Also, the awareness of scale 6 firms that their cost advantage was momentary led them to maximize their profit for the short-run, in other words to sell at P_o (cartel price).

As for the scale 4 firms—the smallest of the large firms in the race for rationalization—$P_4 = MC$ was not a tenable position for any length of time. They either had to drop out of the race or make the transition to scale 5 or 6. The most rational choice under the circumstance was to move to scale 6, and this they did as they were the firms—as Fellner has shown [17]—with the least to lose and the most to gain from this transition.

Firms with scales 2 and 3 were medium-sized firms which were not able to join the race.[18] Their entrepreneurial ability, the possibility of acquiring a market sufficiently large to justify innovation, and most important, the ability to obtain sufficient credit to innovate restricted them from entering the race.[19] The policy of the government during this period was to encourage large firms to rationalize, and this meant that its loan policy was clearly preferential toward large firms. Tax policy also benefited large and growing (in absolute size) firms more than others.[20] It was evident that large firms were encouraged to grow on the theory that they were the ones capable of increasing exports and of revitalizing the Japanese economy. The dissolution of prewar Zaibatsu-bank/Zaibatsu-firm ties enabled formerly non-Zaibatsu large firms to enjoy the same footing, in terms of financing their race for rationalization. No large firms, including postwar firms (non-Zaibatsu connected firms), were barred from the race, provided they were large and were in the race from the beginning.[21]

The foregoing general analysis finds support in the following examination of changes in the trend of value added, contributed respectively by large, medium, and small firms of Japanese manufacturing industries.[22]

---

[17] William Fellner, "The Influence of Market Structure on Technological Change," *The Quarterly Journal of Economics*, LXV (1951), pp. 556–577.

[18] Scale I firms can be considered either "small" or the smallest of "medium" firms.

[19] For further discussion on this point, see chap. 9, pp. 163–165.

[20] This aspect of the policy is discussed in detail in chap. 8.

[21] This point is elaborated in chap. 7.

[22] Since the criteria used for the market classification of JFTC and the Industrial Classification of Markets used by M.I.T.I. are different and data by market and by

The only positive trend coefficient is seen for the large firms, while the coefficients for medium and small firms are all negative. The relatively larger negative coefficients for the medium-small firms indicate that the former, *as a group*, declined more in relative importance over the period. That is, the large firms, as a group, accounted for an increasingly larger share of the value added in the manufacturing industry at the cost of the relative importance of medium-sized firms.[23] The total value added by the large firms increased from 25.3 percent in 1953 and 23.7 in 1954, to 29.8 by 1957.[24] The relatively small negative coefficients for the small firms can be explained as due to the fact that they were either in different (small-scale) industries or not directly competitive with large firms in terms of market share.

In sum, given the government's chief concern during Phase I—to provide inducements for rapid capital accumulation and to enhance what it called the rationalization of technology—the large firms, which

TABLE 10

Time-Trend Equations of Value Added
by Employee Scale of Manufacturing Firms, 1953–1957 *

EMPLOYEE SIZE CLASS	TIME-TREND EQUATION
4–9	$45.32 - 0.18T$
10–29	$56.80 - 0.16T$
30–99	$77.16 - 0.55T$
100–299	$111.22 - 1.46T$
300–499	$143.02 - 1.12T$
500–999	$157.98 - 2.11T$
Over 1,000	$171.02 + 4.65T$

* The calculation was confined to the post-Korean boom period up to the 1958 recession. The equations are calculated for $VA_i = a + bT$, where i is employee size class and T is time. The t-tests on regression coefficients (b's) reveal that all b's are significant at .10 probability level, at $n = 5$.
SOURCE: Computed from 6 volumes (1953–1961) of *Kogyō Tōkeihyō Sangyōhen* (Industrial Statistics, Manufacturing Volume).

employee size cannot be obtained, Table 10 is used instead to show a general trend in value-added data available for the size classification which is used here.

[23] JFTC does not publish concentration ratio data for the 20 largest firms. But for those industries which the author was able to check (14 markets among the sample), it was found that their respective ratios for the 20 largest firms had risen during Phase I. The Statistical Bureau, M.I.T.I., has begun to compile the data for the largest, four largest, eight largest and twenty largest firms. The first results for 1961 were completed in September 1964 for internal use.

[24] Calculated from the source cited for Table 10, the total number of large firms employing over 1,000 in 1957 was 463 as against 387 in 1953, while the firms employing between 100 and 999 increased from 5,424 to 7,173 for the same period.

we consider as consisting of oligopoly sets in the manufacturing markets, were given a privileged place against small-medium firms. The consequence was that the race for rationalization accelerated within these oligopoly sets, causing the apparent trend toward deconcentration for the ten largest firms while markets as a whole became more concentrated. Thus, in the context of postwar Japan (1950–1958), it is perhaps more accurate to conclude that the active and far-from-invisible hand of the government—such as the encouragement of cartels—significantly contributed in bringing about the trend observed.

PHASE II (AFTER 1959)

A cursory examination of the 53 sample markets after 1959 shows a perceptible shift in the pattern of change in concentration ratios

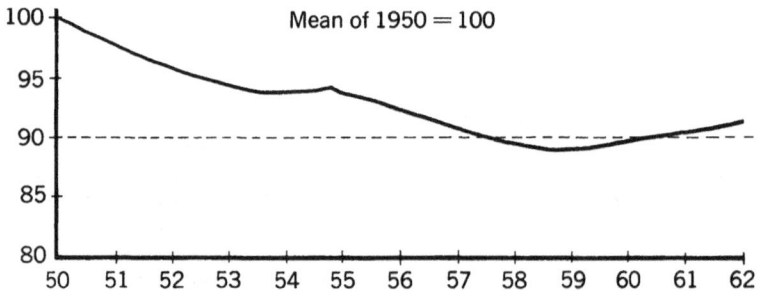

Diagram 2. The Average Concentration Ratio of 45 Markets at the Largest-Five-Firm Level

from what was observed in Phase I. A recent JFTC publication also contains a diagram based on the average ratios of 45 markets, in which concentration ratios are above 70 for the largest five firms, and it shows that there has been an observable shift in the pattern of the changes (see Diagram 2).[25] It can be seen in the diagram that the deconcentrating trend of these 45 highly concentrated markets appears to shift gently upward. However, to observe the shift in the pattern of change as precisely as possible, within the limitation imposed by the available data, the method used for Phase I can be used again. Instead of the earlier $C = a + bT$ for 1950–1958, now this equation is calculated for 1950–1962. (The result of the calculation is seen in Appendix I.) Then, to see the impact of the change in concentration ratios in these four years, a comparison is made between the time-trend coefficients found at

[25] JFTC, *Shuyō Sangyō no okeru Seisan-Shūchūdo* (Concentration Ratios in Major Industries) (Tokyo, 1964), p. 48. The criteria used in selecting these 45 markets overrepresent highly concentrated markets.

the end of this chapter (1950–1958) and those which were just calcu-lated. (The results of the calculation for the entire period, 1950–1962, are also in Appendix I.) If the new coefficient is larger, it is counted as an upward shift, and if smaller as a downward shift. Where both coefficients are negative, a smaller absolute value for the later period counts as an upward shift. In both cases an upward shift means an increase in the rate of concentration in the years after 1958.

Although it is unwise to make any definitive inference on the basis of only a brief (1959–1962) observation, we can suggest that, in more than half of the sample markets for the largest, three largest, five largest and ten largest firms, there has been an upward shift in the pattern of

TABLE 11

Comparison of Time-Trend Coefficients
for 1950–1958 and for 1950–1962

TREND	LARGEST FIRM	THREE LARGEST FIRMS	FIVE LARGEST FIRMS	TEN LARGEST FIRMS
Upward shift	33	30	26	26
Downward shift	20	20	20	19

SOURCE: Concentration ratios for the period between 1959 and 1962 were taken from JFTC, *Shuyō Sangyō ni okeru Seisan Shūchū-do* (Degree of Concentration in Major Industries) (Tokyo, 1964).

change in concentration ratios. It is also significant that the largest number of these shifts is observed for the largest firms. Recalling in Table 9 the largest-firm levels where we noted the largest number of negative coefficients, we can perhaps say that the apparent new trend to increase market share differentials among the largest firms may have been developing since 1958. Examining the types of industries, the upward shifts were contributed to a large extent by two groups, that is, the rapidly innovating industries—such as rayon fabrics, calcium cyana-mide, synthetic dyes, sulfuric acid, vinyl chloride, cement, pig iron, electric copper, and others—and the consumer goods industries—such as milk, butter, soy sauce, beer, sugar, cameras, matches and others.[26]

What, then, accounts for this apparent upward shift just observed? Three main factors can be suggested. The first is essentially an extension of the explanation offered for the deconcentrating trend observed in

[26] Cotton yarn, petroleum refining, and cotton cloth, for example, are markets in which innovation (scale change), changes in distribution methods, and cartel and import restrictions on raw materials have played major roles in influencing their respective market structures. Only a further evaluation of these mutually dependent factors can provide evidence of their relative importance.

Phase I, the rate of innovation. After the 1957–58 recession, which was described as "a temporary slowdown of the overheating investment engine," the race for rationalization was continued with renewed vigor, aided by favorable changes in the world economy as a whole. Firms began to compete for fear of being outrationalized by their competitors in investing for $f_3(P)$, then for $f_4(P)$. As this race continued, however, the total capacity in the market began to outpace the demand at an increasing rate due mainly to the increasing "lumpiness" of technology.[27] The result was as has been popularly termed "excess competition due to surplus capacity."[28] It has become evident to many in the market that the fallacy of composition was a distinct reality in the postrecession economy of Japan. Large firms in the oligopoly set could not continue to outrationalize each other and it was gradually evident to them that the sum total of the expected market share, after the completion of $f_4(P)$ by all the firms, far exceeded the expected demand.

Thus, the result of rationalization by all firms in the oligopoly set was increased excess capacity, and the less-than-optimum operation of $f_4(P)$ spelled a possible higher cost than the case of the near-optimum operation of $f_3(P)$. Added to this consideration was the sharply increased absolute capitol requirement which was necessitated by $f_4(P)$. Some firms in the oligopoly set, which had been straining their credit sources and the asset structure as they innovated from $f_1(P)$ to $f_3(P)$, found it extremely difficult and often impossible to obtain sufficient credit to finance investment in $f_4(P)$.[29] Given the general outlook of excess

[27] See Y. Morozumi's "A Proposal by M.I.T.I.," *Sangyō Taisei no Saihensei* (The Reorganization of Industrial Structure) (Tokyo, 1963). Mr. Morozumi is the Chief of the Industry Section of M.I.T.I.

[28] For example, the index of industrial investment jumped from 190.3 in 1958 to 328.7 in 1959, along with inventory which rose from 156.6 to 199.6 (in both cases, 1953 = 100). Tōyō Keizai Shimpō-Sha, *Keizai Tōkei Nenkan* (Year Book of Economic Statistics) (Tokyo, 1962), pp. 60–64. The following data on excess capacity of all industries in 1955 as equaling 100, increased from 127 in 1957 to 205.8 in 1961, while the rate of operation in respective years was 80.1 and 85.5 percent of the total capacity. The rate of operation of the heavily cartelized chemical fertilizer industry was, for example, 67.5, while capacity index increased from 127.2 in 1957 to 181.2 in 1961. Of course, the amount of absolute excess capacity has risen quite rapidly. Statistics Division, M.I.T.I., *Tsusan Tōkei Geppō* (Monthly Statistics of International Trade and Industry) January 1957 through December 1961, and Tōyō Keizai Shimpō-Sha's *Yearbook of Economic Statistics* (Tokyo, 1962), pp. 60–64. The latest M.I.T.I. *White Paper* reports that the rate of operation of all industry is approximately 67 percent of total capacity. M.I.T.I., *White Paper* (1963), p. 80. One should of course be reminded of the fact that "capacity" is extremely hard to define and disagreements of the meaning of this term exist among economists.

[29] See S. Tsuru, "Formal Planning Divorced from Action: Japan," in E. E. Hagen, ed., *Planning Economic Development* (Irwin, 1963), p. 143. Using figures released by the Bank of Japan, Tsuru found that the ratio of capital costs to value added in manufacturing firms increased from 27.5 in 1955 to 33.1 in the second half of 1961. Also, the ratio of own capital (equity) to borrowed capital (long- and

capacity and the difficulty of financing, some either decided to merge with former competitors or be absorbed by others in the oligopoly set. Data available clearly indicate that mergers among the largest firms visibly increased after the recession, and the network of financial control began to spread at an increasing rate.[30]

The second factor is the government policy which has become increasingly active since the end of 1958 or following the recession, as we saw in chapter 5. The Ministry of International Trade and Industry (M.I.T.I.) observed that frequently attempted investment limitation agreements (*Jishu-Chōsei*) among the large firms failed nearly without exception; and many industries, especially those innovating rapidly, appeared to increase excess capacity if they were left to their own devices. Under these circumstances, M.I.T.I. began to take the initiative to amend the Anti-Monopoly Act further, mainly to gain authority to guide investment decisions of the largest firms in innovating industries. M.I.T.I.'s proposal to amend the act, though it was presented with an explicit plan to increase government loans in exchange for the authority to guide the investment policy of firms, was vigorously protested by medium and large firms alike. The former feared that the proposed change would encourage the growth of larger firms at the cost of their survival, and the latter objected to the "element of prewar-like increase in the bureaucratic control of private industry." [31]

As seen in the preceding chapter, however, this proposal was withdrawn by the Liberal-Democratic party as it faced strong opposition from the industries, the Socialist party and JFTC. Nevertheless, the tone of the policy was set. From 1959 to 1960, the steel industry, for example, was given authorization to practice the "open-price system,"

---

short-term loans) of the manufacturing firms in 1960 was 23 percent, compared to 43 in West Germany (1960), 65 in the U.S. (1961) and 66 in England (1961). These figures are quoted from H. Ouchi *et al*, *Nippon Keizai Zusetsu* (The Japanese Economy in Graphs) (Tokyo, 1963), p. 91.

[30] Mergers among large firms began to increase visibly after 1959. The number of mergers whose post-merger assets were over 500,000,000 yen (approximately 1.4 million dollars) increased as follows:

Assets (in billion yen)	1959	1960	1961	1962	1963
.5–1	7	8	9	10	15
1 –5	8	9	13	23	28
5 –10	0	0	3	3	5
over 10	0	1	2	3	12

Less than 2,000 firms in Japan had assets exceeding 500,000,000 yen in 1963. T. Nomoto, "The Recent Trend of Mergers," *Kōsei Torihiki* (May 1964), p. 4.

[31] R. Kodo, "A Proposal from the Industry," *The Reorganization of Industrial Structure, op. cit.*, p. 116.

which in effect was government-sanctioned price leadership by Yawata, the largest steel producer. The Bank of Japan at the same time pursued the loan policy which de facto discriminated against relatively smaller firms in the oligopoly set. The enforcement of the Anti-Monopoly Act was reduced to a minimum, and the government appeared to let nature take its course—an increase in mergers—even if it meant that the merged firm controlled over 50 percent of a market and had increased financial control over relatively smaller competitors.[32]

The third factor that encouraged the upward shift was what is loosely termed by Japanese economists as the "distribution revolution." As an important postwar phenomenon, those commodities that are sold directly to the household began to be sold on a brand-name basis.[33] This trend, which became manifest around 1955–56, began to accelerate after the recession. Firms often merged to assure a larger market, and their brands were widely advertised. The result of such phenomena was that market-leading firms absorbed or merged with relatively smaller firms in the oligopoly set. In a sense, something analogous to the absorption of new technology has taken place in the method of distribution, namely, economies of scale in advertising and other economic advantages resulting from well-differentiated products were beginning to be exploited at a rapidly increasing rate following the recession. Admittedly, these factors need to be researched further, but it is suggested here that these are the main factors that caused the upward inflection.

GROWTH RATE OF INDUSTRIES AND CONCENTRATION RATIOS

The effects of these three factors, and generally of the policy of the Japanese government since 1953, are also clearly seen in the relationship between the growth rate of output and the concentration ratios of manufacturing markets. If our foregoing analyses are correct, one expects the market structure, observed in terms of concentration ratios at the largest-, three-largest-, and ten-largest-firm levels, to have a negative relationship with the rate of increase of output during Phase I. That is, as industries expand their outputs, under the policy and "mechanism" (Diagram 1, p. 93), the concentration ratios decline.

To evaluate this expectation we have computed correlation coefficients between the time-trend coefficients for 1950–1958 and the growth rates of the sample markets. The results are as shown in Table 12.

Although all coefficients were negative as expected, none of them was

[32] An exhaustive study of recent mergers was made by H. Misonou, *Kigyō Gōdō* (Enterprise Mergers) (Tokyo, 1964).
[33] Brand selling existed before World War II, but not to the degree seen since 1958. *Ibid.*, pp. 65–96.

significant at the .05 level for the ten largest firms. For the largest-, and three-largest-firm levels, approximately 9 percent of the trend of deconcentration was explained by the growth rate of output and less than 12 percent of the trend was explained, even when only growing markets were considered. These results, which indicated that the growth rate of output failed to show a significant relationship with the changes in concentration during Phase I, can perhaps be explained as follows: In this phase (1953–1958), oligopolists vied for newer technology and a larger market share. Thus, when the rate of increase of output was nearly equal for all competing oligopolists, the concentration ratios

TABLE 12

Correlation Coefficients Between Market Growth Rates
and Time-Trend Coefficients of Concentration Ratios [a]
1950–1958

CLASS	R FOR GROWING MARKETS	R FOR ALL MARKETS
Largest firm	−.3324 (49) [b]	−.2812 (52) [c]
Three largest firms	−.3459 (49)	−.3013 (52)
Ten largest firms	−.1953 (44)	−.1367 (47)

[a] Growth data are in terms of unit of output. When data were given in a few cases—in value terms—they were deflated.
[b] Numbers in parentheses indicate sample size which varies because some markets reach a concentration ratio of 100 before the 10-largest firm level.
[c] Output figures are not available for one market (electric locomotives).
SOURCE: JFTC, Nippon Sangyō Shūchū no Jittai (The Reality of Industrial Concentration in Japan) (Tokyo, 1957), and Shuyō Sangyō ni okeru Seisan Shūchō-do (Degrees of Concentration in Major Industries) (Tokyo, 1964).

obtained for the ten largest firms reflected a very "weak" relationship with the rate of increase in output. For the largest-and three-largest-firm levels, this explanation is less tenable, but an explanation for the observed result is found in Table 13.

These are rankings in terms of the value of shipments. What is to be noted is that, in the short period from 1953 to 1958, the ranking observed for these ten randomly selected markets has been fluid. N refers to a new firm which was not one of the top ranking ten in 1953. Except for tires and tubes for vehicles, the relative position of the top five and even the top three firms shifted in the nine remaining markets. This means that, as the oligopolists competed for rationalization in the framework of Diagram 1 (p. 93), the participants in this rationalization race shared the increasing size of total output in their respective markets. Under such circumstances, we observe these weak relationships between the growth rate of output and the concentration ratios.

On the other hand, a similar calculation for Phase II (1959–1962), as shown in Table 14, may be expected to yield different results. This is especially true in light of the increasingly pro-monopoly policy which emerged during the period and the increased lumpiness of newer technology.

TABLE 13

Ranking of Ten Largest Firms in 1958 in Terms of 1953 Ranking

SELECTED INDUSTRIES	RANKING IN 1958 IN TERMS OF 1953 RANKING *									
Paper (western type)	1	3	2	4	N	5	8	N	6	N
Chemical dye	1	2	3	4	5	8	6	7	10	9
Chassis for passenger cars	3	1	2	6	4	5				
Chemical fiber (nylon & rayon)	2	1	8	3	N	4	N	6	N	N
Cotton weaving	2	3	4	1	5	10	7	9	8	6
Ammonium sulphate	1	3	5	4	2	6	8	9	10	7
Regular hot rod steel plate	1	3	2	4	7	5	N	N	N	N
Beer	2	1	3							
Oil refining	1	4	N	8	5	3	6	N	N	9
Tires & tubes for vehicles	1	2	3	4	5	6				

* N refers to a "new firm" which was not one of the top ranking ten in 1953.
SOURCE: Japanese Fair Trade Commission, *Nippon Kogyo no Jittai* (The Reality of the Japanese Industries), Appendix III (Tokyo, 1957), pp. 272–282. For 1958 data, JFTC, *Shuyō Sangyō ni okeru Seisan Shuchu-do* (Concentration Ratios of Major Industries in 1958) (Tokyo, 1960), pp. 2–24.

TABLE 14

Correlation Coefficients Between Market Growth Rates *
and Time-Trend Coefficients of Concentration Ratios

CLASS	1950–1962	1959–1962
Largest firm	−.2748 (52)	−.1171 (52)
Three largest firms	−.2932 (52)	−.0610 (52)
Ten largest firms	−.1336 (47)	−.0110 (47)

* Growth rates for 1959 to 1962 were obtained by calculating b from $I_{62} = ae^{bT}$, where I_{62} is the index of 1962, a is 100 (1959 base) and T is 3. The growth rate from 1958 to 1959 was obtained by backward extrapolation, i.e., by calculating output for 1958 from $I_{58} = 100e^{-b}$. The slopes of the logarithmic trend lines for the entire period were obtained by connecting the midpoints of the two segments (1950–1958 equation and 1959–1962 equation). It was also found that the b's which were calculated by connecting these two segments, by using the index $I_{58} = 100e^{-b}$ as the link (since real output data are available for 1958), were virtually identical to those obtained by the method described earlier. The first two digits of the calculated R's were not affected by the second method.
SOURCE: Concentration and output data for the period between 1959 and 1962 were published by JFTC in April, 1964. FTC, *Shuyō Sangyō ni okeru Seisan Shūchū-do* (Degrees of Concentration in Major Industries) (Tokyo, 1964).

The results of Table 14 are not strictly comparable with those of Table 12, since the output figures for Phase II were released only in index form (1959 as 100), as explained in the Note for Table 14. However, the results in Table 14 clearly indicate that the relationship between the growth rate of output and concentration ratios are even weaker than in Phase I, to the point of presenting a positive coefficient at the ten-largest-firm level.

This, however, is not difficult to explain. During Phase II, the policy began to encourage the market-leading firms—the larger firms among the oligopolists—to rationalize and to merge with or absorb other market-leading firms or oligopolists in the market. In the framework of Diagram 1, a few giant firms were encouraged and aided in their efforts to reach a larger-scale, lower-cost unit of production. Under these circumstances, not only are the coefficients in Table 14 smaller in absolute values vis-à-vis those observed in Table 12, but also the relationship becomes positive in one instance, at the ten-largest level. Also, when the ranking of the ten markets was examined for Phase II, as was done for Phase I (Table 12), in nine markets the ranking of the largest three firms did not change during Phase II. At the five-largest and ten-largest levels, changes in ranking have become an extremely rare event, save for big mergers or absorption. Compared to Phase I, one must conclude that the large firms became entrenched during Phase II.[34]

STRUCTURAL CHANGES

The distribution of employees and value of shipments show a clearly observable trend toward concentration. Table 15 shows that firms employing over 500 began to increase their share of employment after 1958. This was accomplished at the cost of the smallest firms employing fewer than 50. However, a more telling structural change is found in Table 16, which shows that, since 1955, firms employing over 500 began to contribute a rapidly increasing share of the total value of shipments.

In 1961, firms employing over 500 accounted for 43.8 percent of the total value of shipments with 25.6 percent of the total employees. This is an increase of 6.8 percent in the value of shipments as compared with that of 1953, and sharply contrasts with the decline in the value of shipments experienced by firms employing fewer than 50 (−6.3 percent) during the same period. When these tables are considered with Table 10, value added by firm size, the prominent characteristic of the

[34] The source cited in Table 12 no longer identifies the names of firms with concentration ratios of the ten largest firms. The observations made in this paragraph are based on trade journals and magazine articles.

TABLE 15

Distribution of Employees by Firm Size, 1953–1961
(in percentage of total)

	FIRMS EMPLOYING:				
YEAR	1–3	4–49	50–199	200–499	over 500
1953	9.9	39.1	17.3	10.4	23.3
1954	10.3	40.6	16.9	10.2	22.2
1955	10.0	40.5	17.8	10.3	21.4
1956	9.0	39.6	18.7	10.6	22.1
1957	8.5	39.6	19.1	10.7	22.1
1958	8.3	39.3	19.6	10.9	21.9
1959	7.9	37.6	20.3	11.3	23.4
1960	6.9	36.5	20.9	11.5	24.2
1961	6.4	35.1	21.0	11.9	25.6

SOURCE: Based on annual volumes of M.I.T.I.'s *Kōgyo Tōkei-hyō* (The Industrial Statistics).

TABLE 16

Distribution of Value of Shipments by Firm Size
1953–1961
(in percentage of total)

	FIRMS EMPLOYING:				
YEAR	1–3	4–49	50–199	200–499	Over 500
1953	2.9	25.7	19.0	15.4	37.0
1954	3.1	27.0	19.0	16.1	34.8
1955	3.1	26.6	19.5	16.2	34.6
1956	2.5	34.7	19.0	16.3	37.5
1957	2.2	23.6	19.3	15.6	39.3
1958	2.3	23.8	19.6	15.8	38.5
1959	2.0	22.7	19.5	15.4	40.4
1960	1.8	21.2	19.4	14.6	43.0
1961	1.7	20.6	19.3	14.6	43.8

SOURCE: Same as Table 15.

postwar Japanese industry has been that of gradual concentration, however measured.

A revealing fact behind those observed in the preceding tables and a consequence of the policy examined earlier is the rising number of bankruptcies occurring between 1956 and 1964. In 1956, the year of *Jimmu* prosperity [35] and of active investment activity, a total of 1,123

[35] The term "*Jimmu* prosperity" means a prosperity unequaled since the *Jimmu* period. *Jimmu* is the name of the first emperor of Japan.

bankruptcies were recorded.[36] This figure rose to 1,413 in 1957 and 1,480 in 1958 as the recession of 1958 began to take its toll. Next came three prosperous years (1959–1961), in which bankruptcies were in the 1,100's. Then, in spite of the fact that the economy was rapidly growing, the number of bankruptcies rose to 1,779 in 1962 and 1,733 in 1963. In 1964, when the economy began to show signs of recession—including a sharp decline in investment—1,620 bankruptcies were recorded during the first six months.

Analyzing these data further, we discover that, although the small firms (assets of less than five million yen) account for, on the average, nearly 90 percent of the cases, the large firms since 1962, even including a few giant-sized oligopolists, are also going bankrupt at a sharply increasing rate. Among the large firms (assets exceeding ten million yen), bankruptcy cases rose from 64 in 1960 and 65 in 1961 to 174 in 1962, 162 in 1963, and 118 in the first six months of 1964. If the bankruptcies among the small-medium firms can be attributed to monetary policy,[37] increased labor costs, relative inefficiency, and business misjudgment, the increased bankruptcies of the larger firms must be attributed to the rapidly changing technological requirements (in absolute size) and the policy of the government which took an active role in its efforts to achieve rationalization, export, and growth.

CONCLUSIONS

On the basis of the foregoing evidence, it can be concluded that postwar Japanese markets continue to concentrate. During the first phase, the concentration took the form of a larger market share for the large oligopolists at the cost of the medium-small firms, though we note that the concentration ratios of the ten largest firms declined. In Phase II, the rationalization race resulted in in-fighting among the oligopolists rather than against the medium-small firms. The results were reflected in Table 14 and also in Diagram 2, (p. 96).

[36] Before 1956, bankruptcy cases did not exceed 1,000 per year. See T. Kobayashi, "Bankruptcies, Their Patterns and Problems," Kinyū Journal (August 1964), p. 50.

[37] M. Shinohara has shown with a convincing array of data that small firms become victims of a tight money policy because banks stop lending to small firms immediately following or even preceding a tight money policy. Also, when business conditions slacken, large firms, often with little or no warning, curtail subcontracting orders from small firms to control the firm's own inventory. T. Ito has documented the practice of large firms in prolonging the waiting period—"site"—of promissory notes, frequently used for payments to small firms when money is tight, and/or business declines. M. Shinohara, Growth and Cycles in the Japanese Economy (Tokyo: Kinokuniya, 1962), especially chap. 8, "Inventory Cycles and the Dual Structure," pp. 188–202; also see T. Ito, "Structural Peculiarities and Labor Problems of Small Business in Japan," in Small Business in Japan, ed. T. Yamanaka (Japan Times Co., Ltd., 1960). These observations are elaborated in chap. 9.

Although no official data have been released since 1962, there is no doubt that the market structure of Japanese manufacturing industries in 1965–66 was more concentrated than it was in 1962.[38] The available evidence suggests that a rapid reorganization of market structure has been continuing since 1962 and especially during the recession of 1965–66. Late in 1965, the *Japan Economic Journal* noted:

> The pressure of depression has set off a series of corporate mergers at a tempo as yet unmatched. Such moves are eventually headed toward an oligopoly—admittedly a desirable industrial structure for enabling effective competition with major foreign manufacturers.

> The industry in general has favorably watched active recent mergers in the textile machinery, trade and cement industries. It may reasonably be believed that the prolonged depression will further promote such moves.

> Major mergers decided upon in recent weeks included those between Sumitomo Cement and Nozawa Abestos & Cement, Kawasaki Dockyard and Yokoyama Engineering, Marubeni-Iida and Tōsho, Tōyō Spinning (Tōyōbō) and Kureha Spinning, and Tekkōsha, Tōshiba Denkō and Azuma Kadō. Earlier, three heavy industries of the Mitsubishi Group were amalgamated, while Nissan Motor and Prince Motors have decided to merge as from next April.[39]

The journal also noted that this reorganization was encouraged by the government which "favors such moves and has provided such facilities as the rationalization finance system and other preferential arrangements." [40] On this basis, the journal went on to say that "the year 1966 is considered as a year of industrial concentration and merger.[41]

The role of the government was and is to encourage the process of concentration with all the power at its command. Especially after 1958 the government provided the leadership which took varied forms ranging from expressions of desire for increased rationalization by the prime minister to suggesting and then actively participating in the negotiation of a merger between two leading automobile firms.[42] Professor Lock-

---

[38] The writer is prepared to judge that the manufacturing markets of Japan in 1966 were considerably more concentrated than they were in 1953. This is based on the concentration observed during Phase I (an increase in market shares of larger firms though concentration ratios of the largest ten firms were declining) and the concentration which continues at a rapid tempo among the ten largest firms in Phase II since 1962.

[39] *The Japan Economic Journal* (November 30, 1965).

[40] *Ibid.* (November 30, 1965).

[41] *Ibid.* (January 11, 1966).

[42] The Minister of International Trade and Industry, Mr. Sakurauchi, actively participated in merger discussions between Nissan and Prince Motors. Mr. Sakurauchi, who "surprised the automobile industry for his strong desire to see the merger

wood expressed his assessment of the role of government as follows: "The hand of government is everywhere in evidence, despite its limited statutory powers. The Ministers engage in an extraordinary amount of consultation, advice, persuasion, and threat. The industrial bureaus of M.I.T.I. proliferate sectoral targets and plans; they confer, they tinker, they exhort. This is 'economics by admonition' to a degree inconceivable in Washington or in London." [43]

The government was and is providing added pressure to mold the market structure which was and is also following its own momentum generated by the economic forces of postwar Japan (increasing "lumpiness" of technology, needs for rapid capital accumulation, and increased international competitive ability). As these two forces worked together in shaping the market structure, one cannot hope to isolate the government's contribution to the increase in concentration of the market structure. However, descriptions in the preceding chapters and the examination in this chapter establish a fact that few would deny: The hand of government has been and is becoming increasingly heavier and more visible since the policy of SCAP began to vacillate in 1948.

If this pressure from the government did in fact exist as argued here, an inevitable, and extremely thorny, question emerges. Should the government have used pressure and, if so, to the degree that it did? Any M.I.T.I. officer would not only answer the last question affirmatively but would also lament his restricted power. He would point to such accomplishments as seen in Tables 17, 18, and 19 and argue that the measures taken by the government—cartels, open price systems, discriminatory loan policy, and so forth—did in fact raise labor productivity, increase exports, and accomplish rapid capital accumulation. [44]

The success—the high growth rate and numerous indicators of a growing economy—and the accompanying structural changes now need to be examined against the various consequences and parallel changes in other aspects of the economy, such as in taxation, labor, and income distribution. When the observations in chapters 8 and 9 are added to those observed in the preceding chapters, we may be in a position to evaluate the claims of M.I.T.I. and the role played by the government in the postwar Japanese economy.

---

through" stated that this merger would provide "a pattern to be followed by other industries." *Asahi* (June 1, 1965).

[43] W. W. Lockwood, "Japan's 'New Capitalism,'" *The State and Economic Enterprise in Japan*, p. 503.

[44] For an excellent assessment of the M.I.T.I. view by Professor Lockwood, see *The State and Economic Enterprise in Japan*, p. 508.

TABLE 17

Gross Domestic Investment [a]
1953–1962
(in billion yen)

	1953	1954	1955	1956	1957	1958	1959	1960	1961	1962
Gross private domestic capital formation	1,335.2	1,156.9	1,371.6	2,263.5	2,401.6	1,903.7	3,289.4	4,273.6	5,863.9	4,949.1
The above as percentage of gross national expenditure	18.8	15.5	16.7	24.4	23.7	18.3	26.2	29.1	33.1	25.6

[a] Total investment, equipment and inventory.
SOURCE: The Bank of Japan, *Economic Statistics of Japan* (1964), pp. 329–330.

TABLE 18

Labor Productivity (Real Value Added per Employee) [a]
All Industries 1950–1961

	1950	1951	1952	1953	1954	1955	1956	1957	1958	1959	1960	1961
Real value added per employee in 1000 yen	189	378	302	362	400	423	462	489	469	540	636	732

[a] In 1955 prices.
SOURCE: M.I.T.I., *Kōgyo Tōkei-hyō* (Industrial Statistics), the annual volumes of 1950–1961.

TABLE 19

Index of Exports,[a] 1950–1963

	1950	1951	1952	1953	1954	1955	1956	1957	1958	1959	1960	1961	1962	1963
Exports	100	164	154	154	197	248	302	345	347	411	490	512	594	659

[a] Custom clearance basis. The base year (1950) export was 298,021,000,000 yen.
SOURCE: Same as Table 15.

7   THE ZAIBATSU QUESTION

The Zaibatsu are said to be reviving in Japan.[1] In his widely read *Nippon Keizai Nyūmon* (Introduction to the Japanese Economy) Professor Nagasu wrote in 1959: "The Zaibatsu have steadily built their power and have revived. No, more than that. Before the war, the Zaibatsu had to share their hegemony with large landowners and were under the Emperor and the militarists, but now there are no militarists or large landowners. The Emperor, too, has become an accessory. The power of Japan now rests squarely in the hands of the Zaibatsu, the sponsors of the Liberal-Democratic Party." [2] Many authors now share this view.[3]

The purpose of this chapter is to examine the so-called Zaibatsu question, which has often been debated by Japanese economists and is usually misunderstood in the West, and to show that the word *Zaibatsu* as used to describe economic concentration in Japan underwent a marked change in meaning in the postwar period. Recent use of this term is inaccurate and misses many of the fundamental structural changes that have taken place in the Japanese economy since the end of World War II.

The term *Zaibatsu* has been in use for over half a century. Many

[1] Under the caption of "Just Like Old Times," *Time* magazine stated: "The postwar U.S. breakup of Japan's Zaibatsu, the huge and powerful prewar cartels that controlled practically all of Japanese industry, was the most ambitious antitrust action in history. The reemergence of the Zaibatsu has been hardly less ambitious." *Time* (August 20, 1959), p. 10.

[2] Kazusi Nagasu, *Nippon Keizai Nyūmon* (Introduction to the Japanese Economy) (Tokyo, 1959), p. 118.

[3] Many articles and several major works support this view. To list only a few: Sōichiro Giga, *Gendai Nippon no Dokusen Kigyō* (Monopolistic Enterprises of Contemporary Japan) (Tokyo, 1962); Shigeto Tsuru, *Essays on Japanese Economy* (Tokyo, 1958), chap. 4; and Shigeru Aihara, ed., *Nippon no Dokusen Shihon* (The Monopolistic Capital of Japan) (Tokyo, 1959).

economists have defined it, and the following three characteristics are
usually attributed to a member of the Zaibatsu group: [4]

(1) Semifeudal characteristics in that centralized control rests in a
    Zaibatsu family, which extends its power through strategically
    arranged marriages and other personal knight-vassal (dedica-
    tion) relationships.

(2) Well-knit, tightly controlled relationships among the affili-
    ated firms by means of holding companies, interlocking director-
    ships, and mutual stockholdings.

(3) Extremely large financial power in the form of commercial
    bank credit, which is used as the central leverage to extend
    control in all industries.

Stating the above differently, Lockwood observed:

> Each of the Big Four combines remained a family enterprise in
> some degree. The exact pattern of control varied from one to an-
> other. The Sumitomo interests were almost entirely owned and di-
> rected by the single head of the family. The Mitsubishi combines
> were controlled by two Iwasaki families, with common responsi-
> bility vested alternatively by custom in the eldest son of one fam-
> ily, then of the other. The eleven branches of the Mitsui family
> acted as a unit in accordance with formal household rules, last re-
> vised in 1900. They held 90 per cent of their wealth collectively.
> Policies were decided through a family council presided over by
> the head of the elder son's family.[5]

More generally, one economist described Zaibatsu as "a form of
monopolistic *konzern*, but in that its capital controlled an extremely
high percentage of stocks of affiliated firms in many industries and in
that its capital effectively extended its influence into all sectors of the
economy, . . . the Japanese Zaibatsu formed a unique type of
konzern." [6] This was the Zaibatsu of prewar years. How much change
has there been? [7]

---

[4] Ryukichi Minobe emphasizes (1) in his *Sengo Keizai no Saihensi* (Reorganiza-
tion of Postwar Economy) (Tokyo, 1953), pp. 96–99; (2) is stressed by Seijiro
Usami in his *Nippon no Dokusen Shihon* (Monopolistic Capital of Japan) (Tokyo,
1953), p. 17; (3) is mentioned by all those consulted but emphasized most by
Hidemasa Koga, *Nippon Kinyū Shihon Ron* (The Theory of Japanese Financial
Capital) (Tokyo, 1957), p. 87.

[5] W. W. Lockwood, *The Economic Development of Japan* (Princeton: Princeton
University Press, 1954), p. 215.

[6] Mosaburo Suzuki, *Nippon Dokusen Shihon no Kaibō* (Anatomy of the Japanese
Monopolistic Capital) (Tokyo, 1935), p. 37. Professor Edwards, describing the
extensive financial control of Zaibatsu, found it "beyond comparison in the world."
C. D. Edwards, "The Dissolution of Zaibatsu Combines," *Pacific Affairs*, XIX
(September 1946), 213.

[7] Or, in view of the trust-busting measures effected by the Supreme Commander
of Allied Powers (SCAP) immediately following V-J Day, we could ask: Did the
Zaibatsu which were dissolved by the SCAP immediately after the allied occupation
revive?

THE EXTENT OF PREWAR AND POSTWAR ZAIBATSU CONTROL

By the late 1930's financial control by Zaibatsu families was extensive by any standard. This can best be seen by examining the Zaibatsu banks, which acted as the central nerves of their holding-company operations. In 1944, loans made by four Zaibatsu banks amounted to 74.9 percent of all bank loans (see Table 20).[8] The Mitsui family owned 67.6 percent of the Mitsui Bank; the Iwasaki family owned 43 percent of the Mitsubishi Bank; the Sumitomo family, 34.5 percent of the Sumitomo Bank; and the Yasuda family, 30.9 percent of the Yasuda Bank. These percentages do not include shares held by the

TABLE 20

Loans Made by Four Zaibatsu Banks in 1944
(in million yen)

NAME OF BANK	AMOUNT OF MONEY LENT	PERCENTAGE OF ALL LOANS MADE
Mitsui	2,604	29.1
Mitsubishi	1,740	19.5
Sumitomo	1,290	14.4
Yasuda	1,068	11.9
Total of 4 banks	6,702	74.9
Total of all banks	8,943	100.0

SOURCE: Holding Companies Liquidation Committee (H.C.L.C.), *Nippon Zaibatsu to sono Kaitai* (The Japanese Zaibatsu and their Dissolution) (Tokyo, 1950), p. 63.

subsidiaries of each combine[9] and hence understate the degree of Zaibatsu control of each of the banks.

With the assistance of this extensive financial power, each Zaibatsu group controlled numerous firms. For example, the Mitsui on the eve of surrender (see Tables 21 and 22) controlled 46 subsidiaries and 143 affiliated firms.[10] A similar pattern of control can be seen for other

[8] Because of a policy to promote bank mergers adopted in 1927, the four Zaibatsu banks by 1931 jointly had 38.2 percent of the total national deposits in their banks vis-à-vis 22.1 percent which they had held in 1926, just before the policy was initiated. This trend continued until the end of World War II. In this sense, the 1944 figures overstate them as representative prewar figures. Toshihiko Katō, *Nippon Ginkōshi Ron* (The History of Japanese Banks) (Tokyo, 1957), pp. 130–211.

[9] Hiroshi Higuchi, *Zaibatsu no Fukkatsu* (The Revival of Zaibatsu) (Tokyo, 1953), pp. 42–45.

[10] The Holding Company Liquidation Committee stated that, when a Zaibatsu holding company owned at least 10 percent of a firm, the firm was a subsidiary of the Zaibatsu. Affiliates were those firms 10 percent or more of whose shares were held by a subsidiary or subsidiaries of the same Zaibatsu. In reality this minimum requirement was well surpassed. When the Zaibatsu were ordered to report all the firms that they

TABLE 21

Firms Controlled by the Mitsui [a]
in 1945 by Asset Size

ASSET SIZE [b] (YEN)	SUBSIDIARIES	AFFILIATES
Less than 500,000	8	38
500,000–1 million	1	27
1 million–5 million	8	40
5 million–10 million	5	19
Over 10 million	24	19
Total	46	143

[a] In this case "Mitsui" refers to the Mitsui family and the Mitsui Trust, 63 percent of whose shares were owned by the Mitsui family.

[b] Less than 8 percent of firms in Japan in 1940 had assets larger than 500,000 yen, and only 0.75 percent had assets exceeding 10,000,000 yen.

SOURCE: Rearranged from H.C.L.C., Data Volume, pp. 468–472.

TABLE 22

Proportion of Stock Owned by Mitsui in Its
Subsidiaries and Affiliates in 1945

PERCENTAGE OWNED BY MITSUI IN SUBSIDIARIES	NUMBER OF SUBSIDIARIES	PERCENTAGE OWNED BY SUBSIDIARIES IN AFFILIATES	NUMBER OF AFFILIATES
0– 9	1 [a]	0– 9	0
10– 19	1	10– 19	20
20– 29	2	20– 29	20
30– 39	8	30– 39	12
40– 49	4	40– 49	14
50– 59	4	50– 59	20
60– 69	9	60– 69	7
70– 79	6	70– 79	8
80– 89	1	80– 89	8
90– 99	5	90– 99	11
99–100	5	99–100	23
Total	46		143

[a] This was Mitsui Light Metal, but 36 percent of their shares were owned by Mitsui Mining, another subsidiary.

SOURCE: Same as Table 21.

Zaibatsu families. Mitsubishi controlled 28 subsidiaries and 153 affiliates; Sumitomo controlled 19 subsidiaries and 186 affiliates; and the last of the four Zaibatsu, Yasuda, controlled 19 subsidiaries and 18 affiliates. These pyramids of Zaibatsu family, bank, and firms penetrated all

---

considered under their absolute control, these 189 firms were reported by Mitsui to SCAP as belonging to such a group. The subsidiaries and affiliates of other Zaibatsu described below also were so reported by each Zaibatsu combine.

TABLE 23

Financial Control of Zaibatsu in Terms of
Capital Paid in, in Various Sectors
of the Economy in 1942

	TOTAL CAPITAL (IN 1,000 YEN) (A)	4 ZAIBATSU CAPITAL (B)	(B)/(A)
Financial			
Banking	1,006,381	482,836	48.0
Credit	41,000	35,000	85.4
Insurance	168,312	86,250	51.2
Total	1,215,693	604,086	49.7
Heavy industries			
Mining	3,070,750	867,725	28.3
Metal	3,829,681	1,009,355	26.4
Machine tool	6,018,598	2,780,065	46.2
Shipbuilding	1,613,811	81,372	5.0
Chemical	2,968,529	930,554	31.4
Total	17,501,369	5,669,071	32.4
Light industries			
Paper	535,144	24,111	4.5
Cement *	315,486	89,476	28.4
Textile	1,288,869	224,119	17.4
Food (Canning)	1,182,641	32,239	2.7
Others	1,265,722	123,062	9.7
Total	4,587,862	493,007	10.8
Others			
Electric-gas	3,825,574	20,000	0.5
Transportation	933,090	45,611	4.9
Shipping	992,080	603,074	60.8
Land, Building warehouse	599,602	136,264	22.6
Shoji, Exp.-Imp.	2,723,796	369,750	13.6
Total	9,074,142	1,174,699	12.9
Grand Total	32,379,066	7,940,863	24.5

* H.C.L.C. put cement in light industries in the original data.
SOURCE: Computed from HCLC, *The Japanese Zaibatsu and their Dissolution,*
Data Volume, p. 469. The (B)/(A) ratio appearing against the total is the simple
arithmetic average of that sector.

segments of the economy. A tabulation compiled by the H.C.L.C.
clearly shows the power enjoyed by these families (see Table 23).

The postwar Japanese economy presents a drastically different picture. As we have seen in chapter 1, the former Zaibatsu families were

ordered to liquidate their banking interests, and their holding companies were dissolved by order of SCAP.[11] In 1960 the largest banks were
owned by various firms and individuals but not by families. The Mitsui
Bank furnishes an example of the change that took place (see Table
24).

The remaining shares were distributed among individuals, none of
whom owned more than 1 percent of the total. All other former Zai-

TABLE 24

Nineteen Largest Owners of the Mitsui Banks in 1960

OWNERS	PERCENTAGE OF THE TOTAL SHARES HELD BY OWNER
Mitsui Life	2.82
Nihon Life Insurance	2.22
Toyota Motor Car	2.08
Mitsui Trading	1.98
Dai-Ichi Life Insurance	1.94
Tokyo Shibaura Electric	1.67
Taisho Marine Insurance	1.66
Toyo High Pressure	1.44
Nihon Sekiyu	1.44
Onoda Cement	1.22
Fujikura Electric Ware	1.22
Meiji Life Insurance	1.2
Toyota Weaving Machine	1.2
Asahi Life Insurance	1.2
Tokyo Electric Power	1.2
Nihon Mining	1.2
Nihon Milling Industry	1.2
Hokkaido Coal Mining	1.2
Mitsui Mining	1.2

SOURCE: This table was compiled for the author by Mr. Hitoshi Misonou of the
Fair Trade Commission, based upon the unpublished FTC study on concentration
of ownership of legal persons (Hō-jin).

batsu banks were similar in their ownership patterns, and the extent of
loans made by the four in 1958 was much smaller than in 1944, as shown
in Table 25. These former Zaibatsu banks are now publicly owned and
their loans have been considerably reduced.

After the dissolution of the Zaibatsu holding companies and changes
in the ownership of former Zaibatsu banks, the stockholding pattern of
large firms also underwent a visible change. Taking the 120 largest (in

[11] SCAP decrees on Dissolution of Holding Companies, December 1945, and on
Limitation of Stockholding and Other Matters, July 1946. For details, see T. A.
Bisson, *Zaibatsu Dissolution in Japan* (Berkeley and Los Angeles: University of
California Press, 1954), chaps. 5 and 6.

TABLE 25

Comparison of Loans Made by Each Zaibatsu Bank in 1944
and by Each "Resurgent Zaibatsu Bank" in 1958
(percent of total loans made by all banks)

YEAR	MITSUI	MITSUBISHI	SUMITOMO	YASUDA-FUJI
1944	29.1	19.5	14.1	11.9
1958	4.7	7.2	6.8	7.5

SOURCE: 1958 figures were taken from Fair Trade Commission, *Shuyō Sangyō ni okeru Seisan Schūchū-do* (Concentration Ratios of Major Industries) (Tokyo, 1958), pp. 18–21.

TABLE 26

Largest Stockholders Classified According to Holding, 1960
(percentage of total)

| INDUSTRIES | FIRMS IN WHICH THE LARGEST SHAREHOLDER HAD LESS THAN | | | | | | | | TOTAL FIRMS |
	5%	6–10%	11–20%	21–30%	31–40%	41–50%	51–60%	91–100%	
Food	5	2							7
Textiles	8	2	1						11
Pulp & paper	3	7							10
Chemical	15	10	1						26
Petroleum	3	1				4 [a]	1		9
Rubber products					2 [b]				2
Cement & glass	2	1	2						5
Iron & steel	8	2	3		1	1			15
Nonferrous metal		1	1			1		2 [c]	5
Metallic products		1							1
Machine tools	2								2
Auto & other	10	6		2					18
Electric & electronic products	3	5		1					9
Total	59	38	8	3	3	6	1	2	120

[a] The holdings of three foreign companies in the three firms listed as the largest holders boost the average of this industry: Anglosaxon Petroleum Co., 50 percent; Tidewater Petroleum Co., 49 percent; Standard Vacuum Oil Co., 55 percent.

[b] In one firm, the Goodrich Corporation owns 35 percent as the largest stockholder.

[c] Two firms in this industry are owned by the users of their products. Theoretically, they could be considered as their plants, since one of them is totally owned by its user and the other has 97.35 per cent of the shares.

SOURCE: The data for this table were obtained from an unpublished study by Mr. Misonou of the FTC, "Daikigyō niokeru Kabushiki Shoyū" (Stockholdings of the Largest Firms), 1960.

terms of total assets) manufacturing firms which are usually market leaders—that is, those ranking high in each market in terms of concentration ratios—[12] we find that these corporations, in 1960, were no longer controlled by one bank or absolutely owned by a family interest. The percentage of the total shares owned by the largest holders in each of these 120 firms appears in Table 26. The largest stockholder in 59 out of 120 firms owned less than 5 percent, and the largest stockholder in 38 firms owned less than 10 but more than 5 percent.[13] Let us examine the three largest shareholders in the five leading firms of the above-

TABLE 27

The Three Largest Shareholders of Five
Selected Leading Firms, 1960

INDUSTRY	NAME OF FIRM	LARGEST HOLDER	PER-CENT	2ND LARGEST HOLDER	PER-CENT	3RD LARGEST HOLDER	PER-CENT
Coal Mining	Mitsui Mining	Yamato Bank	4.42	Nomura Securities	3.99	Mitsui Bank	1.67
Chem. Textile	Toyo Textile	Mitsubishi Credit	4.92	Yamato Bank	4.60	Japan Life Insurance	2.09
Paper	Jyujo Paper	Mitsubishi Credit	6.50	Yamato Bank	4.24	Sumitomo Bank	4.10
Iron & Steel	Yawata Steel	Japanese Bank	2.82	Yamato Bank	2.47	Mitsubishi Credit	2.07
Electric Products	Toshiba Electric	Industrial Bank International General Electric (U.S.A.)	7.16	First Life Insurance	4.04	Yamato Bank	3.48

SOURCE: Same as for Table 26.

mentioned 120. (These five firms are a biased sample in the sense that they overrepresent holders with Zaibatsu names.) Even if we were to grant for the moment that such stockholders as the Yamato,[14] Mitsui, Mitsubishi, and Sumitomo banks are the so-called Zaibatsu banks, we must note the striking contrast to prewar days (see Table 27).

[12] These concentration ratios are in terms of total value shipments in yen by a firm, divided by the total of shipments in a market. For measures of concentration, see M. Adelman, "The Measures of Industrial Concentration," *Review of Economics and Statistics*, XXXIII (November 1951), 278.

[13] Of course these percentages can be significant in terms of possible control, especially when the stockholding is diffused. Also see fn. 32, below.

[14] Yamato Bank is the former Nomura Bank, which was considered a second-rate (minor) Zaibatsu in prewar years. According to the amount of loans made by this bank, it is not among the ten largest.

The Mitsui, in 1928, owned an average of 69.4 percent of the shares in the ten largest Mitsui-affiliated firms.[15] The Mitsui Bank in 1960 owned only 1.67 percent of Mitsui Mining, and was not even the largest stockholder; the largest stockholder was the Yamato Bank. In prewar days no two Zaibatsu were found together in the list of the largest stockholders of the large firms in Japan. Their relationship was usually,

TABLE 28

Ten Largest Shareholders of Hitachi,
Yawata, and Fuji (1961)
(Shareholding in percentage of the total number of shares outstanding)

HITACHI MANUFACTURING		YAWATA STEEL		FUJI STEEL	
HOLDER	SHARE-HOLDING	HOLDER	SHARE-HOLDING	HOLDER	SHARE-HOLDING
Nippon Life	5.0	Mitsubishi Credit Kogyo	3.0	Mitsubishi Credit Kogyo	3.2
Mitsubishi Credit	4.8	Bank	2.7	Bank	3.0
Meiji Life	2.2	Fuji Bank	2.1	Toyo Credit	2.6
Toyo Credit	1.8	Toyo Marihu Insurance	1.9	Sanna Bank	2.1
Sumitomo Credit	1.7	Sanna Bank	1.8	Kobe Bank	2.1
Dai-ichi Life	1.3	Sumitomo Bank	1.8	Sumitomo Bank	2.1
Nissan Life	1.1	Toyo Credit	1.7	Fuji Bank	2.1
Kogyo Bank	1.1	Mitsubishi Bank	1.5	Tokai Bank	1.8
Nissan Fire	0.9	Japan Ore Mining	1.4	Mitsui Bank	1.8
Hitachi Shipbuilding	0.8	Toyo Can Mfg.	1.4	Mitsubishi Bank	1.8
Total	20.7		19.3		22.6

SOURCE: Based on N. Imai, ed., *Gendai Nippon no Dokusen Shihon* (Monopoly Capital of Contemporary Japan), I (Tokyo, 1965), 107.

as Lockwood put it, dog-eat-dog rivalry,[16] and today there is no reason to believe that these large banks are less than fiercely competitive. Jyujo Paper is a striking example, in that three so-called Zaibatsu are listed as its three largest owners.[17] In the old days of Zaibatsu control, such a

[15] Higuchi, p. 43.
[16] Lockwood, p. 230.
[17] Professor Kenzo Suzuki has very effectively criticized the general and specific weaknesses of this popular thesis of financial control by the revivalists, attacking Miyazaki Yoshiichi's articles in which the latter presented the *keiretsu* thesis. K. Suzuki, "On the Monopolistic Tendencies of Postwar Japan," *Riron Keizaigaku* (Journal of Theoretical Economics), Vol. XIII, No. 2 (February 1962), pp. 48–57.

grouping would have been inconceivable except in the rarest cases of joint ventures. Table 28, which is compiled for the three largest firms in terms of total assets in 1961, makes this point even more clearly.

The major reason for this phenomenon is the increasing absolute capital requirement of modern technology. Many firms including these largest had been and continue to be dependent on outside funds to meet their investment needs. It is noteworthy that the three largest shareholders of the Yawata Steel in 1961 (Table 28) are different in composition and ranking, indicating a fluid relationship of suppliers of funds and borrowers in contrast to the stable relationship prevailing in prewar years. The increasing need of investment funds no longer leaves room for the prewar sort of cohesiveness of the holding-company type, tightly organized and easily identifiable units of financial *lineage* (*keiretsu*).

MUTUAL STOCKHOLDING PATTERNS OF BANKS
AND FIRMS, AND INTERLOCKING DIRECTORSHIPS

In spite of this evidence, Professor Nagasu and others maintain that the large banks are still centers of reemerging Zaibatsu. For example, Giga flatly states that "these financial institutions (banks and other financial intermediaries) are the most important links in their stockholding patterns in *Konzerns* and therefore for 'Zaibatsu revival.' " [18] Professor Nagasu, along with others, bases his argument on the fact that the Zaibatsu-affiliated firms own their respective Zaibatsu banks, and their mutual stockholding pattern is such that these "well-knit" groups are Zaibatsu. Taking the Mitsui Bank as an example, we can examine Giga's data. He found that nineteen so-called Mitsui-affiliated firms jointly owned 16.2 percent of the Mitsui Bank, as of 1960, and that the Mitsui Bank then invested in these firms.[19] The danger lies in not examining these figures a step further. We learn that one of these nineteen firms owned 2.6 percent of the Mitsui Bank, and that this was the largest percentage owned by any firm in this group of nineteen Mitsui-affiliated firms. A firm owning merely 12,000 shares (less than .07 percent), out of the total of 18,000,000 shares of the Mitsui Bank, was also included in this group of nineteen.[20]

Let us now examine how much control the Mitsui Bank had in these nineteen firms. The group included Mitsui Mining, in which the bank

[18] Giga, pp. 265–266.

[19] Data for this paragraph and the two following are obtained from Giga, p. 269, and the Misonou data as identified in the source for Table 26.

[20] As of June 1942, the largest shareholders of the Mitsui Bank were: the Mitsui family (475,977 shares), Mitsui Hō-onkai (200,000), and Mitsui Insurance (16,200); i.e., these three owned nearly 69 percent of the total (one million shares). Higuchi, p. 43.

was the third largest holder, with 1.67 percent of the total shares. In
Mitsui Chemical, another in this group, the bank owned 2.14 percent,
again as the third largest holder; and in Mitsui Shipbuilding, the bank
was not even one of the three largest holders. The control the bank had
in these nineteen firms was, to say the least, extremely tenuous, though
firms were classified as Mitsui-affiliated.

A similar observation could be made for other so-called Zaibatsu
banks. For example, if we take ten Mitsubishi-affiliated firms which had
borrowed over one billion yen or more from the Mitsubishi Bank, we
find that in no case was the Mitsubishi Bank the largest stockholder. In
three firms, the bank was the third largest; in four, the fourth; in one,
the sixth; in one, the ninth; and in one, the fifteenth largest stockholder.
Five of these firms received their largest loans from government banks,
and in five other cases the largest loans were from other "Zaibatsu
banks." [21] In short, what is meant by Mitsui- or Mitsubishi-affiliated
firms is that some portion of their shares (no matter how small) was
owned by one of these formerly Zaibatsu banks. There is no reason to
suspect that these so-called affiliated firms acted according to the will of
these banks. In many cases, one firm can be "affiliated" with several
large banks, which often include one of the government-owned banks.

Along with these bank-firm financial-connection arguments to prove
the Zaibatsu revival, we often find that the Zaibatsu revivalists—if we
can so label them—stress mutual stockholding among "Zaibatsu firms."
One such example can be found in a book by Professor Tsuru: "The
new Mitsubishi Shoji Company came to hold significant parts of shares
of Mitsubishi-related firms, such as the Mitsubishi Bank, Mitsubishi
Marine Transportation Company, New Mitsubishi Heavy Industry
Company, Mitsubishi Chemical Company, and Mitsubishi Electric
Equipment Manufacturing Company. In this manner, the interlocking
ownership of the former Mitsubishi Zaibatsu firms is rapidly becoming
as close as it was before the war." [22]

However, examine the 1960 data on these "significant parts of shares"

[21] A table in the *Oriental Economist* which was to show the interlocking shareholding pattern of "the Mitsubishi Group Affiliates" suffers from the same weakness as
Giga's work. The cross-classification of mutual shareholding of twenty-four firms, upon
further examination, discloses the weakness of the link among these firms rather than
the cohesion implied. In clear contrast to the prewar pattern, we find in the table
that the largest owner of the Mitsubishi Shoji (trading) is Tokyo Marine and Fire,
with 6.95 percent. But the latter holds, as one of the three largest shareholders,
shares in such firms as C. Itoh, Meiden-Sha, and Ataka Sangyo, which are classified
as Sumitomo affiliates by Giga and others. We also note that only 3.75 percent of
the total shares of Tokyo Marine and Fire is owned by the Mitsubishi Bank.
"Zaibatsu Revival?" *Oriental Economist*, XXVI (June 1958), 348–349.
[22] Tsuru, pp. 69–70.

TABLE 29
Stockholdings of Mitsubishi Shoji (Trading) in "Mitsubishi-Affiliated" Firms, 1960

NAME OF COMPANY	TOTAL SHARES	SHARES OWNED BY MITSUBISHI SHOJI	PERCENTAGE OWNED BY MITSUBISHI SHOJI
Mitsubishi Bank	220,000,000	2,277,000	1.25
Mitsubishi Marine Transportation	96,000,000	1,501,000	1.60
Mitsubishi Chemical	200,000,000	838,000	0.42
Mitsubishi New Heavy Equipment	246,960,000	1,103,000	0.44
Mitsubishi	265,000,000	961,000	0.37

given in Table 29.[23] To say that Mitsubishi Shoji owned "significant parts" of "Mitsubishi-affiliated firms" is unwarranted, and the statement made by Professor Tsuru must be interpreted in the light of the above knowledge. Several other cases of mutual holding among large firms recently cited by Japanese writers fail to establish the point intended when examined in more detail.[24]

Interlocking directorship is invariably mentioned by the revivalists as an effective link in the Zaibatsu revival. Some writers are ready to accept all firms that list a former Mitsubishi officer as their director or auditor as members of the Mitsubishi-affiliates. Many others tabulate names of firms having interlocking directors and infer, without further evidence, that these firms are elements of a reviving Zaibatsu whose will is

[23] Computed from Giga, pp. 270–271. The Giga data against which the statement of Professor Tsuru was checked are for 1960, two years after the publication of Professor Tsuru's book.

[24] Examining the so-called proofs of mutual stockholding among "reviving Zaibatsu firms," we discover that the standards used by the revivalists are quite subjective and vary considerably from one author to another. No two authors seem to agree upon the degree of financial connection necessary for two firms to be called "financially connected." There are cases in which a firm is identified as "Mitsui-affiliated" by one author and as "Mitsubishi-affiliated" by another. According to one economist, two giant firms could be considered as financially connected for the purpose of Zaibatsu revival if both of them happen to own a small percentage of the shares (even less than 1 percent) of a third small firm. Another economist grouped all firms whose largest holders were foreigners and called these firms "foreign Zaibatsu." Giga, chap. 6, "Dokusen Kinyūkikan to Dokusenteki Sangyōshihon tono Yugō Yuchaku Kankei no Kyōka" (Monopolistic Financial Organizations and Their Fusion with Industrial Capital), *Monopolistic Enterprise of Contemporary Japan*; Shimazaki Teruo, *Nippon no Ginkō* (Banks in Japan) (Tokyo, 1961); Yonemura Hajime, "Seijyōka Katei ni okeru Keiretsuyūshi no Kentō" (An Examination of Financial Connection in the Stage of Normalization), *Kōsei Torihiki* (May 1956), pp. 2–14.

coordinated by these directors.[25] But in view of the much reduced mutual shareholdings observed earlier and also in view of the drastically changed economic structure of postwar Japan, a careful qualitative study of postwar interlocking directorship is required before one advances what he observes today as evidence for revival of well-knit clusters of firms which are "controlled by monopoly capital." [26] In the absence of evidence, the postwar interlocking directorship must be considered different from that of prewar years.

Before the war, interlocking directors were overseers from *Honsha* (the parent company) and were dispatched to carry out a centralized *Honsha* policy. "So strict was the control over personnel that prior to dissolution all interchanges of employees, both executives and staff, among subsidiaries were directed by Sumitomo Main (*Honsha*), which also undertook the original hiring and assignment." [27] Under such circumstances, interlocking directors possessed power akin to that of a colonel from the office of the inspector general. Interlocking directors of today are far from being overseers or effective coordinators. There exists "a manifest sign of keen competitiveness among the firms in an affiliated group in production of a commodity or in gaining the hegemony in the market," even when interlocking directors are found for the so-called affiliated group. To cite only two well-known cases of "intra-affiliated firm" competition, two "Mitsubishi-affiliated" and interlocked firms are known to have been keenly competitive in the production of chemically processed lead, and three "Mitsubishi-affiliated firms," also interlocked, have engaged in competitive bidding in order to obtain a patent-lease agreement with an American firm.[28]

In this connection, several presidents' clubs are often cited as added evidence of the Zaibatsu revival. Some authors regard these regularly scheduled meetings of presidents of the so-called affiliated firms as equivalent to the top-level meetings of former Zaibatsu combines. But here again, in their anxiety to revive the Zaibatsu, the revivalists often seem to have ignored a clear qualitative difference between these clubs and the prewar metings over which a head of a Zaibatsu clan presided. This difference is well summarized in the *Oriental Economist*:

> The Kin'yo Kai [The Friday Club] serves as a clearing house for information, and also as a consultative organ. It makes no deci-

---

[25] See for example, Higuchi, pp. 46–53.

[26] This is a pet phrase of the revivalists, though never defined.

[27] The *Oriental Economist*, XXVII (July 1959), 414.

[28] These examples and the quotation in this paragraph are from H. Misonou, "Sengo Dokusen Taikei no Tokushitsu" (Characteristics of the Postwar Monopolistic Organization), *Keizai Hyoron* (Tokyo, 1962), p. 27.

sions, and it has no secretarial machinery. Consequently, it would be erroneous to believe that the Kin'yo Kai exercises the authority and power formerly wielded by the Mitsubishi Main [parent] company. This contention, asserted in various ways by Mitsubishi executives, appears to be true. But there is no denying that the Kin'yo Kai does function as an effective pivot for coordination of group-affiliated activities.[29]

How effective a pivot this type of club makes is a question yet to be examined. The "coordination of group-affiliated activities" needs to be established in economically meaningful terms if it is to be used as evidence of the Zaibatsu revival.

DISTRIBUTION OF STOCKHOLDING

All these efforts by the revivalists are intended to show somehow that a behind-the-scene financial control center approximating that of the former Zaibatsu exists. On the basis of the preceding examination, however, we must conclude that such centers no longer exist in Japan. This judgment is further enforced when we consider what is now known as the "Stockholding Revolution of Japan" which has taken place since the end of World War II. If we observe those individuals who owned more than 100 shares of stock for the four selected years as below, we find that the number of such holders has been steadily increasing since 1946 (see Table 30).

TABLE 30

Number of Individuals Owning More Than 100 Shares

	1946	1950	1956	1960
Number of individuals	1,712,650	4,288,545	8,606,889	10,660,260

SOURCE: Tokyo Security Exchange, *Tokyo Shōkenjo Tōkei Nempō* (Tokyo Security Exchange Annual Statistical Report) (Tokyo, 1960), p. 113.

Has there been a tendency for ownership of these shares to concentrate in the hands of a few individuals or a few nerve centers of financial control, as was the case before the Zaibatsu dissolution? Tables 31 and 32 furnish the pattern of changes in stockholding since the end of the war; the following conclusions may be made: (1) Although we observe a gradual trend of concentration of holdings in the hands of the largest holders when the percentage distribution of shares held by size of shareholding is examined, it is evident that these holders have increasingly been institutions rather than individuals; and (2) the holdings of

[29] The *Oriental Economist*, XXVII (July 1959), 414.

TABLE 31

Percentages of Shares Held by Size of Shareholding, 1945–1961

SHAREHOLDING CLASS (SHARES)	1945	1949	1950	1951	1952	1953	1954	1955	1956	1957	1958	1959	1960	1961
Less than 100	8.93	2.61	1.70	1.02	0.81	0.56	0.38	0.29	0.19	0.15	0.13	0.11	0.09	1.13
100–499	17.41	21.23	19.11	16.48	15.43	12.29	10.75	8.59	4.66	3.30	2.57	1.93	1.48	— —
500–999	6.31	11.64	11.05	10.48	10.83	9.55	9.69	9.76	8.85	8.46	7.82	7.06	6.19	4.59
1,000–4,999	13.51	24.22	21.53	21.09	21.03	22.08	22.95	23.38	23.13	24.61	25.05	24.39	23.56	24.37
5,000–9,999	5.10	5.49	4.96	4.75	4.36	4.36	4.49	4.69	5.23	5.26	5.25	5.29	5.62	5.51
10,000–49,999	— —	— —	— —	— —	12.17	10.81	10.04	9.64	8.86	8.26	7.84	7.60	7.49	— —
50,000–99,999	48.74	34.82	41.65	45.83	6.31	5.95	5.29	5.00	4.31	3.78	3.33	3.09	2.81	64.40
Over 100,000	— —	— —	— —	— —	29.06	34.46	36.41	38.45	44.77	46.18	48.01	50.43	52.76	— —

NOTE: This data covers only those firms listed at stock exchanges. The number of firms vary from 631 in 1945 to 785 in 1961, but this covers all giant firms (assets exceeding one trillion yen) and about one-third of the large firms (assets exceeding 100 billion yen).

SOURCE: N. Imai, ed., *Gendai Nippon no Dokusen Shihon* (Monopolistic Capital of Contemporary Japan), I (Tokyo, 1965), 97.

TABLE 32

Percentage of Shares Held by Type of Shareholders, 1945–1961

TYPES	1945	1949	1950	1951	1952	1953	1954	1955	1956	1957	1958	1959	1960	1961
National and local governments	8.29	2.80	3.14	1.76	1.01	0.71	0.53	0.39	0.27	0.23	0.33	0.22	0.20	0.18
Financial institutions	11.17	9.91	12.63	18.64	21.82	22.94	23.65	23.61	25.56	26.11	29.00	29.30	30.62	31.19
Brokerage firms	2.82	12.56	11.90	9.22	8.44	7.34	7.06	7.94	7.10	5.69	4.38	3.74	3.72	2.65
Legal persons (firms)	24.65	5.59	11.03	17.80	11.75	13.54	14.52	14.64	17.04	17.56	16.95	17.33	17.80	17.69
Individuals	53.07	69.14	61.30	56.98	55.79	53.79	54.04	53.15	49.85	50.13	48.93	47.74	46.19	46.63
Foreigners	—	—	—	—	1.19	1.68	0.20	0.27	0.18	0.28	0.29	0.25	0.27	6.63
Foreign legal persons	—	—	—	—	—	—	1.52	1.46	1.30	1.24	1.16	1.19	1.07	1.33
Others	—	—	—	—	—	—	—	—	—	—	0.10	0.10	0.15	—

NOTE: See Table 31
SOURCE: Same as Table 31, pp. 98–99.

individuals and legal persons who could be controlled by individuals have been shown to be either stable or declining. These are sharp contrasts vis-à-vis the prewar pattern. For example in 1960, of 4,769,602 shares issued by the 200 largest firms, 9.5 percent was owned by individuals (4.4 percent by Japanese and 5.1 by foreigners), 16.5 percent was owned by legal persons, and 1.7 percent by others. The remaining 72.3 percent was owned by financial institutions, which are owned, in turn, by numerous legal persons and individuals. Observing the same data, two Japanese "revivalists" concluded that "the controlling shareholders of the large firms in Japan are financial institutions. This means that the controlling shareholders of the large enterprises are large enterprises themselves and that the large enterprises control all of the shareholders." [30] This conclusion is justified only if these financial institutions are still controlled by the same few Zaibatsu families and firms that existed before World War II.

CONCLUSION

Our preceding examination indicates that the term "Zaibatsu," as used in postwar years, is not synonymous with the prewar Zaibatsu. We could perhaps go so far as to say that in prewar terms, Zaibatsu no longer exists in Japan. We must admit that the postwar diffusion of the shareholding pattern may permit the control of large firms with a much smaller percentage of total shares. The large banks, with former Zaibatsu names, are still significant in terms of the loans they make, expressed as a percentage of total bank loans; but shareholding patterns are approaching those of Western nations,[31] and the postwar shareholding pattern is generically different from that of prewar days. It is no longer manipulated by the behind-the-scenes financial power representing a few family interests. In recent years, the absolute control of large firms once enjoyed by former Zaibatsu families cannot be found.[32]

[30] N. Imai, ed., *Gendai Nippon no Dokusen Shihon* (Monopoly Capital of Contemporary Japan), I (Tokyo, 1965), 102.
[31] A recent study by S. P. Florence on the shareholding pattern of the largest English firms provides a useful comparison. The Japanese stockholding pattern, as shown in Table 26, is considerably less concentrated than that of the English firms examined by S. P. Florence, *Ownership, Control, and Success of Large Companies: An Analysis of English Industrial Structure and Policy, 1939–1951,* (London: Sweet and Maxwell, 1961).
[32] In contrast to the U.S. practice, though bankers' ownership of industrial common stocks and the large number and influence of cartels in Japan are to be carefully analyzed, the author ventures an opinion that a markedly similar control mechanism could be observed in view of similarly widespread stock ownership in both countries. In the case of Japan, "the center of gravity" of control is expected to lean more toward banks, but, vis-à-vis the U.S., it is a question of degree and not of kind as it was before the war.

Regardless of postwar Americanization, however, Japan will retain in her economic system some reflection of prewar traits. One such trait could be the relative importance of personal contacts. For example, preferential arrangements among formerly Zaibatsu-connected officers are often explicitly or implicitly suggested as the core of the postwar Zaibatsu. But if such relationships exist, in this case as well as in those cases involving the effectiveness of interlocking directorships and the presidents' clubs, they must be examined and shown to outweigh the evidence given in this chapter before they are used as proofs of be- hind-the scenes financial power or of a Zaibatsu revival.

As shown in chapter 6, the market structure of Japanese industry has become more concentrated since the end of World War II. But an increasingly concentrated market structure, even the emergence of near-monopoly firms, cannot be equated with a Zaibatsu revival.

During the period between 1953 and 1958, Phase I of chapter 6, the ranking of the top ten firms changed visibly. This was a phenomenon that had never existed before in Japanese industry. For example, Lock- wood described the Japanese economy following World War I as fol- lows:

> Japanese governments looked to the Zaibatsu for aid and assistance in financing public budgets, in building foreign trade and colonial enterprise, and in creating heavy industries required by the Army and the Navy. . . . All these political prerequisites and connec- tions worked to the advantage of the great financial houses, and made it the more difficult after 1900 for any upstart to challenge their supremacy. . . . Given the political setting, and the general shortage of capital and experience for large-scale industry, the big combines enjoyed unusual opportunities for employing familiar business devices to concentrate power.[33]

If we confine ourselves to the question of market power, we find that the supremacy of many of the largest firms was successfully challenged by "upstarts." As one newspaper reported, "The biggest gains since the war have been made by those firms with no previous Zaibatsu ties or those which have gotten farthest away from them."[34] The unchallengeable economic hegemony of the Zaibatsu group, which Lockwood seems to be describing, had become a thing of the past as far as market power was concerned.

Even since 1959—a period of pro-monopoly policy (Phase II of chapter 6)—newly emerging market leaders have become more securely entrenched. They enjoy the market power they possess because of size,

---

[33] Lockwood, pp. 221–222.
[34] The Asahi Evening News (Tokyo, March 3, 1962).

efficiency, and other related reasons, in the fashion of Ford, General Motors, and General Electric. This power is distinctively different from the power enjoyed by Zaibatsu which Lockwood described above.

Any discussion of the Zaibatsu must be made in full cognizance of the basic changes that have taken place in the economy since the end of World War II. The postwar Japanese economy is increasingly geared to mass production and mass distribution to a degree unknown in prewar years. This has necessitated numerous changes in interfirm relationships. Technological changes require a closer coordination of the activities of firms; inputs and outputs must now flow smoothly; and sales must be made under a well-known brand name.[35]

The postwar changes in interfirm relationships, which are rooted in the rapidly increasing optimum size of production units and mass distribution, have received and continue to receive the direct and indirect blessings of the government. The policy makers, who are anxious to foster growth and, especially the competitive ability of Japanese firms in international markets, can ill afford to discourage the emerging pattern of interfirm relationships.

It would be a mistake, however, to conclude that the Japanese government aided "the revival of Zaibatsu" in its anxiety to achieve rapid growth. To denounce the large firms as monopolistic capitalists and Zaibatsu is a serious error of naïve Marxists who fail to distinguish the fundamental differences between the prewar-type interfirm relationships and the postwar developments resulting from "the Second Stage of the Industrialization." [36] Many of the socially desirable aspects of the functions once performed by the prewar Zaibatsu are now performed by large firms. The government, as discussed in chapters 5 and 6, adopted policies to encourage these socially desirable functions (which Lockwood discussed) of the prewar Zaibatsu to be performed by large postwar firms.

Although this chapter argues that the Zaibatsu (as defined in Webster's New Collegiate Dictionary "the few, especially four, wealthy families owning and controlling most of the Japanese industries") has been dissolved and has not revived, this is not to endorse all the means by and the extent to which the government has been and is fostering these replacements for the prewar Zaibatsu. We shall attempt to evaluate these policies of the government in the final chapter, following examinations of two other aspects of postwar Japanese economic policy.

[35] Some of these so-called affiliated groups, when examined, turn out to be relationships cemented by the participating firms' desire to assure their supply of input or sale of their output.

[36] *The Economist* (London, September 8, 1962), pp. 907–936.

8 TAX POLICY FOR ECONOMIC GROWTH

REVISIONS IN 1953–1954

Like the Anti-Monopoly Act, the tax laws underwent a series of revisions following the Korean War. In 1953 the government was anxious to reduce the pace of inflation, which followed the Korean War boom, in order to "rectify the seriously unbalanced international trade and to aid rapid capital accumulation for the sake of rationalization." Thus, along with the full-scale 1953 amendment of the Anti-Monopoly Act, six fundamental revisions were made in the tax laws. These clearly indicated the policy goal and the extent to which the Japanese government was departing from the principles recommended by the Shoup mission.[1]

The wealth tax introduced by the Shoup mission was eliminated entirely on the grounds that assessing the value of wealth was exceedingly difficult to administer and evasions were relatively easy by such means as hoarding jewels or other types of assets that could escape assessors' eyes. Along with this change, the maximum tax rate for personal income tax was raised from 55 percent for income exceeding two million yen, to 65 percent for income exceeding five million yen. But this increase was mere formality, as the following will reveal.

The capital gains tax, which enjoyed a partial exemption, was eliminated for gains resulting from share trading. A new share-trading tax was levied as shares were sold *independent* of all other incomes. The new tax

---

[1] Factual observations in the first half of this chapter are based on: Japan Tax Research Association, *Zeisei Kenkyū Sankō Shiryō-shu* (Collected Data for Research in Taxation) (Tokyo, 1965); H. Matsukuma, ed., *Sengo Nippon no Zeisei* (The Tax System of Postwar Japan) (Tōyō-Keizai, 1959); and Y. Hayashi, *Sengo Nippon no Sozei Kōzō* (The Tax Structure of Postwar Japan) (Tokyo, 1958).

was to be paid by the seller on the value of the shares sold. The two major reasons advanced at the time were: (1) to avoid more capital gains due to share trading than other forms of capital gains (land, forest, and other types of assets which already enjoyed exemptions); and (2) to increase the inflow of capital into the stock market.

Under the tax laws of 1953, capital gains that resulted from the dissolution or mergers of firms were taxed on individuals receiving such gains, at the rate applicable on the personal income tax schedule. However, the 1953 amendment made such gains taxable at the corporate level before these gains were distributed to individuals. The tax rate was a flat 46 percent, on the basis that this would simplify tax collection and keep the tax burden on dissolution gains in line with other changes made in 1953, especially the elimination of the capital gains tax on share trading.

The accessions tax, which was introduced by the Shoup recommendation, was divided into inheritance and gift taxes. The inheritance tax was to be paid on an "as inherited" basis and not cumulatively as it was under the accession tax. The exemption, also, was raised from 300,000 yen to 500,000 yen. The rate ranged from 15 percent for an inheritance below 200,000 yen, to 70 percent for an inheritance exceeding one hundred million yen.

The final and most important revision, in the sense that this was the course that the Shoup mission had explicitly opposed, allowed all interest income to be taxed *independently* of all other incomes at a flat rate of 10 percent. This measure dramatically demonstrated that Japanese tax policy was to follow a path of encouraging capital accumulation, though it could mean a significant reduction in the progressivity of the income tax. In the same spirit, for the official reason of controlling inflation, the sugar tax was raised rather sharply.[2]

In the free corporate sector, a tax exemption of 50 percent for profit earned from exports was granted. This became the first of a series of special exemptions and reductions which have been granted in rapid succession to the corporate sector since 1953. The Tax System Examination Commission (*Zeisei Chōsa Kai*) was established in August 1953 as an advisory body to the cabinet. The first report of the commission, issued early in 1954, stated, "A reduction of the tax burden must be continued with emphasis on direct taxes, especially on the personal income tax. However, we cannot reduce taxes without meeting our revenue needs; therefore, an increase in revenue as the result of increased

[2] The sugar tax rose from 1,950 yen per *kin* to 2,350 yen per *kin*. One *kin* is 0.6 kilogram.

economic activities which are motivated by tax reduction and revenues from taxes on luxury items and other indirect taxes must be increased. A decrease in the income tax is helpful in providing stability of the economy and a hope for tomorrow's life; thus an increase in indirect taxes at this juncture [of our economy] is inevitable."[3] At the time of the report, the Consumer Price Index was rising and one of the reasons for the above quotation was to "check inflation" by means of higher excise taxes. However, as the last sentence of the quotation makes clear, the commission in effect endorsed the government policy of rapid capital accumulation.

In 1954 a 300-million-yen deficit in the international trade balance and steadily rising price levels, which were encouraged by the easy money policy of 1953, threatened the trade balance further. Thus, a policy of "tax reform without tax reduction" was adopted and this appeared in the 1954 revisions in the form of a significant increase in indirect taxes, further increases in special tax reductions, and exemptions benefiting legal persons (firms), especially the larger firms.[4]

The changes in the personal income tax schedule were minor, but they were directed toward reducing the progressivity in the schedule. The amount of reduction in the personal income tax was relatively small (32 billion yen), but it was offset by an increase in indirect taxes (27.5 billion yen) on tobacco, sugar, sake, automobiles, television sets, and gasoline. Also, the tax rate on interest income was reduced from 10 to 5 percent. In the corporate sector, the 1954 revision allowed a new 5 percent tax reduction on profits earned by exporting plants (building plants and equipping them), and the conditions for tax exemptions for price fluctuations were relaxed so that firms could now reserve funds during boom years in anticipation of future price decreases. In short the expression "tax reform without tax reduction" applied to taxpayers as a whole, but not to a particular class of taxpayers who either benefited by the decreased progressivity in the income tax schedule and added special provisions or suffered by increases in indirect taxes.

REVISIONS IN 1955–1957

The Liberal-Democrats' new cabinet, which was formed in March 1955, promised during the election campaign that 1955 would be a year of large tax cuts for everyone. The total tax reduction carried out was 34 billion yen, a figure smaller than the 50 billion promised during the campaign; the cabinet, however, was able to deliver its campaign prom-

[3] Quoted in Matsukuma, ed., *Sengo Nippon no Zeisei* (The Tax Systems of Postwar Japan), p. 128.

[4] Quantitative evidence is presented in Tables 43 and 44 in this chapter.

ise of a tax reduction for all, mostly because of a upturn in economic activity. By 1955, the international trade balance was back in the black, due to an improved world market and the success of the tight money policy. Industrial expansion began with renewed vigor. It was estimated that GNP would rise by 10 percent in 1955. Three major tax reduction measures were carried out:

(1) *Income tax cut.* The personal income tax schedule of 1955 was designed to benefit all but the top three income classes in the tax schedule. A comparison of the 1954 and 1955 tax schedules makes this evident (see Table 33).

TABLE 33

Personal Income Tax Schedule
1954 *vs.* 1955 (percent)
(income in 1,000 yen)

Income class 1954	Below 20	20–70	70–120	120–200	200–300	300–500	500–1000	1000–2000	2000–3000	3000–5000	Above 5000
Income class 1955	Below 25	25–75	75–135	135–250	250–400	400–650	650–1100	1100–2000	2000–3000	3000–5000	Above 5000
Tax rate	15	20	25	30	35	40	45	50	55	60	65

SOURCE: Japan Tax Research Association (Collected Data for Research in Taxation) (Tokyo, 1965), pp. 48–49.

(2) *Abolition of the tax on interest income and tax rate reduction for dividend income.* These two 1955 revisions were significant changes which, in effect, reduced the existing progressivity in the personal income tax schedule. The interest income was made tax-free for two years (1955–1956) as "a measure for capital accumulation." Also, for the same reason, the tax rate on dividend income was reduced from 15 to 10 percent, and the exemption for dividend income was increased from 25 to 30 percent for a two-year period (1955–1956).

(3) *Reduction of the corporate profits tax.* This tax, which has stood at 42 percent since 1952, was reduced to 40 percent for firms where profit exceeded 500,000 yen and 35 percent for those below that amount. The differential rates were introduced to compensate for the increasingly large tax privileges enjoyed by larger firms.

Although it was suggested during the election campaign that the tax reductions might necessitate an increase in indirect taxes, no significant increase was made in the latter. As a general observation, one could say that the 1955 revision distributed the benefit of economic growth to all, though the distribution of this benefit clearly favored continued growth rather than increased equality of income distribution.

The tax law changes carried out in 1956 were minor. The so-called *Jimmu* Prosperity[5] of 1956 enabled the government to maintain a balanced budget, which was based on the optimistic forecast of the economy envisioned during the adoption of the 1955 tax revisions.[6] A change was made to reduce the tax relief granted for entertainment costs, which until then had received a minimum of control. This was the result of public criticism of lavish tax-supported expenditures by firms. Tax exemptions that were allowed for the funds reserved for retirement payments were also restricted, not to exceed the amount needed if one-half of all employees retired at the same time. The sugar tax was raised slightly, but the basic exemption was increased and a family of five (husband, wife, and three children) was now exempted from the personal income tax if their income did not exceed 20,000 yen per month.

The economy continued to maintain its high rate of growth throughout 1956. Realizing a larger-than-expected increase in tax revenue (190 billion yen), the Liberal-Democratic party in 1957 adopted a campaign slogan: "Tax reduction by 100 billion, and service increase by 100 billion."[7] Increased service meant that the government would increase investment in social overhead (roads and port facilities, and so forth), housing, and other welfare expenditures. Although the total tax reduction was 72 billion instead of 100 billion yen, the largest budget on record (1.375 trillion yen) promised increased highway construction and housing. Two major revisions made in 1957 were as follows:

(1) *Reduction in the personal income tax.* The personal income tax was reduced for all income classes, as shown in Table 34.

The 1957 revision was characterized by the facts that the tax rate for all income classes, except for those earning above 50 million yen, was lower than that which had been effective in 1956, and the rate of reduction was larger for higher income classes due to wider income class intervals. Considering the fact that the income class earning over 50 million yen consisted of only a handful of households, we can safely conclude that this revision reduced the progressivity of the tax schedule, though it reduced the tax rates for all income classes. Along with this

[5] See fn. 35, chap. 6.
[6] For the estimated 10 percent, the real growth rate was 10.3 percent.
[7] Matsukuma, p. 132.

TABLE 34

Personal Income Tax Schedule, 1956 vs. 1957 (percentage)
(income in 1,000 yen)

Income class 1956	Below 30	30–80	80–150	150–300	300–500	500–800	800–1200	1200–2000	2000–3000	3000–5000	Over 5000
Rate	15	20	25	30	35	40	45	50	55	60	65

Income class 1957	Below 50	50–200	200–500	500–1000	1000–1500	1500–2500	2500–4000	4000–6000	6000–10,000	10,000–20,000	20,000–30,000	30,000–50,000	Over 50,000
Rate	10	15	20	25	30	35	40	45	50	55	60	65	70

SOURCE: Same as Table 33.

change, the 1957 revision also extended the effective period of the provisions making interest income tax-free for an additional two years (1958–1959); and dividend income, which enjoyed a 10 percent flat tax rate and a 30 percent exemption after 1955, was also given the same extension.

(2) *Revisions in "special" reductions and exemptions.* The provision providing for a partial tax exemption of profits from exports was continued for an additional two years (1958–1959). However, some exemptions, such as for funds reserved for possible loss by export trading and expenditures made in establishing overseas branch offices, were abolished. The tax exemption granted for funds reserved for price fluctuation was restricted, but regulations pertaining to depreciation allowances were relaxed for the mining and forestry industries.

REVISIONS IN 1958

By March 1957, signs of "overheating" began to appear, and soon the 1958 recession was on. Following two increases in the discount rate in March and May, industrial output began to decrease. The Wholesale Price Index fell 15 percentage points by September 1958, compared with the all-time peak it reached in May 1957. The tax revisions reflected this change, and the government reacted to strengthen the industries. Thus, this was the year in which for the first time since 1950 there was no reduction in basic exemptions and changes in the personal income tax schedule. The revisions were concentrated in those areas that the government considered most effective in realizing its goals.

The corporate profits tax was reduced from 35 to 33 percent for small firms, and from 40 to 38 percent for large firms. Small firms were defined as those earning less than one million yen in 1958. (The 1959 revision raised it to two million yen.) As an emergency measure for capital accumulation, the 1958 revision allowed 3 percent of saving to be deducted from income tax payments, provided the 3 percent did not exceed 6,000 yen. Also, the minimum taxable inheritance was raised from 500,000 yen per heir to 1.5 million yen plus 300,000 yen multiplied by the number of heirs, and the rate was made less progressive. The gift tax, too, enjoyed a doubling of exemption levels from 100,000 yen to 200,000 yen.

REVISIONS IN 1959

In spite of increasing basic exemptions, the tax law revisions in the years preceding 1959 had undeniably favored the rich, that is, reduced effective progressivity in the income tax schedule. In 1959, however, we find a pause in this trend. The reasons for this are many, the most important being that the general election of 1959 was, for the first time, a confrontation of two major parties, the Liberal-Democrats and the Socialists. Splinter parties on the left and on the right had been absorbed, and the ground had been laid for a political struggle between the two major parties. Another important reason was that the recession of 1958 had ended and the economic outlook was for prosperity; also the Liberal-Democratic party, conscious of the 1958 revisions that favored the corporate sector and the higher income classes, was under pressure to adjust the distribution of tax burdens.

During the election campaign against the socialist platform, the Liberal-Democrats promised (1) to raise the basic exemption to 25,000

TABLE 35

Personal Income Tax Schedule Changes
Made in 1959 (percent)
(income in 1,000 yen)

Income class – (1957) below 50 – (1959) below 100	50–200 100–200
Rate (1957 & 1959) 10	15

SOURCE: Same as Table 33

yen per month for a family of five, from the prevailing 21,000 yen, to lighten the tax burden of wage earners; (2) to reduce indirect taxes to aid the lower income classes; and (3) to reduce local taxes, which were in many instances regressive or proportional to income. If progressivity existed in some types of local taxes, it was much less so when compared with national taxes—a condition that had become more and more prevalent due to the increased revenue needs of local governments. In all, the party promised a tax reduction of 70 billion yen.

The measures carried out by the victorious Liberal-Democratic party included an increase in the basic exemption that exceeded the amount it promised. The revision allowed for a basic exemption of 300,000 yen for a family of five. The changes made in the personal income tax schedule, too, realized the campaign promise. While no change, either in rates or in income class intervals, was made for those earning over 200,000 yen, the revisions shown in Table 35 were made for the lowest income classes.

Also, the tax exemption allowing for retirement income was raised from 500,000 yen to one million yen, and the 1959 revision introduced a provision which provided for an additional exemption according to age at retirement and length of service. Although the gasoline tax was raised for the purpose of meeting the increasing need for highways and their maintenance, taxes on sugar, entertainment, some categories of *sake*, and a dozen items in the Commodity Tax List were reduced.[8] Upon the expiration of the 1957 revision, interest income again became taxable at a flat 10 percent independently of all other income. But the prevailing provisions on dividend income (30 percent exemption and a flat 10 percent rate) were continued for an additional two years until 1961. On the other hand, except for the extension of a provision allowing for a fractional exemption of export income, there were only minor changes in the tax laws pertaining to the corporate sector.

TAX LAW CHANGES IN THE 1960'S

The tax law changes made during the period from 1960 through 1965 have been predictable. In those years of prosperity, the fruits of economic growth were distributed to all income classes; and especially when the corporate profit rates were high (1961 and 1962), the government carried out a revision in personal income taxes to reduce the tax burden on the lower income classes. In those years when the economy was in recession (1964–1965), the government effected changes which lightened the tax burden on the corporate sector.

The personal income tax schedule was changed twice in 1961 and 1962, and the 1962 rates were still in effect as of May 1965. As is noted in Table 36, the revisions of 1961 concentrated tax reductions in the lower income classes, while the 1962 revisions lowered the tax rates in all income classes except those earning above six million yen. (Only .1 percent of total taxpayers were earning over this amount in 1960.)

The tax on interest income, previously a flat 10 percent, was reduced in 1963 to a flat 5 percent for a period of two years. Also, the tax on dividend income was given the same reduction in rate, with an exemption of 30 percent for a period of two years. These measures were taken on the theory that such changes would aid industry, which was beginning to experience a downturn, because an increased inflow of capital to industry was needed to prepare it for the liberalization of international trade. In 1965 the tax rate on interest income reverted to 10 percent, and the tax on dividend income was raised to 15 percent. These changes were made primarily to offset other revisions which reduced the corpo-

[8] *Commodity Tax List* refers to items listed for excise taxes. Items listed are consumer durables and luxury items.

TABLE 36

Personal Income Tax Schedule (percentage), 1961 vs. 1962

1961 Income class	Below 15	15–40	40–70	70–100	100–150	150–250	250–400	400–600	600–1000	1000–2000	2000–3000	3000–5000	Over 5000
Tax rate	10	15	20	25	30	35	40	45	50	55	60	65	70

1962 Income class	Below 10	10–20	20–50	50–80	80–120	120–180	180–250	250–400	400–600	600–1000	1000–2000	2000–3000	3000–4000	4000–6000	Over 6000
Tax rate	8	10	15	20	25	30	35	40	45	50	55	60	65	70	75

SOURCE: Same as Table 33.

rate taxes. But a series of special "time laws" (*jigen-hō*) of two-year periods were continually enacted after 1953 to retain the special status of interest and dividend incomes. What began as a special measure in 1953 thus acquired permanence in the tax laws of postwar Japan.

Taxes on corporations were reduced by means of rate reduction and the introduction of a lower tax on distributed profits, and by changing the definition of small and large firms (see Table 37). These changes reflected the recession of 1963, the government's desire to accelerate the rate of investment, and a willingness to accommodate the demands of industries which were made in the name of "rationalization for the sake of facing increased international competition."

TABLE 37

Changes in Corporate Taxes (percentage)
(The figures in parentheses are the tax rates applicable to distributed profits)

	1961	1964	1965
Tax rates on large firms	38 (28)	38 (26)	37 (26)
Tax rates on small firms	33 (24)	33 (22)	31 (22)
Maximum profit to qualify for the small-firm rate	2 million yen	3 million yen	3 million yen

SOURCE: Same as Table 33.

The major reason for the continued differential rate for large and small firms of the corporate profits tax has, of course, been that the larger firms enjoy a far greater share of special deductions and exemptions. It is true that a firm earning less than three million in 1965 is an extremely small one, and the partial intent of this differential rate is undoubtedly to reduce the tax burden on these small firms to the level enjoyed, for example, by wage earners of similar income. But, as will be shown shortly, seventeen special provisions benefited the larger firms much more than the differential rates might suggest. In 1963 and 1965 the time limits of most of the existing special provisions were extended.

IMPACT OF THE TAX LAW REVISIONS

The foregoing is a brief outline of the changes in tax laws, in order to provide a glimpse of the basic policy. Our task in the remainder of this chapter is to evaluate the consequences of the changes summarized above. We can begin with an analysis of the revisions to the personal income tax burden. Due to the lack of data on all taxpayers,

TABLE 38

Exemptions for a Five-Person Household (in 1000 yen) and the Ratio of Annual Average Wage of Manufacturing Workers to Exemptions

YEAR	1953	1954	1955	1956	1957	1958	1959	1960	1961	1962	1963
Exemption [a]	208	222	241	249	275	283	325	328	371	363	364
Wage/exemption [b] (Japan)	108.1	102.8	100.7	105.3	98.8	94.3	86.6	89.2	81.9	86.7	86.4
Wage/exemption [c] (U.S.)	108.8	108.9	116.0	120.2	123.8	125.4	132.7	134.6	137.9	143.4	142.7

[a] The Japanese exemptions were calculated on the basis of the laws effective in that year.
[b] Wage data are based on The Ministry of Labor, *Maigetsu Chingin Tōkei Sōgō Hōkoku-shū* (Aggregate Report of Monthly Wages) (Tokyo, 1963), and are deflated by the Bank of Japan deflator.
[c] U.S. data are based on the *Economic Report of the President* (January 1965).

this examination of the incidence of the personal tax is made using the data available on wage earners, though an attempt will be made to evaluate the incidence on all types of income earners.

First, let us observe the gradual increase in basic exemptions made during the period between 1953 and 1963. To obtain a meaningful yardstick, the annual basic exemptions for a family of five (husband, wife, and three children) were calculated using the exemption criteria of the respective years and were compared to the annual average wage of manufacturing workers.

Of course, the wage/exemption ratio of less than 100 does not mean that typical households earning an average wage are exempted from the income tax, since in many instances it is likely that they have more than one wage earner and/or some asset income. Table 38, however, serves to show that, compared to the United States, the magnitude of Japanese exemptions measured in real terms has increased perceptibly over the years. Given the knowledge that postwar economic growth has indeed been effective in lowering the tax burden as a percentage of rising real income, what should one expect for the tax burden as a whole if we consider the total impact of changes in the personal income tax schedule, numerous revisions in indirect and excise taxes, and measures that gave preferential treatment to some types of income?

To pursue this question, we can make use of the data collected by the prime minister's office. This is a family budget study of urban wage earners (blue- and white-collar) who comprised nearly 54 percent of the total labor force in 1960. The data for the month of July have been chosen from each year under examination.[9] Table 39 gives the results of the computation which was made for indirect (sales) taxes on tobacco and alcoholic beverages and for direct (income) taxes, the income tax on earned wages, and the local income tax. (For explanations and the method of calculation, see Appendix II.)

Although data for the periods of 1953–1958 and 1959–1962 are not strictly comparable as the identification of income classes differs, a glance at Table 39 reveals that the tax paid by each income class, except the lowest, was smaller in 1962 than it was in 1953. Comparing the data for the period between 1953 and 1958, the decreasing trend of the tax burden becomes clearly visible for the income classes above 16,000 yen and the rate of decrease increases as the level of income rises. For the

[9] If the total annual earning figure is divided by 12, it will be larger than the monthly earning figure due to a large bonus paid in December. Many firms pay a small bonus through June and July, thus making the earnings in these months closer to the annual average.

TABLE 39

Tax Burden of Alcoholic Beverages, Tobacco, Local, and Income Taxes as a Percentage of Total Income
(1953–1962)

INCOME CLASS * (1000 YEN)	LESS THAN 4	4 TO 8	8 TO 12	12 TO 16	16 TO 20	20 TO 24	24 TO 28	28 TO 32	32 TO 36	36 TO 40	40 TO 44	44 TO 48	48 TO 52	52 TO 56	56 TO 60	60 TO 64	64 TO 68	68 TO 72	72 TO 76	76 TO 80	80 & OVER
Year																					
1953	3.79	5.01	4.36	5.08	6.63	7.61	8.84	9.85	12.54	11.74	12.20	15.54	14.06	15.18	19.43						
1954	35.09	3.85	3.42	4.10	4.74	5.51	6.28	7.46	8.83	10.90	11.82	10.60	15.97	12.18	13.68	20.41					
1955	70.34	3.40	3.56	3.07	3.68	4.65	5.30	6.52	7.99	8.99	10.07	11.17	12.16	13.52	12.57	15.12	15.70	16.38	14.45	17.35	21.75
1956	75.35	5.70	3.47	3.67	3.42	4.47	5.46	6.54	6.69	8.21	8.83	8.78	11.26	11.48	13.64	14.10	14.30	15.65	11.22	14.94	23.42
1957	49.77	2.74	3.60	2.95	2.95	3.86	3.95	4.52	5.47	6.13	6.14	6.28	7.75	8.23	7.13	7.58	9.01	10.26	8.47	10.03	13.59
1958	41.37	5.32	2.89	3.11	3.11	3.28	3.57	4.74	5.47	6.42	5.69	6.27	7.10	7.90	7.12	8.85	8.30	9.35	11.15	11.08	14.31

INCOME CLASS (1000 YEN)	LESS THAN 5	5 TO 10	10 TO 15	15 TO 20	20 TO 25	25 TO 30	30 TO 35	35 TO 40	40 TO 45	45 TO 50	50 TO 60	60 TO 70	70 TO 80	80 TO 90	90 TO 100	100 & OVER
1959	38.98	3.62	3.83	2.76	3.00	3.41	3.39	4.97	4.48	5.35	6.37	7.53	8.19	8.62	9.72	15.17
1960	31.36	5.20	3.09	2.80	3.27	3.26	3.72	4.44	4.81	5.16	6.41	7.03	7.67	7.78	8.02	12.68
1961	61.31	2.98	2.97	3.10	2.94	3.33	3.47	3.60	4.59	4.38	5.30	5.42	6.36	6.85	6.80	11.50
1962	86.47	4.28	3.55	2.60	2.52	3.16	3.36	3.85	4.48	5.62	4.86	5.69	5.96	7.09	6.65	10.06

* Each income class does not include the upper boundary. For example, 4 to 8 is 4,000 to 7,999 yen.
SOURCE: The Prime Minister's Office, *Kakei-Chosa Hōkoku* (The Family Budget Study Report), monthly volumes.

years between 1959 and 1962, the same observation holds true, but only for the income classes above 50,000 yen.

Considering the changes in the mid-points of quintile income distribution during the period, as shown in Table 40, we may conclude that the lowest 20 percent income recipients during the 1953–1958 period and the lowest 60 percent income recipients during the 1959–1962 period experienced virtually no change in their tax burden. On the other hand, during the 1953–1958 period, the second, third, and fourth quintiles in the urban wage earner class saw their tax burden fall nearly 50

TABLE 40

The Mid-Points of Quintile Monthly Income Distribution
Urban Wage Earners, 1953–1962
(in yen)

YEAR	1ST QUINTILE	2ND QUINTILE	3RD QUINTILE	4TH QUINTILE	5TH QUINTILE
1955	11,255	19,533	25,728	33,816	55,516
1957	12,543	21,766	28,452	37,239	63,331
1959	14,178	24,676	32,570	42,322	70,703
1961	17,008	29,621	38,915	51,494	88,629

SOURCE: Toyo Keizai Publishing Co., *Year Book of Economic Statistics*, from the 1956 to 1962 volumes. Estimates made by the Ministry of Finance differ only in the last two digits.

percentage points, and the fifth quintile about 30 percentage points. In the 1959–1962 period, the fourth and fifth quintiles enjoyed further reductions in their rates by 20 to 30 percentage points.[10]

From Table 39 and the foregoing observation, one can expect that the combined tax burden of these four taxes has become over the years less progressive. This can be easily shown by a simple statistical method. Leaving the explanations and results of this procedure to Appendix III, let us summarize the results of this calculation.

What we find is that the rate of progressivity was reduced, as ex-

[10] As noted in Table 40, changes in the midpoints of quintile income distribution warn us that the tax burden of each household must be considered along with the changes in pattern of income distribution. For example, the 11,000-yen income class (first quintile) paid approximately 4 percent of their income for taxes considered here in 1955 (Table 39). But if a household experienced an increase in income along with changes in the first quintile figures, the household in 1961 received 17,000 yen and paid less than 3 percent of its income. For the fourth quintile the median income was 33,816 in 1955, but it rose to 51,494 by 1961. The tax rate in Table 39 indicates that, if a household enjoys increases in income while keeping its relative position to others constant, the rate falls from about 8 percent to 5 percent.

pected, from slightly over .25 percent of monthly income per 1,000 yen in 1953 to .06 percent per 1,000 yen by 1962. Although most of this was caused, as we have seen in earlier tables, by changes in the income tax schedule, we also find that indirect (sales) taxes can be shown to have contributed to this result by a noticeable decline in their absolute magnitude of regressivity. Namely, the rate of regressivity of two indirect taxes (tobacco and alcoholic beverages) changed from −.03 percent per 1,000 yen in 1953 to −.01 percent per 1,000 yen in 1962. This means that the income taxes and indirect taxes joined their forces—one reducing their progressivity and the other increasing their regressivity—to decrease the progressivity of the tax burden of these four taxes over the ten-year period. The only inconclusive result of this set of calculations

TABLE 41

Reported Earning and Percentage of
Total Tax-Paying Population in Each Class, 1960
(Annual earnings in million yen)

Earning class	BELOW .2	.2–.3	.3–.5	.5–.7	.7–1.0	1.0–2.0	2.0–5.0	OVER 5.0
Percentage of population	24.3	21.4	33.2	12.4	5.3	2.7	0.6	0.1

SOURCE: H. Ohuchi, ed., *Nippon Keizai Zusetsu* (The Japanese Economy in Graphs) (Tokyo, 1963), p. 197.

was obtained when the impact of the local income tax on the tax burden was measured independently. This tax, which is known to be less progressive than the income tax on earned wages, provided no statistically clear trend, indicating that this tax is subject to a multitude of forces that make its relationship with the income level less significant in some years.

Before interpretations of these observations can be provided, it is essential to place the urban wage earners in the strata of income distribution in Japan. In this regard, the highest quintile of the wage-earning class falls in the 90th to 95th percentile of the income distribution of the total population. Taking 1960 as an example, of all the tax-reporting units, the total earning level and the percentage of the total in each class are given in Table 41.

This means that, since the mid-point of the fifth quintile of the wage-earning class in 1960 was 954,480 yen (annual earnings), it is safe to assume that the fifth quintile is in the upper half of the annual earnings of the .7–1.0 million yen class. The accumulated percentage of the population earning below 1.0 million is 96.5 percent. In brief, the data examined can be considered to reflect nearly all of the population [11] except the top 3.5 percent.

THE CORPORATE INCOME TAX

In analyzing the impact of the changes in the tax laws relating to corporations, a few observations are needed in addition to those discussed in the first half of this chapter. Although sufficient data are not available to carry out an extensive examination of time series and cross-sectional analysis of the tax burden by the size of firms and by industry, tables 42, 43, and 44 eloquently demonstrate the course of the policy.

As was suggested earlier, one of the measures that most clearly indicated government concern for capital accumulation by corporate entities was the special exemptions and deductions, which were granted to firms after 1952.[12] As shown in Table 42, the annual total of corporate income exempted from the corporate income tax shows a clearly increasing trend. The total for 1963 (1,374,714,000,000 yen) exceeds the total indirect taxes collected in 1963 (1,149,072,000,000 yen).

Also significant is the following observation on the distribution of these exempted incomes and reserve funds by the asset size of firms. The observation is based on a very small sample and requires a qualified interpretation; but inasmuch as the major point to be made is supported by the studies of Professor Hayashi and Mr. Taniyama,[13] it is believed that Table 43 reflects the general pattern of distribution of these special exemptions. The average percentage of the taxed earnings for

[11] However, since the data examined here are for urban wage earners, one should be cautious in evaluating the tax burden of "employers" in small-scale, family-owned firms and professional groups. Professor Komiya found that an average annual income of "employers" in small firms was only .45 million yen and in the professional groups .57 million yen in 1959. Though it is true that these groups come under the 1.0 million yen class, the proportion of asset income in their earnings is expected to be higher than for the urban wage earners. This means that if the data observed in Table 39 applied to these groups, they overstate their tax burden. R. Komiya, *Sengo Nippon no Keizai Seichō* (Tokyo, 1963), p. 180. [English edition, *Postwar Economic Growth in Japan*, trans. R. S. Osaki (Berkeley and Los Angeles, 1966).]

[12] On the corporate tax vis-à-vis capital accumulation, see H. Hayashi, "Capital Accumulation and Taxation in Japan," *National Tax Journal*, XVI (June 1963), 174–192; and S. Davidson and Y. Yasuba, "Asset Reevaluation and Income Taxation in Japan," *National Tax Journal*, XIII (March 1960), 45–48.

[13] Professor Hayashi supports this observation, basing his examination on the data up to 1955. Hayashi, p. 363. H. Taniyama observed that "of the total deductions and exemptions between 1950 and 1963, 15.8 percent was exclusively for the largest firms, 48.5 percent was mostly for the largest firms though small-medium firms shared somewhat, and 5 percent was exclusively for the small-medium firms." The remainder, he observed, was shared by all firms. H. Taniyama, *Zeikin ni Mesu o ireru* (Dissection of the Tax System) (Tokyo, 1964), p. 97.

TABLE 42

The Amount of Income and Reserve Funds
Exempted from Corporate Taxes (in million yen), 1952–1963

	1952	1953	1954	1955	1956	1957	1958	1959	1960	1961	1962	1963
Income exempted [a]	7,445	11,514	17,775	33,473	51,324	80,561	52,294	47,208	49,310	69,125	37,283	57,647
Deduction for reserve funds [b]	89,585	190,591	301,194	405,356	531,046	627,972	719,706	833,665	967,097	1,107,728	1,194,533	1,137,067
Total	97,030	202,105	318,969	438,829	582,370	708,533	772,000	880,873	1,016,407	1,176,853	1,231,816	1,374,714

[a] Exempted incomes are those portions of income from export earning, producing "important products" (electricity and machine tool are two major ones) and the profits paid out as dividends for the flotation of new shares.
[b] Deductions include funds reserved for bad debts, price fluctuations, retirement payments, special repairs, export losses, water shortage, breach of contract losses, and extraordinary risks.

SOURCE: Japan Tax Research Association, *Collected Data for Research in Taxation*, p. 83.

TABLE 43

Special Tax Deductions for Firms, 1960–1962 [a]

The Small Firm Sector

FIRM	INDUSTRY	ASSETS (MILLION YEN)	SPECIAL DEDUCTION [b] (PERCENT)	SPECIAL EXEMPTION [b] (PERCENT)	SPECIAL DEPRECIATION [b] (PERCENT)	TAXED EARNINGS [b] (PERCENT)
A	Cement	80.0	2.9	15.4	3.4	78.3
B	Coal, wholesale	50.0	11.6	12.8	...	75.6
C	Antenna producers	40.0	...	...	...	100.0
D	Chemicals	20.0	...	15.3	0.3	84.4
E	Glass bottles, wholesale	15.0	...	13.6	...	86.4
F	Export	15.0	20.3	1.9	...	77.8
G	Camera, wholesale	10.0	4.3	11.0	...	84.5
H	Chairs, retail	9.0	0.1	5.6	...	96.3
I	Machine repair shops	6.0	...	3.9	...	96.1
J	Propane gas, retail	6.0	...	8.0	...	92.0

The Large Firm Sector

FIRM	INDUSTRY	ASSETS (BILLION YEN)	SPECIAL DEDUCTION [b] (PERCENT)	SPECIAL EXEMPTION [b] (PERCENT)	SPECIAL DEPRECIATION [b] (PERCENT)	TAXED EARNINGS [b] (PERCENT)
A	Mining	4.8	1.0	15.4	4.8	78.8
B	Textile	1.6	17.8	4.5	6.8	70.9
C	Chemical-textile	12.0	30.8	3.5	9.5	56.2
D	Paper	2.3	7.2	14.2	4.8	73.8
E	Oil products	7.2	38.3	4.5	8.3	48.9
F	Iron and steel	23.0	12.7	5.1	29.3	52.9
G	Electric products	22.5	3.8	9.0	8.0	79.1
H	Export	5.0	20.3	16.4	8.0	63.1
I	Electricity	30.0	8.2	31.4	...	60.5
J	Banking	5.5	1.9	31.4	1.0	65.7

[a] All figures in this table are means of five semiannual reports from the last half of 1960 to the last half of 1962.
[b] Figures in columns 4 through 7 are percentages of respective deductions as percentage of total taxable earnings.
Source: These data were obtained for the author by Mr. Hauo Taniyama of the Japan Tax Research Association. Samples of firms were chosen to represent ten industries and their data were obtained from unpublished sources available at the Ministry of Finance.

firms possessing total assets of one billion yen or more was 54.09 percent, as against 87.14 percent for firms whose assets totaled less than 100 million yen. If this result accurately reflects the general pattern, it must be concluded that the large firms were clearly favored over the small. In fact the 1960 Report of the Tax System Commission found that the effective rate of the corporate tax was considerably higher for the firms possessing assets of 10 million or less, compared to those having assets exceeding 10 million yen, as shown in Table 44.

The report of this cabinet-appointed Tax System Investigation Commission concluded: "The most undesirable aspect of the current [1964] tax laws is in relation to the taxes on asset incomes. In recent years, Japan's rates of saving and capital accumulation have been the highest in the world and are approaching what could be considered a ceiling.

TABLE 44

Effective Rates of the Corporate Taxes,[a] 1958–1963

	1958	1959	1960	1961	1962	1963
Large firms (assets exceeding 10 million)	31.4	30.2	29.0	28.5	31.0	31.3
Small firms (assets below 10 million)	42.7	42.0	37.7	41.1	40.0	38.0

[a] This includes the Corporate Income Tax, business tax (state, which is about 5.4 per cent of the corporate tax, and business inhabitant's tax [city], which is about 8.1 percent of the corporate tax).

Moreover, for these rates, this is not particularly desirable. Special laws [relating to interest and dividend incomes and exemptions for corporations] must be discontinued." [14]

CONCLUSION

It can safely be said that the central and prime goal of the tax policy after 1953 was to achieve a high rate of growth, and this goal was pursued by such changes as were necessary to increase saving, that is, to aid rationalization. The results of this policy appeared as a gradually less progressive direct tax burden and an increasingly more regressive indirect tax burden. It appears also clear that this policy was enhanced by

[14] Tax System Investigation Commission, *Tax Commission Report of 1960*, p. 112.

giving a preferential tax treatment to the larger firms vis-à-vis the small ones by means of numerous special exemptions.

One must, however, keep in mind that this policy has contributed toward achieving the world's highest growth rate, and as we have observed, the tax burden as a percentage of real income has indeed decreased over the years. Government officials would be able to argue that the growth enabled a lower tax for all taxpayers over the years. If one ignores for the moment the tax burden in the sense of equity for all, this argument appears convincing.

Although declining, the corporate tax rate is significantly higher than the weighted (reporting units by the respective effective rate of taxes) average of income tax. As observed in Table 39, the rate of decrease in the tax burden was largest during the period between 1953 and 1958, and this is also the period in which the percentage figures for the corporate tax (Table 45) increased from 21.1 in 1953 to 25.89 in 1958 (the less-than-30-percent figures for 1958 and 1959 are the effects of a recession). Further, it is clear from Table 45 that since 1960 the corporate tax has been responsible for over 30 percent of total national taxes, while the income tax has not exceeded the 25 percent mark. In brief the general reduction in tax rates, while maintaining the burden of taxes on national income relatively stable, was made possible by rapidly rising corporate profits.

If we are to examine the impact of growth-oriented, postwar tax policies on "equity and justice," however, one cannot fail to conclude that they have scored poorly. Vivid evidence to this fact is seen in Table 46, in addition to what we have already observed in this chapter. Although the pattern of income distribution is not determined by tax policies alone, we could consider that many of the changes, especially the asset income, have been significantly influenced by those tax policies examined.

Perhaps the following observation made by Professors Kogiku and Bronfenbrenner is appropriate as our general conclusion: "Partisans of economic growth concerned themselves rather with dynamic or historical problems of extending the range of resources and technologies available. Their argument often implies acquiescence toward a considerable degree of inefficiency in resource allocation, and of 'maldistribution' of economic power at any time, if this inefficiency and maldistribution accelerate economic development, somehow defined." [15]

[15] M. Bronfenbrenner and K. Kogiku, "The Aftermath of the Shoup Tax Reform," *National Tax Journal*, X (December 1957), 354. This is Part II of their very useful article which examined pre-1957 tax rates and policy in Japan.

TABLE 45

Income Tax and Corporate Tax as a Percentage of Total National Tax

	1953	1954	1955	1956	1957	1958	1959	1960	1961	1962	1963	1964
Income tax	31.01	30.58	29.73	28.05	20.94	21.77	20.25	21.68	22.26	24.25	24.27	24.86
Corporate tax	21.10	21.43	20.50	23.90	30.29	25.89	28.44	31.82	32.06	40.98	30.97	32.67

SOURCE: Calculated from the data by the Institute of Economic Statistics, Japan, *Economic Indicators* (*Keizai Shihyō*) (Tokyo, 1964) and annual *White Paper*, *op. cit.*

TABLE 46

Distribution of Wage and Asset Income for Nonagricultural
Households ^a by Decimal Class

INCOME CLASS	WAGE INCOME			ASSET INCOME		
	1956	1959	1962	1956	1959	1962
1	3.1	2.6	2.8	1.3	0.7	0.4
2	4.7	4.3	4.6	2.0	1.0	0.7
3	5.9	5.7	5.8	2.4	1.4	1.1
4	6.9	6.8	6.5	3.7	1.9	1.3
5	8.1	8.0	7.9	4.7	2.6	1.8
6	9.2	9.2	8.9	5.2	3.2	2.3
7	10.7	10.5	10.3	7.0	4.3	3.8
8	12.3	12.2	12.1	8.4	6.2	6.7
9	14.8	15.5	15.0	16.8	11.1	10.6
10	24.7	25.2	26.1 ^b	48.5	67.6	71.3

^a More accurately, the data excluded those households in agriculture and forestry (Nōrin Sangyō).

^b The large wage income for the highest decimal class is due to the high income of officers of firms and professional employees.

SOURCE: T. Ishizaki, "Dual Structure and Income Distribution," *Nijyu Kōzō no Bunseki* (Analysis of the Dual Structure), eds. Y. Tamanoi and T. Uchida (Tokyo Keizai, 1964), p. 160.

9 LABOR AND WAGE IN
THE POSTWAR GROWTH

INTRODUCTION

Prewar Japanese economic development was achieved, as Lockwood put it, in a "perpetually crowded labor market," [1] and the familiar growth model which assumes an infinitely elastic supply of labor has often been discussed using the Japanese case.[2] Industrial wage rates, which "remained tied to the general level of wages in comparable urban employments and ultimately to the plane of living of the peasant," [3] undoubtedly played an important role in prewar Japanese economic development. How much change has there been since the end of World War II?

The purpose of this chapter is to show how the rapid economic growth of the postwar years affected the Japanese labor market, wages, and the labor share of national income and to what extent the growth-conscious policies of the government influenced the wage structure and the labor share.

SOME BASIC CHANGES IN THE POST-WORLD WAR II PERIOD

The supply-demand condition of the postwar Japanese labor market, observed through available indexes, has little resemblance to that observed for the prewar years. Compared to the prewar pattern, the

---

[1] William W. Lockwood, *The Economic Development of Japan* (Princeton: Princeton University Press, 1954), p. 494.

[2] See for example W. Arthur Lewis, "Economic Development with Unlimited Supplies of Labor," *The Manchester School of Economic and Social Studies*, Vol. 22, No. 2 (May 1954), and especially G. Ranis and J. C. Fei, "Innovation, Capital Accumulation, and Economic Development," *American Economic Review*, LIII (June 1963) and their recent *Development of Labor Surplus Economy: Theory and Policy* (Irwin, 1964).

[3] Lockwood, p. 494.

postwar rate of population increase shows a wide fluctuation, as shown on Table 47. The large increase in the labor force between the ages of 15 and 59 for the 1945–1950 period was to a large extent due to the estimated five million returnees from Japan's ex-colonies and those who were demobilized immediately following the end of World War II. This large influx of 5 million out of 7.7 million, which was the increase of the 15–59 age group between 1945 and 1950, was the equivalent of a natural increase for a ten-year period for this age group at the rate which prevailed between 1914 and 1935. In the 0–14 age group, except for a brief baby boom immediately following the war, the rate of increase

TABLE 47

Rate of Population Increase by Age Group
per Quintennial Period Indicated (percentage)

	0–14	15–59	OVER 60
1920–25	7.4	7.5	−0.3
1925–30	7.3	8.7	4.2
1930–35	8.4	6.9	7.7
1935–40	3.3	3.4	10.2
1940–45	2.4	0.2	2.6
1945–50	10.0	19.5	11.2
1950–55	1.3	10.3	13.0
1955–60	−6.0	9.1	15.0

SOURCE: Based on the census reports of 1950 and 1960, published by the Census Bureau, the government of Japan.

dropped sharply and the group declined in absolute number by 1.77 million, or −6.0 percent, between 1955 and 1960.[4]

After 1955, along with the decline in the rate of population increase, the participation rate began to fall, reflecting a rising standard of living.[5] The participation rate in 1960 was 66.1, against 72.3 in 1920 and 69.0 in 1930. In terms of the population pyramid, the percentage of those over 60 increased from 8.1 in 1955 to 14.5 in 1961. The Ministry of Welfare estimates that this figure will reach 29.5 by the year 2000. A decreasing

[4] The net increase in population in 1960 was 9.3 per 1,000 population. This was one of the lowest in the world.

[5] Umemura has fit a regression equation in the form of X (participation rate) $= a + bY$, where Y is the income expressed in constant yen for a six-year period between 1955 and 1960 (twelve observations—January and December of each year). The results of his calculations were: $X = 90.449 - 0.0261Y$ ($R^2 = .957$) for males and $X = 63.111 - 0.0402Y$ ($R^2 = .981$) for females. Mataji Umemura, Sengo Nippon no Rōdō-Ryoku (The Labor Force in Postwar Japan, Hitotsubashi University Economic Research Paper, No. 13 (Tokyo, 1964), p. 110.

TABLE 48

Index of Labor Force, Nonagricultural Employment, Total Employment (1953 = 100), and Rate of Unemployment (percentage), 1953–1962

	1953	1954	1955	1956	1957	1958	1959	1960	1961	1962
Labor force	100.0	101.5	106.3	107.4	109.5	110.1	109.4	113.1	114.5	115.4
Nonrural employment [a]	100.0	104.8	107.8	115.2	126.8	134.8	149.1	168.8	185.0	198.2
Unemployment [b]		1.73	1.56	1.52	1.15	1.41	1.25	.91	.85	.82

[a] Nonrural employment refers to employment in mining, manufacturing, and service industries.
[b] Definition of unemployment changed in 1953. Figures after 1953 use essentially a definition identical to that used in the U.S.A.

SOURCE: Index of employment was obtained from *Maitsuki Kinrō Tōkei Chōsa, Sōgō Hōkokusho* (Monthly Labor Statistics Study, an Aggregate Report), published by Labor Statistics Research Bureau, the Ministry of Labor, March, 1961; and, *Maigetsu Kinrō Yōran* (Monthly Labor Statistics Report), 1964, published by the same.

rate of population increase and a falling rate of participation characterized the supply side of the postwar Japanese labor market.

The general trend of the demand side of the labor market vis-à-vis the index of supply (labor force) since 1953 is shown in Table 48. The indexes in this table indicate that nonrural employment— manufacturing and service sectors—has risen much more rapidly than the labor force. This result is seen in the declining rate of unemployment. The general picture of the postwar labor market is one that has

TABLE 49

Indexes of Hourly Real Wage and Labor Productivity (1953 = 100) and the Labor Share of National Income (Percentage)

	1953	1954	1955	1956	1957	1958	1959	1960	1961	1962	1963
Hourly real wage index	100	106	109	120	126	125	136	148	162	167	162[a]
Labor productivity[b]	100	107	113	119	128	123	150	173	197	198	216
Labor share[c]	47.7	49.9	48.5	48.8	49.8	52.7	50.7	49.8	50.9	53.3	53.9

[a] The decline of this index for 1963 is due to a recession and a sharp increase in the price index.

[b] The Labor Productivity index is a composite index obtained by combining labor productivity indexes by type of industry, on the basis of the value added weights as used in calculating the M.I.T.I.'s 1960 standard production indexes. For details see sources cited below.

[c] Labor share is the ratio of the total compensation of employers to the total national income by distributive shares.

SOURCES: Statistics Department, the Bank of Japan, *Economic Statistics of Japan*; Economic Planning Agency, *White Paper, 1964*; and Bela Belassa, "Recent Developments in the Competitiveness of American Industries and Prospects for the Future," *Facts Affecting U.S. Balance of Payments*, Joint Economic Committee, U.S. Congress (Washington, D.C., 1962), Table 3, p. 36.

gradually become a seller's market. This is a consequence of the demand-supply pattern in the labor market brought about by economic recovery, growth, and a decrease in the rate of population increase and the participation rate.

Table 49 gives rise to two observations. One is that the rates of increase of real hourly wages and labor productivity differ appreciably, and the other is that the labor share of income is significantly lower (though one can sense an upward pressure) compared to any other industrial nation (U.S., 71.1; West Germany, 63.5—both in 1962). How much do these observations reflect consequences of postwar growth per se and how much can be attributed to government policies? Or, stating it differently, how much of the foregoing is to be expected as the result of the rapid economic growth Japan underwent during the period after the war and to what extent did the growth-conscious government accentuate these results?

Our attempts to answer these questions must begin with the recollection of the rapid rate of technological change. This—what Lockwood called the "technological dynamism"[6] of postwar Japan—was the process of rationalization described in chapter 6 which required rapid capital accumulation. The effects of and requirements for this rationalization are clearly seen in tables 50, 51, and 52. Table 50 shows the changes in labor productivity (gross value added per employee is used as an approximation), Table 51 shows the labor share (cash payment divided by gross value added), and Table 52 shows the wage rate of these respective industries between 1951 and 1960.

These three tables show that in those industries in which technological change was rapid and large capital investments were made, as shown in the increasing productivity of labor, the labor share tended to be smaller, though the monthly nominal wage earnings were higher than in other industries. For example, the chemical and petroleum products industries, which saw the most rapid increases in labor productivity (Table 50) due to the adoption of a series of capital-intensive technologies, showed the lowest labor shares (Table 51). Exactly the opposite case is seen for the textile, printing, and machine tool industries.[7] When a rank correlation coefficient was calculated between the annual average rate of increase in productivity of labor and the labor share, the result was an expected negative value of $-.205$. These results, however, are hardly surprising. The major reason for the level of labor share has been due, along with the relatively favorable supply of labor up until 1960, to the rapid rate of capital investment. Table 52 should be evaluated with Table 49: a slower rate of increase in wages relative to the rate of increase in productivity is a prerequisite for rapid capital accumulation in order to carry on the process of rationalization.

However, a further examination of what we could perhaps call

[6] W. W. Lockwood, "Japan's 'New Capitalism,'" *The State and Economic Enterprise of Japan*, p. 460.
[7] The classification of M.I.T.I. data does not correspond with the usual classification of industries. Thus, in interpreting these data, we must, for example, note that the textile industry may include products that should be classified in the chemical industry. For the purpose that these data are used here, however, the M.I.T.I. classification is sufficient in providing the general pattern of each industry. For details of industry classification of the M.I.T.I. data, see Tōyōkeizai, Shimpō-sha, *Yearbook of Economic Statistics*, 1962, pp. 178–183.

TABLE 50

Productivity of Labor (Gross Value Added per Employee) in Manufacturing Industries, 1951–1960
(in 1000 yen)

INDUSTRY	1951	1952	1953	1954	1955	1956	1957	1958	1959	1960
Textile	281	261	701	316	350	368	353	366	424	476
Paper & pulp	720	612	680	647	674	752	766	723	866	916
Pub. & printing	401	492	535	636	676	726	748	946	766	869
Chem. products	517	499	694	785	878	945	884	1008	1240	1478
Petroleum & coal products	1006	966	1237	1044	1375	1272	1587	1585	2519	2608
Rubber products	271	373	419	569	558	538	560	548	508	625
Iron & steel	434	375	536	550	672	1040	973	760	962	1098
Metal products	307	326	409	417	426	416	529	489	503	610
Machines	258	326	348	418	418	453	545	604	626	738
Electric tools & appliances	337	417	493	560	528	504	577	782	696	756
Transportation equipment	227	357	442	456	411	514	601	897	834	987

SOURCE: Calculated from M.I.T.I. *Kogoyō Tōkei-hyō* (Industrial Statistics), Annual Volume, 1951–1960.

TABLE 51

Labor Share (the Ratio of Cash Payments to Gross Value Added), 1951–1960
(in Percentage)

INDUSTRY	1951	1952	1953	1954	1955	1956	1957	1958	1959	1960
Textile	30.7	40.9	35.9	37.4	34.5	34.8	38.5	39.2	35.2	35.6
Paper & pulp	25.2	34.1	31.6	36.2	34.6	32.4	33.2	34.3	30.2	30.2
Pub. & printing	37.4	34.7	36.5	33.6	33.3	34.6	35.8	30.3	39.1	39.0
Chem. products	31.7	37.2	28.7	29.3	27.8	27.8	31.2	29.0	24.5	22.0
Petroleum & coal products	16.2	20.5	18.2	24.2	19.9	23.5	19.9	21.6	14.5	15.6
Rubber products	48.1	36.0	37.9	28.3	29.4	31.1	29.8	32.0	34.8	31.9
Iron & steel	46.5	60.3	45.3	51.1	43.4	34.1	35.6	46.5	37.7	35.4
Metal products	43.0	43.9	44.3	42.5	41.1	42.8	37.4	40.2	41.7	38.2
Machines	54.7	51.0	52.3	48.8	48.1	47.0	44.1	40.2	41.4	39.1
Electric tools & appliances	41.7	40.9	38.0	37.4	37.9	39.1	36.8	27.5	30.0	30.5
Transportation equipment	72.4	57.0	51.3	55.1	61.1	53.7	50.8	35.0	38.2	33.0

SOURCE: Same as Table 50.

TABLE 52

Nominal Average Monthly Cash Income of Manufacturing Wage Earners, 1951–1960
(in Yen)

INDUSTRY	1951	1952	1953	1954	1955	1956	1957	1958	1959	1960
Textile	7,677	8,697	9,630	10,215	10,497	11,388	11,638	11,546	12,820	14,343
Paper & pulp	16,192	19,170	20,490	21,331	22,089	23,094	23,793	21,894	23,580	25,196
Pub. & printing	12,027	15,097	17,213	18,452	19,179	20,829	22,470	23,102	25,335	28,055
Chem. products	13,224	15,284	17,479	19,198	20,326	22,073	22,708	24,114	26,009	28,342
Petroleum & coal products	15,911	17,237	20,699	24,329	24,303	25,669	28,243	26,823	29,872	33,575
Rubber products	10,355	11,702	13,667	14,110	14,328	14,826	14,546	14,356	15,225	16,256
Iron & steel	17,010	18,654	20,501	21,886	22,945	26,536	27,223	29,522	31,722	34,282
Metal products	11,614	12,899	14,918	15,517	16,357	17,650	18,590	17,182	18,606	20,666
Machines	12,134	14,159	16,029	16,352	16,412	19,078	20,623	20,605	22,349	24,663
Electric tools & appliances	12,516	15,673	17,434	17,636	18,025	19,696	20,428	19,662	20,644	21,520
Trans. equip.	14,074	17,321	19,905	20,866	21,374	24,201	25,723	26,161	28,237	30,219

SOURCE: Calculated from Labor Statistics Bureau, The Ministry of Labor, *Maigetsu Kinrō Tōkei Chōsa, Sōgō Hōkokusho* (Collected Reports of Monthly Labor Statistics Investigation) (Tokyo, 1961).

"usual" (that is, to be expected in any process of economic development) observations reveals the special features of the postwar Japanese economic growth. The first of such features was suggested by Professor Nakamura who, after examining the labor share, wage level, and total output of manufacturing industries between 1952 and 1959, observed, "In those industries in which technological advance has been rapid, and which enjoyed boom conditions and whose concentration ratios were high, the labor share clearly showed a decline. Of course, in such industries, wage rates were relatively high, but it was evident that the labor share has been slow to respond to the rapid economic growth." [8]

The interactions among technological changes, market structure, and the role of government have been discussed in chapter 6. However, Professor Nakamura's observation, which is well established theoretically,[9] can be examined further—more explicitly in terms of large firms vis-à-vis small firms—to grasp the full weight of the technological dynamism and the possible impact of the government policy.

We begin by observing the relative rate of increase in capital intensity between large and small firms and viewing consequent changes in value added per worker for firms of different size. Table 53 shows that between 1955 and 1961, capital per worker increased more rapidly for the largest firms, with assets exceeding 100 million yen ($277,777), than for firms below that asset size. This is clearly seen when one compares the indexes, as defined in Table 53, for 1955 and 1961. Table 54 tells the same story for value added per employee for firms of various sizes measured by the number of employees. Beyond the observation made by Nakamura, it is evident that the rapid technological changes significantly altered the relative position of large and small firms. This noticeable change in so short a period was the product of composite forces of technological dynamism and the policies of the government in those areas we have discussed earlier.

An examination of the so-called *shiwayose* [10] demonstrates how the government policy directly and indirectly contributed to the widening of the technological gap and the rapid capital accumulation which made the technological changes in large firms possible. In an economy that obviously gave preferential treatment to large firms by means of taxa-

---

[8] Takahide Nakamura, "Income Distribution and Consumption Structure," *Nippon-gata Chingin-Kōzō no Kenkyū* (A Study of the Japanese Wage Structure), eds., N. Funahashi and M. Shinohara (Tokyo, 1961), p. 70.

[9] It should be recalled that the postwar rationalization is capital using and the Japanese labor market before 1959–60 was as we observed in Table 48.

[10] The exact translation of the term is "wrinkling up," but the English phrase "passing the buck" conveys the meaning precisely.

TABLE 53

Amount of Capital Investment per Worker (in 10,000 Yen),[a] 1955–1961

(Index is 100 for over-100-million-yen firms)

ASSET SIZE OF FIRMS	1955 CAPITAL PER LABOR	1955 INDEX	1956 CAPITAL PER LABOR	1956 INDEX	1957 CAPITAL PER LABOR	1957 INDEX	1958 CAPITAL PER LABOR	1958 INDEX	1959 CAPITAL PER LABOR	1959 INDEX	1960 CAPITAL PER LABOR	1960 INDEX	1961 CAPITAL PER LABOR	1961 INDEX
Less than 5 million	13	15.7	15	17.4	13	12.0	15	11.7	18	12.9	23	13.9	19.7	11.1
5–10 million	23	27.7	22	24.4	22	20.4	27	21.1	30	21.6	32	19.9	37	20.8
10–50 million	33	37.8	32	35.6	34	31.5	46	35.7	42	30.2	45	27.2	48	27.0
50–100 million	46	55.4	45	50.0	54	50.0	61	47.7	61	36.5	61	36.8	71	37.7
Over 100 million	83	100.0	90	100.0	108	100.0	128	100.0	139	100.0	166	100.0	178	100.0

[a] Liabilities and net worth divided by the number of employees at the end of each period.
SOURCE: Calculated from Analytical Statistics Division, the Ministry of International Trade and Industry, *Kōgyo Tōkei-hyō, Sangyō-hen* (Industrial Statistics Table, Industrial Part), Annual Series from 1955 to 1962.

TABLE 54

Value Added per Employee in Manufacturing Industries (in 10,000 yen = 27.78 dollars), 1955–1961
(Figures in parentheses are ratios of the value added for specific scale of employment as a percentage of value added at 1000 or above)

EMPLOYEES	VALUE ADDED [a] 1955 (10,000 YEN)	VALUE ADDED 1956	VALUE ADDED 1957	VALUE ADDED 1958	VALUE ADDED 1959	VALUE ADDED 1960	VALUE ADDED 1961
30–49	30.3 (42.4)	31.6 (39.0)	34.5 (37.9)	34.8 (41.7)	36.5 (37.1)	43.3 (37.1)	51.5 (39.5)
50–99	36.4 (50.9)	37.0 (45.7)	41.1 (45.1)	39.3 (47.1)	43.1 (43.8)	49.2 (42.1)	57.1 (43.8)
100–199	44.9 (62.8)	46.1 (56.9)	49.8 (54.7)	47.1 (56.5)	50.2 (51.1)	58.9 (50.4)	67.0 (51.4)
200–299	53.1 (74.3)	55.9 (69.0)	60.2 (66.1)	56.8 (68.1)	60.4 (61.4)	68.6 (58.7)	75.0 (57.5)
300–499	59.5 (83.2)	67.6 (83.5)	68.3 (75.0)	61.4 (73.6)	70.0 (71.2)	73.7 (63.1)	83.8 (64.3)
500–999	68.4 (95.7)	72.8 (89.9)	76.5 (84.0)	63.9 (76.6)	78.1 (79.5)	93.5 (80.1)	99.5 (76.3)
over 1000	75.5 (100.0)	81.0 (100.1)	91.1 (100.0)	83.4 (100.0)	98.3 (100.0)	116.8 (100.0)	130.4 (100.0)

[a] Value added is the value of shipments minus the cost of materials.
SOURCE: Same as Table 53.

tion, anti-monopoly, and loan policies, one of the forms by which large firms gained increasing dominance over small firms, or by which medium-small firms were made to serve the interests of the large firms, was the so-called financial and inventory *shiwayose*.

The financial *shiwayose* takes the form of a delayed payment to subcontractors to reduce the interest costs of large firms, especially when business conditions slacken. To indicate the prevalence of this practice, terms such as "typhoon bill" and "childbirth bill" came into existence in the postwar years. The former can be cashed in 210 days after goods are delivered [11] and the latter after nine months. Of this practice, Professor Ito remarked: "Such prevalence of long-term bills was not found in prewar Japan—it is a phenomenon peculiar to postwar Japan. This delayed payment is closely connected with the cutting of subcontract unit prices in the sense that both involve the shifting of burdens to small- and medium-size enterprises. This is an important fact which must be borne in mind in considering small business problems in Japan." [12]

This practice must also be considered with the fact that the interest costs of the small firms are significantly higher than that for the large firms, as observed in Table 55. The pressure of high interest costs on the small firms forces them to practice their own *shiwayose* on the wage level of their own employees. [13]

Table 55 also indicates that the effects of the business cycle are felt more keenly by the small firm than the large. Compared to the differentials of interest rates among firms of different sizes in the boom year of 1956, the differentials observed for the recession year of 1958 are appreciably larger. When business conditions begin to slacken, the smaller firms are the first to suffer a reduction in the amount of available credit. They are often forced to resort to credit which is available at higher

[11] According to an old wives' tale in Japan, typhoons come after the 210th day in a year. There exists a law that prohibits delayed payments to subcontractors, *Shitauke Daikin Chien Bōshi-hō*, but the enforcement of this is extremely difficult because complaints must be made by subcontractors, whose business depends on maintaining good terms with the parent firms. *Asahi* reported that in the recession of 1964–65, some large firms resorted to delaying the inspection of goods delivered in order to delay the effective date of goods delivered. *Asahi* (September 4, 1965).

[12] Taikichi Ito, "Structural Peculiarities and Labor Problems of Small Business," *Small Business in Japan*, ed. T. Yamanaka (The Japan Times, 1960), p. 158.

[13] For example, the loan rate of credit associations and mutual loans and savings banks was in the 10.75–12.43 percent range in 1957, as against the 7.98–8.54 range for city and local banks. The largest sources of credit for the small-medium firms are the former and they can borrow from the latter only rarely. The pattern is reversed for the large firms. Interest rates are taken from the Bank of Japan, *Hompō Keizai Tōkei* (Economic Statistics of Japan), 1957.

TABLE 55

Average Level of Interest Rates * on Borrowings by Size of Firms
1956–1958 (Percentage)

	SIZE OF CAPITAL PAID IN (MILLION YEN)					
YEAR	2 OR BELOW	2–5	5–10	10–50	50–100	OVER 100
1956	15.36	14.52	14.28	14.19	13.35	12.24
1957	12.79	15.11	14.40	14.79	12.59	10.23
1958	17.38	17.80	13.83	13.84	13.62	11.15

* The average interest rate in the manufacturing industry is defined as the sum of interest payment discount divided by the total of short-term borrowings from financial institutions, plus long-term borrowings and corporate debentures.

SOURCE: The calculation was made by Professor Kenichi Miyazawa, using data published by the Ministry of Finance. See K. Miyazawa, "The Dual Structure of the Japanese Economy," *The Developing Economies*, II (June 1964), 158.

prices and/or suffer bankruptcy.[14] In a comprehensive study of the consequences of this aspect of the dual structure, Professor Shinohara observed:

Increments in loans outstanding from financial institutions are depicted by industry for large and small firms. By big firms, we mean those with paid-up capital of more than 10 million yen, and by small firms, those with less than that figure. Year-to-year increments in outstanding loans, both operating and equipment, are [examined] for five industries, *viz.*, textiles, chemicals, primary metals, electrical machinery, and other machinery. We have disaggregated the series into industries to avoid the possibility that a lead on the part of small business loans for industry as a whole might reflect differences in the cycle between industries. But the lead of loans to small business is evident in each industry except electrical equipment, and even there, if four-quarter moving averages of quarterly series were to be depicted, some lead could be found. In the 1954–55 depression, the small firm troughs are all found in 1954, while those of the big firms, except in electrical machinery, are all in 1955.[15]

[14] According to a study made by Mr. Kobayashi of the Tokyo Chamber of Commerce, the causes of bankruptcy during the first half of 1962 among the medium-small firms were: (a) decline in business (28.5 percent); (b) difficulty in collection of payments due (24.9); (c) laxity in business management (13.7); (d) increased inventory (11.4); (e) excess capacity (11.0); and (f) insufficient operation funds (10.5). He then observed that "it cannot be denied that tightness of credit is directly related to bankruptcies. Shortage of credit appears in many forms." Takehiko Kobayashi, "Bankruptcies; Their Patterns and Problems," *Kinyū Journal*, V (August 1964), 52–53.

[15] M. Shinohara, *Growth and Cycles in the Japanese Economy* (Tokyo: Kinokuniya Bookstore Co., 1962), p. 191. The word in brackets was "illustrated" because Shinohara has an accompanying diagram.

Shinohara, also finding a similar pattern in inventory, concluded that "the lead of the small firms in both credit and inventory cycles is almost beyond doubt, and seems to be a pronounced trait of the Japanese economy." [16]

These phenomena are clearly fostered, directly and indirectly, by government policy. Loans to large firms are given preferential consideration by the government banks [17] to protect important customers, and the fact that the larger firms are relatively better risks vis-à-vis small firms was a part of this consideration. Inventory reductions are often initiated at the outset of a recession by the government-sponsored "administrative cartels" or so-tans (output limitation) for the benefit of the oligopolistic firms, as we saw in chapters 4 and 5. The result is that the small firm subcontractors are penalized most, as they are used for cushions in such cases.[18]

The shiwayose of inventory reduction hits the subcontractors hardest. This is possible due to the extremely weak position of small firms in the rapidly rationalizing and growing economy, in which technological changes and an increased strain on the capital market have become the order of the day.[19] As absolute capital requirements for newer technology became larger, the government aided—directly and indirectly as we have seen in the earlier chapters—the process of capital concentration. This of course was a highly effective process in increasing exports and in achieving the policy goal of rapid growth. Professor Shinohara concurs with this view when he says:

> Capital concentration has . . . stimulated industrial growth. The existence of the dual economy makes it possible for the relatively large firms to employ cheap labor (relative to labor cost in more advanced countries) in combination with highly advanced technological production methods. The combination of cheap labor and high-level technology tends to reduce costs and raise profits, thus leading to greater capital financing from internal funds, on the one hand, and a lowering of product prices on the other, which in turn helps to expand the foreign market.[20]

[16] Ibid., p. 193.
[17] There have been government loan programs for small firms. But due to the amount of the loans and the conditions attached to them, they are generally considered of little significance. See for a detailed discussion of government loans for small firms, Kōichi Hosono, "Finance and Co-operatives, Outline of Small Business Financing in Japan," in T. Yamanaka, ed. Small Business in Japan, pp. 321–349.
[18] Even in normal periods, small subcontractors often become a safety valve for inventory control. When a recession starts, however, many subcontractors naturally face sudden curtailment of all orders by the parent firm.
[19] See fn. 22, chap. 5, for changes in the ratio of owned capital to borrowed capital ratios.
[20] M. Shinohara, p. 21.

Such a process of concentration of capital encouraged by the government is clearly a policy to favor a selected few for the sake of rapid growth. Professor Ito states this rather bluntly:

> The secret of Japan's high economic expansion lies in helping only efficient and growing industries and offering no assistance to stagnant or small enterprises, the primary consideration being the efficiency of economic policies. It seems that the Government's stand is to eliminate the "dual structure" while accelerating the natural selection of the "survival of the fittest" in a capitalist society. Such a policy would produce many victims and its pressure on society would be extremely grave.[21]

Some consequences of these pressures—the composite forces referred to earlier and the forces of *shiwayose*—are found in the following evidence. Table 56 shows the wage differential between large and medium-small firms. The relative wage rate of firms employing fewer than 400 shows a revealing pattern for the period observed. In all cases the wage level, expressed as a ratio of the wage level of firms employing over 500, for the medium-small firm employees is lower in 1960 than in 1950, in spite of the increasingly tighter labor market of postwar Japan.[22] Setting aside the observable cyclical variations, one cannot fail to note that the relative wage level of the employees of medium-small firms failed to close the gap. This must be considered with the fact that, as we saw in Table 56, the wage level of large firms lags appreciably behind labor productivity.

More revealing evidence is found in a 1963 publication of the Ministry of Welfare.[23] In discussing poverty in Japan, this document defined "poverty" as an annual income below 220,000 yen (approximately $611) for a household of 3.8 persons. This is about $160 per person annually or 45 cents per person per day. The findings on poverty are shown in Table 57.

In addition to the fact that 20 percent of all Japanese households are poor by this definition, Table 57 discloses an important fact. Except for the catch-all group of "others," the three largest contributors of poor

[21] T. Ito, *The High Growth of the Japanese Economy and the Problems of Small Enterprises*, Management and Labor Studies Series, No. 9, Keiō University English Monographs, 1964, p. 25.
[22] Beginning in 1959, the wage differential between large and medium-small firms began to narrow due to the developing labor shortage. However, impacts of this new development remain to be seen. In analyzing the postwar economic growth of the period we are discussing here, we cannot yet consider this development to be a significant factor. For a further discussion of this development and possible implications, see K. Yamamura, "Wage Structure and Economic Growth in Postwar Japan," *Industrial and Labor Relations Review*, 19 (October 1965), 58–69.
[23] See *Source* for Table 57.

TABLE 56

Levels of Wages of Smaller Scale Firms, 1950–1960
(Wage level of firms employing over 500 = 100) [a]

		1950	1951	1952	1953	1954	1955	1956	1957	1958	1959	1960
Scale of firms by employee 100–400 class	All industries [b]	89.1	86.9	85.4	86.2	87.1	85.2	83.7	83.2	82.9	82.6	82.7
	Manufacturing industries	83.1	79.5	79.1	79.3	77.8	74.3	72.1	73.5	73.5	73.1	73.6
Scale of firms by employee 30–99 class	All industries	76.8	74.0	73.4	75.0	75.8	72.6	69.9	73.2	72.9	73.0	74.3
	Manufacturing industries	67.3	61.7	58.8	59.8	60.0	58.8	56.1	62.4	61.6	63.0	65.8

[a] The wage level of firms employing over 500 is calculated out of universe and for 100–400 and 30–99 classes is based on samples covering 1/1 to 1/12 of the total in 29 subcategories. For example, the total sample size was 82,695 firms in 1960.
[b] Excluding agriculture, fishery, and forestry but including mining and service sectors.
SOURCE: Same as for Table 50.

TABLE 57

Households Earning Less than 220,000 Yen
by Indicated Grouping, 1963

	NUMBER OF HOUSEHOLDS (1,000)	"POOR" HOUSEHOLDS AS A PERCENTAGE OF TOTAL HOUSE- HOLDS IN THE RESPECTIVE GROUPS
Total	4,510 (100.0) [c]	20.0
Small firm employees [a]	849 (18.8)	14.8
Temporary employees [b]	759 (16.8)	49.2
Family operated businesses	714 (15.8)	64.3
Farmers	682 (15.8)	27.4
Unemployed	619 (13.7)	76.1
Others [d]	895 (19.8)	12.2

[a] Defined as firms employing less than 1,000.
[b] *Hiyatoi*, usually work on a day-to-day basis.
[c] The number of poor households as a percentage of total poor households.
[d] Include all others not listed, such as the disabled, widowed, aged, etc.
SOURCE: Based on data provided in: The Ministry of Welfare, *Kokumin Sēkatsu Jattai Chōsa* (Examinations of the Reality of the National Living Standard), 1963 volume.

households are small firm employees, temporary employees and those engaged in family-operated businesses.[24] The reason why 18.8 percent of the total of poor households are composed of the employees of small firms has been suggested (the medium-small firms for our usage are defined in Table 57 as firms employing less than 1,000). This group does not include the family operated business, which also is one of the largest contributors to the poor.

When we examine the second largest contributor to the poor households—the temporary employee group—we discover that their existence and magnitude contribute to the growth of large firms and are the result of the government policy which has failed to act to mitigate the problems of these temporary employees. That is to say, there exists the growing problem of "permanent" temporary employees, such that the

[24] In this group, it should be noted that 64.3 percent of the households are poor and this is second only to the unemployed group, with an expected high proportion of 76.1 percent. Many factors undoubtedly contributed to this distribution of the poor. The high proportion of the poor in family operated businesses, for example, can partially be explained by the fact that those business units are in the service sector and operated with little capital and skill. As with "corner grocers" in the U.S., their income level is low for many reasons. As in the U.S., many family operated retail stores in Japan have come to face, at an increasing rate, competition by chains of outlets which are organized by large producers. This phenomenon became much more manifest since the "distribution revolution" referred to in chap. 6.

existing laws for the protection of their rights of labor are effectively violated. Although available data on this increasingly serious problem are limited, studies show, for example, that in 1961, 12.2 percent of blue-collar employees of manufacturing firms employing over 500 were permanently employed as temporary employees.[25] There is also evidence to show that this figure has increased rapidly since 1954 and continues to do so.[26] Examining this problem, Professor Imura concluded: "By such means, the large enterprise can avoid costs involved in all types of

TABLE 58

Wage Payment to Regular and Permanent Temporary Employees
in Firms Employing over 100, April 1961
(in Yen)

INDUSTRY	REGULAR EMPLOYEES (A)	TEMPORARY EMPLOYEES (B)	B/A
Total manufacturing			
(male)	28,075	14,678	52.3
(female)	10,935	8,411	76.9
Iron and steel			
(male)	35,005	16,454	47.0
Machinery			
(male)	27,295	14,159	51.9
Electrical equipment			
(male)	22,155	11,980	54.1
(female)	10,181	8,138	79.9
Transportation equipment			
(male)	30,972	17,310	55.9

SOURCE: Calculations are based on the Ministry of Labor, *Collected Investigations on the Reality of Wage*; K. Imura, "Several Considerations on the Theory of Wage Differential by Firm Size," *Mita Gakkai Zassi* (June–July 1963), p. 164.

fringe benefits, and pressure of the labor unions, thus enabling employment [of permanent temporary employees] at a lower cost [than regular employees]. This practice permits firms to increase or decrease the number of employees without incurring the costs of retirement benefits, and difficulties relating to such a practice vis-à-vis labor unions."[27] In fact, wage levels of permanent temporary employees are significantly lower than those of the regular employees, as shown in Tables 58 and 59.

[25] In 1961, this amounted to 27,417. Of the total temporary employees, firms employing over 500 accounted for 60.9 percent, firms employing 100–499, 29 percent and firms employing 30–99, 10.1 percent. Kyōko Imura, "Several Considerations on the Theory of Wage Differential by Firm Size," *Mita Gakkai Zassi* (Keiō University, June–July 1963), p. 150.

[26] *Ibid.*, p. 150. Also see seven articles which deal with "The Postwar Wage Policy and Wages" in *Keizai Hyōron* (February 1964).

[27] Imura, p. 153.

These tables make it evident that this practice, enjoyed primarily by the large firms, must be considered an important factor in explaining the high incidence of poverty among the temporary workers.[28] In spite of the repeated demands of labor unions and a large majority of Japanese labor economists who consider this to be the most vital labor issue, no effective law remedying this growing problem has been enacted.[29]

Before concluding this chapter, one vital observation, which summarizes the significance of what has been described above, must be added. It is Table 60 on income distribution which reflects—directly and indirectly—the impact of the increasingly manifest "dual structure" of firm

TABLE 59

Cash Payments Made in 1960 in Addition to Wages
(Bonuses and Other Benefits) by Firms Employing over 1,000
(in Yen)

INDUSTRY	REGULAR EMPLOYEES (A)	TEMPORARY EMPLOYEES (B)	B/A
Iron and steel			
(male)	88,813	15,913	17.9
Machinery			
(male)	77,012	16,082	21.9
Electrical equipment			
(male)	69,100	9,260	13.4
(female)	33,027	9,990	30.2
Transportation equipment			
(male)	91,172	24,629	27.0

SOURCE: Same as Table 61.

size, *shiwayose*, permanent "temporary employees," and so forth, as well as of those factors examined in earlier chapters.

This table shows the income earned by each of ten equal numbers of households from the lowest one-tenth to the highest one-tenth. The figures show the total income earned by each one-tenth of the total households as a percentage of total income. What is observed is a discernible decline in the share of total income by the first five income groups, against a visible trend of increase in the share of the highest tenth. When the percentage figure for the highest income class is

[28] For the ineffectiveness of the minimum wage law enacted in 1961, see the author's article cited in fn. 22, this chapter.

[29] The large firm sector, led by the Association of Large Firm Executives and Financial Leaders (*Keizai Dōyu Kai*), now asks "a reexamination of existing laws" for the purpose of affording a free hand to employers who wish to exercise "the rights of management without labor problems." *Asahi* (May 31, 1965).

TABLE 60

Income Distribution for All Households by Decimal Income Class [a]
(Percentage)

DECIMAL CLASS	1952	1956	1959	1962
1	2.0	1.8	1.5	1.4
2	4.8	3.8	3.3	3.3
3	6.2	5.1	4.6	4.7
4	6.5	6.4	5.9	5.9
5	8.0	7.6	7.2	7.2
6	8.5	9.1	8.8	8.6
7	11.0	10.9	10.5	10.3
8	12.5	12.6	12.8	12.6
9	14.8	16.0	16.3	16.2
10	25.7	26.7	29.9	29.8

[a] Data is for cash income. This calculation, made by Prof. Ishizaki, is based on the Ministry of Welfare, and is widely used as the best available data.
SOURCE: T. Ishizaki, "Dual Structure and Income Distribution," in Y. Tamanoi and T. Uchida, Nijū Kōzō no Bunseki (Analyses of The Dual Structure), eds. Y. Tamanoi and T. Uchida (Tōyō Keizai, 1964), p. 157.

divided by that of the lowest, we observe that the ratio has risen from 12.85 in 1952 to 21.28 in 1962.[30]

CONCLUSION

The "natural" process of economic growth—to exploit the economies of scale and related prerequisites to accomplish it—was and is being achieved at the "cost" [31] of those who were not favored to lead the postwar economic growth. The costs, as we have seen in this chapter, appeared in the form of an increasingly unequal distribution of income, a relatively small (vis-à-vis other industrialized nations) labor share of income, a slower rate of increase in real wage than that of labor productivity, and low wage levels of employees of medium-small firms,

[30] When calculations were made for the distribution of wage and salary incomes using Family Budget Study Report, the following results by quintile income class were obtained:

Class	1953	1954	1955	1956	1957	1958	1959	1960	1961
I	8.63	8.40	8.37	8.47	8.12	8.01	8.03	8.08	7.81
II	14.46	14.35	14.25	14.28	13.92	13.82	13.80	13.74	13.45
III	18.55	18.43	18.41	18.34	17.95	17.91	18.01	17.76	17.51
IV	23.52	23.52	23.50	23.17	23.04	23.01	23.12	22.95	23.31
V	34.85	35.30	35.46	35.71	36.97	37.17	37.04	37.47	37.87

Class I refers to the total disposable income (total income minus all taxes) of the lowest 20 percent of households. Class II refers to the next 20 percent, and so on. When the percentage figures for Class V are divided by the Class I figures, we obtain 4.0:1 in 1953 and 4.7:1 in 1961. Also see Table 46, chapter 8.
[31] The concept of "cost" will be discussed in the next chapter.

and of permanent "temporary employees." The "natural" forces of the postwar growth, it could be said, were fed upon these "costs," and were nurtured in the climate that encouraged *shiwayose* and other important ingredients in the economy.

The climate, to a large extent, was created by the government policies. The policies encouraged rapid growth with all the power at its command. Some of its power was translated into tangible sets of inducements for rapid capital accumulation and adoption of new technologies, while others worked to create an atmosphere of a hothouse in which the growth consciousness of the policy-makers stimulated, energized, and guided the rapid economic growth. The government policies, we must conclude, functioned as powerful catalysts in the "miraculous" accomplishments of the Japanese economy after the end of World War II.

But these costs must be evaluated against the accomplishments, the fruits of the economic growth. Are these costs justified in some sense of the term? Are they a necessary price for economic growth? We shall attempt to examine these questions in the next chapter.

10 *CONCLUSION*

Since the end of World War II, the economic democratization policy of the Supreme Command of the Allied Powers was significantly modified and was replaced by the growth-oriented economic policies of the Japanese government. If our observations in the preceding chapters have been correct, we can conclude that the central focus of the policy goal shifted from exclusive emphasis on economic democracy—as envisioned by the SCAP officials—to sustained emphasis on rapid economic growth.

The reasons why the SCAP policy had to be revised and abandoned in substance are not difficult to discover. The policy, which began as a policy of punishment for Zaibatsu and other economic institutions of the enemy of yesterday, began to be subjected to strong pressures for change almost as soon as it was implemented. The rapidly changing nature of international politics, the Cold War, and mounting criticism of SCAP policies in Washington (charges of antibusiness, of making Japan a ward of the United States, and even of socialism) were significant parts of this pressure.

The most important reason for the decline of the economic democratization policy, however, was its professed unconcern for the recovery and economic growth of the devastated Japanese economy. During the initial phase of the program, SCAP was able to dissolve the Zaibatsu, impose a rigid Anti-Monopoly Act, overhaul the tax system, and so on, because the possible impact of these measures on economic recovery and growth was ignored. However, as politico-economic necessities began to make the economic recovery of Japan "essential to the peace of Asia" and her economic growth "desirable," the SCAP policy was forced to retreat.

Even before the beginning of the Korean War, the wall of economic democracy began to crack. The government loan policy, the Weighted Production Policy (*Keisha Seisan Hōshiki*), and the 1949 amendment of the Anti-Monopoly Act were a few signs of the retreat. These were admissions by SCAP and Washington that economic democracy, as envisioned in 1945–1946, was not congruent with, and was perhaps even contradictory to, the recovery of the Japanese economy. Then, when the Korean War came, the already flaccid economic democratization policy began to erode rapidly to open the way for the policies of the Japanese government.

In the course of our examination, we have come to the view that the economic policies of the Japanese government significantly aided the rapid economic growth of Japan, but with the consequences we have seen. A crucial question which one must raise in this concluding chapter is: Has the Japanese policy been successful? Or, are these consequences—one might call them "costs"—somehow justified when considered against the benefits derived from the policies?

In the strictest sense such questions are unanswerable. As has been made clear in earlier chapters, one cannot hope to isolate that part of costs or benefits due to the policies from those due to "natural" economic forces of growth. Perhaps more fundamentally, even if such an identification were possible, the question is impossible to answer as we possess no means of measuring either benefits or costs objectively. In addition we should be reminded that any distinction between costs and benefits may be questioned, as such a distinction often is a reflection of our own values; for example, some people even refuse to consider increased inequality of income a cost.

Realizing this unavoidable link between one's evaluation of a policy and one's values, let us observe four *positions*, rather than answers, to the questions posed above. These are four discernible positions, as the author evaluates them, taken by the Japanese on the postwar economic policies.

THE MARXIST POSITION

The first position is that of the Marxists, a vocal group by virtue of the fact that a large number of academic economists and professional economic writers enunciate their position in a stream of books and articles. Although this group does not command any significant political power, theirs is a position with which all three other groups must contend in academic discussions and in popular dialogues.

The Marxist position is clear-cut and the most definable of all groups. From its point of view, both the SCAP policy and the policies of the

Japanese government were and are policies for, of, and by monopoly capital. The former carried out measures in order to make the Japanese economy weak and incapable of competing in international markets, in other words, servile (*jūzoku*) to American monopoly capital; and the latter continues to adopt policies to exploit the masses for the gains of giant corporations and financial interests.

Their view at first glance appears illogical or at best curious, as they denounce both the economic democratization policy of SCAP and the policy of the Japanese government which undid much of the SCAP policy. A standard explanation for this apparent contradiction is that the American monopolists instituted the economic democratization policy to enslave the Japanese economy, but when the Cold War became an undeniable reality, the Japanese monopolists were encouraged to serve as an arm of capitalist imperialism.

All this is based on the Marxist orthodoxy and requires little elaboration. Even in discussing specific issues, this group begins with pat generalities and familiar phrases and ends with expected conclusions which are far less illuminating. In discussing the Anti-Monopoly Act, for example, their premise is that this was enacted by U.S. monopolists to make the Japanese economy servile, and the Japanese government (monopolistic capital) mereley goes through the motion of respecting it, and amends or ignores the act if necessary in the interest of "monopoly capital." In either case, the Anti-Monopoly Act in capitalism is meaningless at best, and a tool of deception at worst. Also, even in discussing such questions as export and trade balance, economies of scale, structure of economy, wages, and so forth, the party line is faithfully followed.

In spite of the above, this group finds its audience because of the academic positions held by Marxist scholars, the sheer volume of literature and repetitive restatements expanding their position, and their straightforward and uncompromising conclusion. At times, this group can spearhead a dedicated, though small, group of followers into actions such as the antitax movement of 1948–1950 and the anti-"price hike" demonstrations of 1965. The resentment, mistrust, and frustrations of those who consider themselves left out of the postwar prosperity and benefits of the economic growth find an outlet in the vocal position which this group continues to take.

THE ANTI-CONCENTRATION POSITION

The second group is also composed of critics and opponents of the government policies. This group includes various subgroups whose views on some issues differ in degree of intensity and scope of opposition to the government policies. One segment of this group might find the general trend of the growth-oriented government policies unwise or undesirable, while other segments might find only some specific policy or the extent to which the policies were carried out detrimental to the "true" interests of the economy. This is the position which, though differing in degree, emphasizes the "just and equal" aspects of economic policy, compared to the policies of the government which emphasize growth. The common denominator of this group is their belief that the government, in its anxiety to promote rapid growth, caused the economy to concentrate to a degree unjustified by the benefits derived from the government policies.

More specifically, by "unjustified concentration," this group means such changes as increasing inequality of income distribution, highly oligopolistic-monopolistic market structure and power, and diverging real burden of taxes in favor of asset-owning groups. Their attacks on pervasive and increasingly entrenched cartels, price rigidity, lagging real wages, financial *shiwayose*, and discriminating corporate taxes and loan policies are only another way of criticizing the increasing concentration of the postwar Japanese economy.

The intellectual force of this position is supplied by the majority of the so-called *kinkei* (modern) economists—non-Marxists who are well versed in theories and tools of "bourgeois" economics. These economists, unlike the Marxists, begin with a critical evaluation of a specific governmental policy, using theoretical tools and statistical data, and find themselves arguing for, or recommending, specific-to-sweeping changes in government policy or policies. Their analyses differ in quality and academic objectivity, but the points made by their position are clear.

This group recognizes the need for rationalization and thus capital accumulation on the bases of economies of scale, international competitive ability, and economic growth in general; but they question and attack the means and extent these were encouraged and stimulated by the government. Although *grosso modo*, the central position of this group could be elaborated as follows:

The government policies significantly aided economic growth by encouraging rationalization and capital accumulation. This emphasis on growth must be credited with playing an important role in raising living standards, increasing exports, accomplishing technological improvements, and contributing to the prosperity of the postwar Japanese economy. However, the costs of these achievements have been (1) increased inequality of income due to several direct and indirect consequences of government policies; (2) increased excess capacity denoting a high degree of misallocation of resources, which could be alternatively allocated for redistribution of income and for increasing expenditures on welfare and public goods; and (3) increased instability of economy as the constant excess capacity, encouraged by cartels and other measures of industry protection, necessitated periodic adjustments of supply and demand. The periodic cycles which the postwar Japanese economy experienced must be considered to have been fostered, to no small degree, by the policies of the government.

Thus, the initial phase of the Japanese government policy to amend the naïve SCAP policy of economic democracy—an unrealistic transplant of American folklore on Japanese soil—was a correct policy. But the Japanese policies thereafter overcompensated for the rigid ideals of the SCAP policy, and these three major undesirable consequences of the Japanese policies which we observe today demonstrate that the degree to which these policies have been effected is clearly "unjustified."

Some economists make the points summarized above with subtlety and quantitative sophistication, often including detailed analyses of terms of trade, effects and impact of changes in rate of interest, lagged multiplier effects of investment demands on consumption, and so forth. But the resulting criticisms, intended (more often than not) and unintended, are unmistakable. Rare is the American economist who finds no fault with the policies of Washington, but rarer still is the "modern" (kinkei) Japanese economist who supports the policies of the Japanese government.

Encompassing the various shades of views—though their central position is the same—this group presents a blurred picture of alternative plans to the government policy. Their recommendations range from nationalization of selected industries to partial changes in tax laws or more stringent enforcement of the Anti-Monopoly Act. In spite of the lack of definiteness in their policy recommendations, this group performs the indispensable task of opposition and provides a counterpressure against the policies of the government.

The political force of this group rests in those who consider themselves victims—a subjective feeling, to be sure—of the government policies. The wage earners and medium-small entrepreneurs form the core of this force. How much of this force influenced the course of the government policies? Answers differ, depending on the position taken by each individual. The "victims" would argue that the policy-makers ignored or discounted their interests, while the government would argue the contrary, as seen below.

THE GOVERNMENT POSITION

This position, which we have examined in preceding chapters, has been to encourage, stimulate, and aid rationalization of the Japanese economy in order to achieve rapid economic growth. If our earlier observations have been correct, this process entailed extensive revisions of the economic democracy policy as envisioned by SCAP. The government position does not deny the necessity for amending the SCAP policy, but it does deny that any "unjustified costs" were imposed on the economy and that "equality and justice" have been sacrificed.

As this position has been discussed in earlier chapters, let us briefly recapitulate. Given the necessity of rationalization for the sake of economic recovery and growth, the means taken to encourage capital accumulation were necessary. The measures taken by the government, beginning with the revisions of SCAP-initiated programs, were all for the purpose of building a viable, prospering, and growing economy. The living standard of the people, as seen in real wage, per capita income, Engel index, or the level of consumption, has steadily increased as the successful result of these policies. The Japanese economy accomplished an internationally recognized, miraculous recovery and growth in the brief period of twenty years.

Some measures have been unpopular. Cartels, for example, were severely criticized; but in order to accomplish rationalization and capital accumulation they were necessary. Considered with the nearly excessive competition existing in the market, the alternative would have undoubtedly been ruinous competition, detrimental to the interests of the economy. Excess capacity observed for the short run is an inevitable fact of rapid technological progress and growth. The fruits of a dynamic economy can only be harvested when the policies have the foresight to see the need for temporary sacrifices. International competition is growing keener. When the nations in the European Economic Community and the United States enjoy a larger and more efficient scale of production in larger markets than those enjoyed by Japanese firms, the interest of the Japanese economy is served by taking all means necessary to assure that its industries become or remain competitive in the international market. The largest firms of Japan should be seen as struggling members of the highly competitive international market rather than monopolists in the domestic market. The Japanese economic policies have met the tests of success. First, the living standard of the Japanese has risen; and second, the policies are supported by the people who retain the Liberal-Democratic party in power. In view of the government the policies followed were the best of two possible worlds—the prewar-type economic policies and institutions and the centrally planned socialist economy. On these grounds the government position maintains that the benefits of the postwar economic policies have clearly exceeded the costs.

THE OLIGOPOLIST POSITION

In postwar Japan, to equate the interests and views of large firms with those of the policy-makers is to make a serious error. These two positions are separate, as has become increasingly clear to all but doctrinaire Marxists. It is perhaps accurate to state that in the early stages of postwar growth the policies appeared to reflect the views of this group as the policies coincided with the oligopolist position. However, as we observed in chapters 5 and 6, when these two views began to diverge, especially after 1958, the oligopolist position on some fundamental issues came into direct conflict with that of the policy-makers.

The oligopolist position argues that government policies should continue to encourage technological progress and to strengthen the international competitive ability of Japanese firms. To this end this group seeks the financial support of the government (loans and tax policies), revival of holding companies, virtual elimination of the twice-amended Anti-Monopoly Act, and so forth—but continued and increasing aid without an increase in governmental control.

The group argues that increased governmental intervention in such forms as government-decreed output cuts and coordination of investment plans seriously threatens the revival of the prewar-type bureaucratic economy. What is needed, this position maintains, is not a carrot-and-stick type of policy, but a policy of allowing the large firms of Japan to achieve "a higher order of economic organization." Like the government, this group emphasizes the international evaluation of firm size; but unlike the government, its concern ends with considerations of relative prices, amount of export, and cost differentials, as this is a one-sided position representing large firm views and their interests.

In spite of the basic difference between this position and that of the government, the former will continue to succeed in winning concessions from the policy-makers in periods of "emergency" or "as a transitional necessity." When liberalization of international trade became the major "emergency" for the competitive ability of Japanese firms, and when the "recession" of 1964–65 "endangered the supply and demand [excess capacity] condition of the industries," existing cartels asked for extensions, new ones were admitted, and other aids in the form of tax, loan, and monetary policies were demanded of the government.

It can safely be concluded of this position that it has been successful in forcing the government to adopt the measures it demanded. Failing to gain the support of this group, the government was unable to gain the power to control and adjust investments in 1963, and in the recession of 1964–65, pleading "the largest excess capacity and inventory since the end of the war," industry, for example, succeeded in raising the number of cartels and inter-giant-firm mergers. The degree to which this position can influence government policies has been large, especially when "emergencies" arose. In spite of this fact, one should not assess that the economic policy of postwar Japan was and is dictated by the oligopolists, Zaibatsu, or monopoly capital.

The future of the Japanese economy and the success of democracy depend on successfully finding a set of economic policies that can satisfy the needs of growth and "equality and justice." Or more realistically, answers must somehow be found to such questions as: Can the Japanese economy have both growth and equality and justice? Should one be sacrificed? If so, which one and to what degree? As usual, no easy answer to these questions can be found in the voluminous literature on economic growth and policy.

ASSESSMENTS AND REFLECTIONS

Recalling our discussions in the preceding chapters and the views advanced by the four positions, let us venture our assessments of and reflections on the postwar economic policies and the future course of the Japanese economy. As was made clear in earlier chapters, we can join with the anti-concentration position in assessing that the *direction* taken by postwar Japanese economic policies was essentially "correct." The imposition of the original economic democracy—an American dream of competitive capitalism—was a punitive measure which, though idealistically motivated no doubt, reflected the immediate postwar public sentiment against Japan. When economic recovery and growth had to be considered, the SCAP measures, because of their incongruence with the specific growth needs of Japan, rapidly eroded. For example, the original Anti-Monopoly Act of 1947, which prohibited any type of exclusive agreement with foreign firms even in the case of exclusive franchise of technology and numerous activities that were necessary for a capital market of an industrial nation, was severely detrimental to growth. Although the original act would have kept Japan innocent of cartels, it would have resulted in a much lower rate of economic growth and a slower rise in living standards. This comment must apply to the tax laws as well. An increased depreciation allowance was needed to hasten the rate of absorption of new technology and to maximize the supply of capital, and a sacrifice in the progressivity of the income tax was an obvious means of doing so.

Agreeing with these measures, however, is quite different from agreeing with the *extent* to which these measures were carried out by the postwar Japanese government. The central contention of our doubt concerning the extent to which the government policies were carried out has been well stated:

> It has sometimes been suggested that faster growth, with the improved standard of living it implies, can be taken as an overriding economic objective. This, however, cannot seriously be claimed. It may be, and I believe it is, a reasonable objective in this country at the present time to speed up the rate of growth, but this is not to say that in deciding on a rate of growth other objectives of policy should be ignored. To take one example among many, the degree to which it is necessary to abstain from consumption now to give a higher output in the future is a decision which has to be carefully weighed. There is certainly a limit to which such abstention would be willingly chosen.[1]

This is from Sir Robert Shone's 1965 lecture, and "in this country" refers to England whose growth rate has not been high. Although it is not conceptually as well defined as in the case of a firm's production function, what is suggested in the quotation is that economic growth is also subject to a decreasing return and an increasing cost. What we hope to argue here is that the Japanese economic policy dedicated to growth has passed the break-even point.

As the well-known Harrod-Domar model shows, the growth rate equals the ratio of saving to income (s/Y) times the efficiency of investment ($\Delta Y/I$).[2] The Japanese case, however, is best examined by a slightly altered model suggested by Professor Harrod. In this version, $GC = s - k$, where G is the growth rate, C is the capital coefficient ($I/\Delta Y$), s is the ratio of investment to income (I/Y) and k is "current addition to capital (the value thereof to be expressed as a fraction of current income) the worthwhileness of which is not deemed to have any immediate relation to current requirement. k is in fact the capital outlay which no one expects to see justified within a short period."[3]

The Japanese economy, wishing to maximize the growth rate (G) sought to increase saving (s) which is necessary to take advantage of more productive technology. At an early stage, saving and productivity

---

[1] Sir Robert Shone, "Problems of Planning for Economic Growth in a Mixed Economy," *Economic Journal*, LXXV (March 1965), 2.

[2] Growth rate is $\Delta Y/Y$, thus s/Y. $\Delta Y/I$ is $\Delta Y/Y$ since all savings are assumed to be invested ($s = I$) in this growth model.

[3] R. F. Harrod, *Toward Dynamic Economics* (London, 1956), p. 79.

increased hand in hand. However, as growth continued, k grew in the form of excess capacity. This meant that to keep the growth rate at the level desired and politically committed, it was necessary to increase saving at a greater rate. This was accomplished by taking measures to increase corporate profits and income in the hands of savers. As the rate of increase in saving grew, however, it began to increase k (excess capacity) at an even more rapid rate. The recourse was to increase savings (s) further if the desired growth rate (g) was to be maintained. This process is effective, using Keynes' analogy, in keeping a high rate of growth in the same fashion that Egyptian monarchs maintained prestige and full employment by building more pyramids which were useless to those who toiled to build them.

This exercise in symbols and analogy serves to make the point that, if growth is to be achieved at the increasing cost of benefiting only a limited sector of an economy much more than others by means of less progressive taxes, by preferred treatment of giant firms in taxation, by monetary policy, and by cartels and mergers which set prices and production quotas in broad daylight, the social value of growth must be viewed as having become increasingly doubtful.

However, showing that the economic policy for growth is becoming less and less desirable is not sufficient to establish that the break-even point referred to earlier has been passed. Since, as Sir Robert Shone's article and others make clear, the task of establishing that the Japanese economic growth has entered into a phase of diminishing returns cannot be based totally on objective criteria even ignoring such elements as psychological factors and "values which are difficult to bring into the economic calculation," [4] we must endeavor to argue that the Japanese economy no longer requires the growth policy.

The major reason in assessing that the growth-oriented economic policies outlived their justified usefulness is to point out that the technological advances, often "lumpy," have been made to a level that is competitive in the world market, and there no longer exists a need for continued sacrifice in economic democracy. After 1958, industries matured one after another, and such industries as iron-steel, chemical, automobile, machine tool, electronics, electrical equipment, cement, fertilizer, paper and pulp, textile (chemical and natural), shipbuilding, and heavy machinery became fully competitive in international markets. Some achieved this in the late fifties and others during the "rationalization wave" of 1961–1962.

In iron-steel, chemical fiber, shipbuilding, cement, ammonium, and some lines of machine tool, it is generally agreed that these industries

[4] Shone, p. 3.

have been internationally competitive since 1962 and some much earlier. Cameras, electric appliances, and light machinery are areas in which Japan's international competitive ability is unquestioned. Debates on further need for government protection are heard for the automobile, some machine tool, and heavy industries. As can be determined by export data, however, the export of buses, trucks, and small passenger cars has been increasing; and in the heavy equipment areas, such as generators and transportation equipment, Japanese firms are winning an increasingly large number of international bids.

If one examines Japanese industries during the period of 1961–1964, when investment activities were at their postwar peak, and analyzes increases in efficiency-cost reductions, one is forced to realize that the government reports which showed the relative inefficiency of several of the Japanese industries up to this period were rapidly becoming outdated. M.I.T.I.'s comprehensive Report of the Industrial Structure Commission (the so-called Arisawa Commission Report) compared plant scale curves of the largest Japanese firms in 28 industries to the best estimates of those Western firms, and found that "in nearly all cases a significant cost reduction could be achieved by enlarging the scale of production to that of the Western level." Especially in nine industries (passenger car, ball-bearing, coal-tar derivatives, chemical fibers, cement, petroleum refining, lathe, aluminum, and chemical fertilizer), they found that at least a 20 to 10 percent cost reduction could be achieved if further rationalization were carried out. Also, of the 1,036 largest firms in Japan, the commission reported that 841 were in need of "enlargement of scale." [5]

A careful examination of technical and trade journals, however, reveals that 1961–1964 investment activities rapidly changed this condition. For example, in those areas still debated, the machine tool industry and the automobile industry effected mergers and enlargements of scale of production in 1963 and 1964.[6] Judging from the published data, then,

[5] M.I.T.I., *Report of Industrial Structure Commission* ("Arisawa Commission Report") (Tokyo, 1963), pp. 10–25.
[6] Even for those industries rated to be behind "the international level" in the Arisawa Commission Report, little effort is required in accumulating evidence that they have now reached the international level. For example, in the recent issues of *Japan Economic Journal*, one finds explicit statements that the iron-steel, electric appliances, and cement industries have, in the past, reached the international level and the problem faced is not the scale-efficiency question but rather that of excess capacity. On the cement industry, the *Journal* wrote, "However, an annual production of 35 million is only 64 percent of the full production capacity (55 million) and each manufacturer is still operating at no more than 60 percent of capacity. As long as the operational scope remains at this level, the industry is still in a state of depression. The normal rate of operation is between 70 and 80 percent." The *Japan Economic Journal* (May 3, 1966 and March 22, 1966).

the remaining problems are large excess capacity and methods of financing expansion rather than technological problems. Although pockets of technological inferiority cannot be denied, as in any industrial nation no matter how advanced, the writer believes that the level of Japanese technology today can no longer be considered inefficient by international standards. In spite of often claimed fears that liberalization of international trade would cause the largest firms in Japan to suffer reduced market shares in the international and domestic markets, such has not been the case.

In short, the long-maintained position of the government—rapid, stimulated process of rationalization for the sake of export—no longer has its force.[7] No rational firm can suffer prolonged "ruinous competition" based on industry-wide excess capacity and, at the same time, want to expand its capacity continuously. However, many a Japanese business leader claims the former and continues the latter with vigor and the certain knowledge that the government will continue to increase protection as "emergencies" arise. Here, it should be recalled that the government forced the willing firms to overinvest by allocating the market share of each firm according to its rated capacity, or its ability to overinvest.

The situation is similar to that of an arms race running uncontrolled. For the sake of "international competitive ability, rationalization and necessary profit," the growth-oriented policies continue. This is a process which can end with monopolies, a total negation of the economic democracy of 1945, just as an uncontrolled arms race could result in a stockpile of deadly weapons and little butter. Firms demanding larger capacity, with the help of the government, absorb a larger share of "purchasing power," slow the rate of increase of domestic demand, and therefore create a greater need for export markets.

To create competitive ability in the world market, these firms in turn require more protection. This is a circle which appears to be forming more obviously since the 1958–1959 recession. If one could measure the "undesirableness" of the increasing disparity in income distribution and economic power in general, one could at least conceptually predate the break-even point before the circle began to form. Even before 1958, when the second rationalization plan launched in 1956 ended in a recession, price rigidity, increasing excess capacity, intricate dumping mechanisms, the widening disparity of income, and so forth could have

---

[7] Along with the source cited in fn. 5, for a detailed examination of the state of Japanese technology, see Imai, Misonou, Miyazaki and Nakamura, eds., *Gendai Nippon no Dokusen Shihon* (Monopoly Capital of Contemporary Japan). Vol. 4, subtitled "Technological Innovation, International Dissemination" (Tokyo: Shiseido, 1965).

cast serious doubts as to the desirableness of a high growth rate. It must be remembered that the prewar Zaibatsu were forced to seek export markets because the policy-makers accommodated their desires too well in an economy known for its cheap labor. The postwar governments, it appears, are wondering why there exists a visible failure for demand to keep pace with supply after robbing the tax structure of its progressivity.

In continuing the type of policy the Japanese government followed, the greatest danger lies in making its point too well. A simple and direct extension of M.I.T.I. arguments prompts the question: Why not nationalization of monopolist firms to give them the maximum economy of scale and supply them with capital? This question, which in fact is raised by socialists and communists, suggests a definite limit to the type of reasoning currently adopted by M.I.T.I. officials. Policy-makers, and especially those who take the oligopolist position, should be constantly reminded of the fact that public opinion in the 1960's is more articulate and educated than that of prewar years. Much of this education, the author believes, was provided by the otherwise unsuccessful SCAP interlude. *Democrashii, anchi-monopolii, ikōlitii* and many other words of English derivation—and more importantly, the concepts—were assimilated into daily Japanese conversation during the brief period of a few years following the war. The Japanese public had been given points of reference—"What economic democracy ought to be . . ."—and any departure from these reference points can no longer go unnoticed. For the government and oligopolist positions to ignore or neglect the voice of the educated is to court serious political consequences. The dipping plurality which the Liberal-Democratic party has been experiencing in general elections ought to indicate the potential danger that could result from a continuation of the course of the postwar economic policies.

In conclusion we must recognize that some sacrifice in economic democracy was required in postwar Japan for the sake of growth. This was especially true in view of the rigid economic democracy imposed on Japan by SCAP whose major concern was reform rather than growth. No one can deny that there existed a critical need to reaccumulate capital in postwar Japan. However, like a military organization which sacrifices some democratic rules for the sake of efficiency, an economy in sacrificing economic democracy must keep a constant eye on efficiency—the desirableness for the economy as a whole. When ill-effects multiply because of the policy and begin to cancel the benefits brought by it, the policy has lost its *raison d'être*.

If the government presently is concerned with growth in the midst of what appears to be a recession, it can stimulate the economy by investing more in public goods, along with making an effort to redistribute the income more equally. The sum budgeted for social welfare in Japan was only 16.3 percent of the total budget of 1964, one of the lowest among nations enjoying per capita income of over $400.[8] The critical need, it appears to the writer, is not to add excess capacity by such means as tax steps to help industries, which are already efficient by any standard, but rather to increase the maximum welfare payment for nearly twenty percent of the Japanese population from 16,147 yen ($45) per month, for a family of four, to a higher figure and to budget a much larger sum for badly neglected housing, education, and other areas of public welfare.[9]

In 1964 a government publication closed its discussion on public welfare by saying: "The catchword in the future should be 'Improve Welfare Through Increasing the Nation's Capacity to Export.' " [10] But the time has come for the government to reexamine the political and economic costs of this reasoning. The third largest producer of steel in the world can boast of that fact only when the nation has regained some elements of the economic democracy it has sacrificed.

No one would deny the fact that the Japanese today enjoy the fruits of the postwar economic growth in which the government played a major role. These consist of higher real wages, improved welfare measures, and much more. Life in Japan is better and easier now than it was in 1945 or 1950 or even in 1955, and far better than it was before World War II. This, however, is not the issue in our evaluation of the recent policy of the government. The issue is, how could a different policy from that being pursued for the past several years still be more desirable in a fuller sense of the term.

---

[8] This figure was 22.1 in the U.S., 28.3 in England, and 18.7 in West Germany in 1962. This must be considered vis-à-vis the fact that the military expenditure is much smaller in Japan than in these countries. Per capita outlay is at the level of Tunisia and Ceylon. Yoshida Hiroshi, "Conditions and the Policy of Social Welfare," *Ekonomisuto* (March 16, 1965), p. 15. In the words of the Economic Planning Agency: "The benefits per capita of social security in Japan, based on studies by the international Labor Organization are still low compared with other countries." For example, in France the per capita benefits for social security were $152, West Germany $148, Italy $58, but Japan only $26 (figures for Japan based on 1962 and those for foreign countries, 1957) which may be said to be quite low even in comparison with Japan's income level. The ratio of transfer income in the national income was 15.7 percent for France, 14.5 percent for Italy, but only 5 percent for Japan (the ratio for Japan based on 1962 and that for foreign countries on 1960). Japan Economic Planning Agency, *Economic Survey of Japan* (Tokyo: Japan Times, Ltd., 1964), p. 85.

[9] This figure is for Tokyo which enjoys the highest welfare payments, and the calculation is based on the Engel Index of 53.6. The allowance for one meal for an adult is approximately ten cents. "Poverty in the Midst of Prosperity," *Ekonomisuto* (October 10, 1963).

[10] The Economic Planning Board, pp. 91–92.

TABLE I–1

Regression Coefficients and t-values for 1950–1958
(t-values appear in parentheses)

INDUSTRY	LARGEST FIRM	3 LARGEST FIRMS	5 LARGEST FIRMS	10 LARGEST FIRMS
Coal	−.327(9.233)	−.838(6.779)	−.807(6.332)	−.622(4.218)
Milk	−.223(.717)	.883(1.622)	.976(1.516)	.883(1.255)
Powdered milk	.332(.194)	2.588(.621)	3.445(.826)	3.695(.887)
Butter	.455(.180)	−.698(.079)	−.173(.117)	−.055(.045)
Soy sauce	.500(19.97)	.433(20.02)	.445(16.25)	.597(14.64)
Monosodium glutamate	.613(2.605)	−.658(3.571)	−1.011(1.294)	.038(40.51)
Wheat flour	1.196(3.603)	1.795(1.545)	2.131(1.502)	2.251(1.602)
Sugar	−1.060(4.687)	−2.543(2.019)	−2.896(2.197)	−2.810(3.553)
Beer	.770(3.465)	−.196(11.87)	—	—
Sake	−.003(15.12)	.050(25.19)	−.068(22.68)	−.140(21.17)
Shochu	−.318(7.396)	−.075(2.919)	.032(1.109)	.152(4.273)
Yeast	−.120(1.034)	.015(.043)	.006(1.865)	1.953(4.006)
Edible vegetable oil	−2.596(4.039)	−3.980(2.212)	−4.148(1.227)	−1.761(.729)
Silk thread	−.268(9.078)	−.592(9.065)	−.687(12.73)	−.545(15.05)
Cotton yarn	−.787(5.517)	−1.978(2.535)	−3.008(1.758)	−4.416(.991)
Carded wool yarn	−1.393(8.928)	−3.281(2.707)	−4.456(2.409)	−4.893(1.783)
Cotton Cloth	−.442(13.10)	−1.323(5.800)	−2.013(3.885)	−3.153(2.218)
Rayon cloth	−2.225(2.377)	−5.661(.817)	−8.365(.491)	−13.850(.308)
Carded wool cloth	.050(.560)	.027(.029)	−.100(.041)	−.177(.323)
Paper pulp	−.602(3.142)	−1.348(4.485)	−1.666(4.309)	−1.255(3.672)
Western paper	−.618(3.915)	−1.995(1.533)	−2.146(2.402)	−1.796(2.223)
Ammonium sulphate	−.052(1.547)	−.358(5.847)	−.505(4.152)	−.461(3.973)
Calcium cyanamide	.932(1.516)	.182(.413)	.120(2.512)	.000
Superphosphate	−.608(7.205)	−.210(2.345)	−.267(3.385)	−.902(18.21)
Sodium hydroxide	−.353(3.519)	−.045(.066)	−.433(.565)	−.485(1.332)
Sulfuric acid	−.375(4.623)	−.453(6.823)	−.573(7.921)	−.582(6.014)
Coal tar	−.755(6.791)	−.295(1.635)	−.270(1.422)	.127(.574)
Synthetic dyes	−1.498(2.859)	−1.261(6.149)	−.938(5.358)	−.515(5.196)
Vinyl chloride resin	−1.748(3.099)	−3.845(4.303)	−3.976(1.901)	−.731(.967)
Celluloid material	−.142(4.477)	−.025(3.44)	.118(1.364)	.338(7.735)

(Continued)

INDUSTRY	LARGEST FIRM	3 LARGEST FIRMS	5 LARGEST FIRMS	10 LARGEST FIRMS
Synthetic fibers	−1.538(1.788)	−1.675(1.646)	−1.333(2.517)	−.065(20.58)
Film	.288(2.011)	.000		
Petroleum refining	−2.015(2.077)	−4.938(.607)	−3.101(1.552)	−1.766(1.878)
Automobile tires & tubes	−.205(5.194)	−.832(8.057)	−.300(12.83)	.000
Plain glass	.043(.178)	.000		
Cement	−.677(21.29)	−1.168(3.809)	−1.546(3.825)	−1.433(4.842)
Fireproof brick	−.003(.089)	−.367(4.476)	−.685(4.701)	−.722(4.001)
Pig iron	−11.066(3.210)	−2.255(4.158)	−.913(3.541)	.238(2.914)
Ferroalloys	−.447(1.072)	−.408(.354)	−.332(.312)	−.483(.505)
Ordinary hot-rolled steel products	−.053(3.806)	.153(4.288)	.135(3.490)	.338(4.491)
Galvanized sheets	−.323(1.858)	.917(2.250)	1.091(1.585)	.867(.750)
Cast iron pipes	−.162(.829)	.322(.177)	−.155(1.010)	−.500(4.286)
Electric copper	−.105(1.853)	−.608(4.285)	−.327(5.191)	.000
Aluminum	−1.923(3.086)	.000		
Handling internal combustion engines	.520(.647)	1.796(.884)	1.823(1.145)	1.500(1.712)
Bearings	−.685(3.186)	−.867(7.263)	−.150(3.977)	.128(11.49)
Passenger cars	.297(1.347)	−1.055(1.419)	−.477(4.945)	.000
Electric locomotive	−1.288(.947)	−1.750(1.085)	−.560(5.460)	.000
Freight car	.392(.204)	.972(.405)	.620(.303)	.573(.679)
Steel vessel	−.073(.394)	−1.116(2.014)	−2.158(1.590)	−3.186(1.391)
Camera	−1.028(1.471)	−1.358(.809)	−1.145(.594)	.137(.086)
Wrist watch	2.563(.765)	4.855(.626)	4.870(.092)	−13.320(.269)
Matches	−.348(6.891)	−.313(15.37)	−.265(4.660)	.010(.148)

SOURCE: See sources cited for tables 8 and 11.

TABLE I–2

Regression Coefficients and t-values for 1950–1962
(t-values appear in parentheses)

INDUSTRY	LARGEST FIRM	3 LARGEST FIRMS	5 LARGEST FIRMS	10 LARGEST FIRMS
Coal	−.126(2.641)	−.449(5.395)	−.349(3.708)	−.345(4.538)
Milk	.228(1.857)	1.745(3.460)	1.887(3.259)	1.509(3.283)
Powdered milk	.134(.268)	1.903(1.275)	1.850(1.232)	2.097(1.376)
Butter	1.186(1.044)	1.050(.321)	.541(.906)	.716(1.450)
Soy sauce	.574(33.18)	.708(15.48)	.848(9.712)	1.002(9.707)
Monosodium glutimate	−1.167(4.232)	−.631(8.245)	−.351(1.384)	.013(33.84)
Wheat flour	.814(6.097)	1.383(3.275)	1.615(3.029)	1.732(3.184)
Beer	.837(7.384)	−.246(27.82)	—	—
Sugar	−.458(2.857)	−1.232(2.090)	−1.329(1.825)	−1.240(1.622)
Sake	.002(16.03)	−.009(9.435)	−.011(7.029)	−.040(11.26)
Shochu	.265(4.073)	1.007(3.540)	1.367(3.003)	1.489(3.071)
Yeast	−.375(5.769)	−.908(2.337)	−.812(1.536)	1.501(6.06)
Edible vegetable oil	−.937(1.749)	−1.471(1.128)	−1.207(.660)	.008(.007)
Silk thread	−.473(15.54)	−.655(18.86)	−.674(23.12)	−.474(23.57)
Cotton yarn	−.482(8.493)	−1.211(3.702)	−1.781(2.398)	−2.735(1.528)
Carded wool yarn	−1.081(11.30)	−2.586(4.052)	−3.567(3.391)	−3.883(2.780)
Cotton cloth	−.301(20.02)	−.924(7.951)	−1.372(5.005)	−2.034(2.841)
Rayon cloth	−1.378(3.382)	−3.789(1.335)	−5.767(.829)	−9.655(.536)
Carded wool cloth	−.210(5.121)	−.433(1.373)	−.684(.857)	−1.230(.650)
Paper pulp	−.250(3.818)	−.292(1.005)	−.366(1.241)	−.634(4.148)
Western paper	−.541(9.068)	−1.129(2.367)	−1.291(3.254)	−.936(2.855)
Ammonium sulphate	−.309(10.52)	−.787(8.868)	−1.212(5.327)	−.841(8.018)
Calcium cyanamide	.982(3.600)	.561(3.080)	.330(9.449)	.000
Superphosphate	−.951(10.49)	−1.049(4.560)	−1.223(4.265)	−1.482(8.190)
Sodium hydroxide	−.675(8.599)	−1.391(2.121)	−1.768(2.293)	−1.891(1.446)
Sulfuric acid	−.365(11.64)	−.630(13.81)	−.838(12.65)	−.810(11.15)
Coal tar	−.247(3.640)	−.047(.799)	−.484(5.203)	.362(4.14)
Synthetic dyes	−1.161(5.369)	−1.473(7.494)	−.910(7.726)	−.630(8.054)
Vinyl chloride	−1.320(5.488)	−2.803(4.021)	−3.186(3.324)	−1.025(3.166)
Celluloid material	1.152(2.182)	.869(2.516)	.545(4.340)	.431(11.73)
Synthetic fiber	−1.720(4.103)	−2.585(2.687)	−2.115(3.472)	−.398(12.42)
Film	−.046(.844)	.000		
Petroleum refining	−1.241(3.144)	−3.244(1.112)	−2.649(3.146)	1.529(4.006)
Automobile tubes & tires	.335(2.078)	−.937(7.605)	−.723(6.625)	−.199(19.87)
Plain glass	−.107(1.386)	.000		
Cement	−.423(16.16)	−.970(7.493)	−1.141(6.335)	−1.092(7.648)
Fireproof brick	.226(8.387)	.151(2.196)	−.140(1.638)	−.319(4.302)

(Continued)

INDUSTRY	LARGEST FIRM	3 LARGEST FIRMS	5 LARGEST FIRMS	10 LARGEST FIRMS
Pig iron	−1.004(7.290)	−2.159(8.154)	−.976(6.992)	.027(.984)
Ferroalloys	−.480(3.250)	−1.035(2.056)	−.975(2.049)	−1.011(2.341)
Ordinary hot-rolled steel products	−.127(7.052)	−.005(.413)	.162(9.755)	.313(11.49)
Galvanized sheets	−.113(2.081)	.734(4.920)	.913(3.712)	1.001(2.405)
Cast iron pipes	.308(2.625)	.458(.868)	−.013(.301)	−6.079(.308)
Electric copper	−.057(2.637)	−.504(9.593)	−.029(1.112)	.000
Aluminum	−.021(3.469)	.000		
Handling-internal combustion engines	.324(1.327)	.996(1.472)	.938(1.720)	.427(1.170)
Bearings	−.945(5.889)	−.944(10.02)	−.563(8.445)	−.239(7.452)
Passenger car	−.738(2.740)	−1.629(3.697)	−.731(10.31)	—
Electric locomotive	−.566(1.314)	−.624(.810)	.428(3.485)	—
Freight car	.095(.173)	1.844(1.489)	2.428(1.472)	1.085(2.777)
Steel vessel	−.116(1.958)	−.553(2.314)	−1.223(2.054)	−1.938(1.670)
Camera	−.401(1.328)	−.540(.812)	−.644(.868)	.172(.296)
Wrist watch	1.948(1.659)	3.300(1.167)	2.205(.104)	−10.230(.530)
Matches	−.224(13.04)	−.281(31.90)	−.275(13.15)	−.053(2.684)

SOURCES: See sources cited for tables 8 and 11.

APPENDIX II

METHODS AND EXPLANATIONS FOR TABLE 39, CHAPTER 8
This table was calculated as follows:

$$
\begin{array}{l}
\text{Burden of} \\
\text{selected taxes} \\
\text{as percentage} \\
\text{of mean income}
\end{array}
=
\frac{\left[\dfrac{\sum\limits_{j=1}^{n} A^t_{j_i}}{n}\right] r_{at} + \left[\dfrac{\sum\limits_{j=1}^{n} T^t_{j_i}}{n}\right] r_{tt} + \dfrac{\sum\limits_{j=1}^{n} LT^t_{j_i}}{n} + \dfrac{\sum\limits_{j=1}^{n} YT^t_{j_i}}{n}}{\dfrac{\sum\limits_{j=1}^{n} Y^t_{j_i}}{n}}
$$

The first term in the numerator is the product of the average expenditure on alcoholic beverages by individuals ($j = 1$ to n) in the ith income class in year t and the tax rate of alcoholic beverages (r_a). r_{at} is a non-weighted average tax rate on five major alcoholic beverages in year t. The second term applies to the tobacco tax, and r_{tt} is calculated in an identical manner to r_{at}. In both cases it is assumed that the total burden is shifted to the consumer. These two taxes account for, on the average, nearly 50 percent of the total indirect tax collected by the national government. The tobacco tax is a composite of national and local tobacco taxes. The rate of the latter is the same throughout the country by law. For example, in 1962 the tax on *Peace*, which retailed at 40 yen, was 25.91 yen. The tax rate, therefore, for *Peace* is 64.8 percent. This process was repeated for the five most popular brands (*Peace, Hi-Lite, Ikoi, Shin-sei, Golden Bat*), and their rates were averaged. The same method was used for alcoholic beverages. Five popular beverages were chosen (*sake*, special, first, and second class; artificial *sake* known as *gōsei-seishu*; sweet potato wine known as *shōchu*; beer; and the most popular brand of whiskey). Since cigarette prices are government determined and prices for alcoholic beverages are cartelized and government controlled, the process of tracing price changes over the period was made relatively easier.

The weakness of this method is that the rates calculated tend to overstate the tax burden on lower income classes and understate that for the higher income classes, assuming that higher income classes buy those cigarettes or alcoholic beverages which are more expensive and subject to a higher tax rate and vice versa for the lower classes. For example, tax rates for special class *sake* was 56.7 percent, and for second class *sake* 35.1 percent in 1962.

The third term in the numerator is *LT*, standing for local taxes paid directly to the local governments. The most important among the local taxes is the inhabitant's tax which uses the national income tax as standard. Recently, however, many variations have been introduced to weaken the pro-

gressivity existing in the national income tax. Some versions of the inhabitant's tax in the municipal districts (*ku*) in cities, levied in addition to the
prefectural inhabitant's tax, are often a flat sum per head. Most of these local taxes are withheld at the source from monthly wages.

The last term is the tax on earned income withheld monthly at the income source on the basis of earning and exemption. The denominator is the
average income of the sample in i^{th} class. Income here is the total of income
earned by the family members, returns from assets, social security benefits,
and gifts but does not include a carry-over from the preceding month, savings withdrawn in the month, debts, and so forth.

APPENDIX III

THE RESULTS AND EXPLANATIONS FOR REGRESSION
COEFFICIENTS CALCULATED FOR THE TAX BURDEN OF FOUR
TAXES DISCUSSED IN CHAPTER 8

TABLE III-1

Regression Coefficients Between Tax Burden and Income Level, 1953–1962

YEAR	REGRESSION COEFFICIENT (b)	STANDARD ERROR OF (b)	t-VALUE *	COEFFICIENT OF DETERMINATION R^2 †	NUMBER OF INCOME CLASSES
1953	.2522	1.661	15.181	.9388	15
1954	.2622	2.419	10.839	.8867	15
1955	.2273	1.075	21.147	.9571	20
1956	.2015	1.953	10.317	.8418	20
1957	.1164	.848	13.742	.9042	20
1958	.1214	.858	11.002	.8582	20
1959	.1057	1.101	9.599	.8600	15
1960	.0836	1.019	8.192	.8173	15
1961	.0717	.798	8.984	.8432	15
1962	.0611	.799	7.946	.8080	15

* All t-values are significant at .01 level at given sample size.
† All R^2 are significant at .01 at given sample size.

Regression coefficients $(b$'s$)$ were calculated for the tax burden (as a percentage of mean income within each income class) as a dependent variable and the level of income as an independent variable. In the form of $(T/Y) = a + bX$, where T is the total of the four taxes under examination, Y is the mean income, and X is the level of income class measured in 1,000-yen units. Since all income classes do not have an identical class interval, the distance between income classes was measured in units of 1,000 yen. For example, for the 1952–1958 data, the distance between the ith and $i + 1^{th}$ income class is four, while for the post-1959 data distances of five and ten were used. For the purpose of calculating regression coefficients, the lowest income class was omitted. An extremely small income and a large monthly debt make the data for this class result in what is shown in Table 39. As expected, the regression coefficients showed a smooth decline between 1953 and 1962.

A weakness in this method is that these regression coefficients do not account for taxes paid on asset income, while the denominator of the equation used in calculating Table 39 includes asset income in the total income. This means that the regression coefficients calculated can understate progressivity of the tax burden, since the higher income classes enjoy a larger asset

TABLE III–2

Tax Burden of Alcohol and Tobacco Tax as a Percentage of Income, 1953–1962

YEAR	REGRESSION COEFFI- CIENT (b)	STANDARD ERROR OF (b)	t-VALUE *	COEFFICIENT OF DETERMINA- TION R^2 †	NUMBER OF INCOME CLASSES
1953	−.03090	.5050	− 6.1183	.7139	15
1954	−.03262	.4454	− 7.3245	.7815	15
1955	−.02438	.3014	− 8.0890	.7659	20
1956	−.02538	.6928	− 4.089	.4553	20
1957	−.02226	.1776	−12.533	.8870	20
1958	−.02525	.4735	− 5.336	.5871	20
1959	−.01186	.1796	− 6.6173	.7448	15
1960	−.01348	.2536	− 5.3141	.6531	15
1961	−.01352	.2271	− 5.9543	.7029	15
1962	−.01184	.1998	− 5.9276	.7008	15

* All t-values are significant at .01 level at given sample size.
† All R^2 are significant at .01 at given sample size.

TABLE III–3

Tax Burden of Local Taxes as a Percentage of Income, 1953–1962

YEAR	REGRESSION COEFFI- CIENT (b)	STANDARD ERROR OF (b)	t-VALUE *	COEFFICIENT OF DETERMINA- TION R^2 †	NUMBER OF INCOME CLASSES
1953	.02947	.5515	5.344	.6556	15
1954	.04575	.6697	6.831	.7567	15
1955	.04080	.3825	10.393	.8437	20
1956	.02648	.8816	3.004	(.3108)	20
1957	.01838	.4691	3.9192	.4344	20
1958	.02460	.3477	7.0765	.7146	20
1959	.01307	.3454	3.7848	.4885	15
1960	.02836	.4035	(0.7029)	(.0318)	15
1961	.01389	.3608	3.8510	.4971	15
1962	.02194	.3933	5.5782	.6747	15

* All t-values, except the one in parentheses, are significant at .05 level at given sample size.
† All R^2, except two in parentheses, are significant at .05 level at given sample size.

income than the lower income classes. However, a further examination of data showed that the understatement of progressivity of the tax burden is minimal, since our data deal with the urban wage earners whose asset income is very small. For all the years under examination, the asset income for the highest income class amounted to less than 2 percent of the total income. (For other income classes this figure is lower and approaches the neighborhood of .06 percent for the lowest income class.)

This means that, for example, in some years the total tax burden (including taxes on asset incomes) is understated by up to .02 percent for the highest income class in Table 39. This assumes that the tax rate on asset incomes is 10 percent. For two years (1953 and 1962), regression coefficients were recalculated after adjusting the data in Table 39 for asset incomes. The results obtained had virtually no effect on the magnitude of respective regression coefficients, that is, .2483 for 1953 and .0630 for 1962.

LAW RELATING TO PROHIBITION OF PRIVATE MONOPOLY AND METHODS OF PRESERVING FAIR TRADE

Law as enacted in 1947

Law as amended in 1953 (present law)

CHAPTER I. GENERAL RULES

Article 1. This Law, by prohibiting private monopolization, unreasonable restraint of trade and unfair methods of competition, by preventing excessive concentration of power over enterprises, and by excluding undue restrictions of production, sale, price, technology, etc., through combinations and agreements, etc., and all other unreasonable restraints of business activities, aims to promote free and fair competition, to stimulate the initiative of entrepreneurs, to encourage business activities of enterprises, to heighten the levels of employment and national income and, thereby, to promote the democratic and wholesome development of national economy as well as to assure the interest of the general consumer.

Article 2. The term "entrepreneur" as used in the Law shall mean a person, natural or juridical, who operates a commercial, industrial, financial or any other business enterprise.

CHAPTER I. GENERAL RULES

Article 1. This Law, by prohibiting private monopolization, unreasonable restraint of trade and unfair business practices, by preventing the excessive concentration of power over enterprises, and by excluding undue restrictions of production, sale, price, technology, etc., through combinations, agreements, etc., and all other unreasonable restraints of business activities, aims to promote free and fair competition, to stimulate the initiative of entrepreneurs, to encourage business activities of enterprises, to heighten the level of employment and national income, and, thereby, to promote the democratic and wholesome development of national economy as well as to assure the interest of the general consumer.

Article 2. The term "entrepreneur" as used in this Law shall mean a person, natural or juridical, who carries a commercial, industrial, financial, or any other business enterprise. Any officer, employee, agent or any other person who acts for the benefit of any entrepreneur shall be deemed to be an entrepreneur in regard to the application of the provisions of the following paragraph and of Chapter III of this Law.

2. The term "trade association" as used in this Law shall mean any grouping or federation of groupings of two (2) or more entrepreneurs having the principal purpose of the furtherance of their common interest as entrepreneur, and shall include the following form:

Provided, however, That any organization which is a grouping or federation of groupings of two (2) or more entrepreneurs, and has the capital or the invested funds from the constituent members, and whose principal purpose is to operate and is actually operating a commercial, industrial, financial or any other business enterprise on the basis of profit, shall not be included therein,

(1) Any juridical associational entity (*Shadan Hojin*), or any other non-juridical associational entity (*Shadan*) in which two (2) or more entrepreneurs are members (including any position similar thereto);

(2) Any juridical foundation (*Zaidan Hōjin*) or any other non-juridical foundation (*Zaidan*), two (2) or more entrepreneurs of which control the appointment or dismissal of its directors or administrators, the execution of its business, or its existence.

(3) Any association (*Kumiai*) in which two (2) or more entrepreneurs are members, or any grouping of two (2) or more entrepreneurs through contract.

3. The term "officer" as used in this Law shall mean RIJI, directors, unlimited partners who execute business, KANJI or auditor, or any person corresponding thereto, managers, or business executives of the main or branch office.

The term "competition" or "competitor" as used in this Law shall include potential competition or potential competitor.

4. The term "competition" as used in this Law shall mean situation in which two (2) or more entrepreneurs do or may, within the normal scope of their business activities and without undertaking any significant change in their business facilities or practices, engage in any one (1) of the following acts: Provided, That such act as mentioned in item (2) shall not be included within the meaning of competition as provided for in Chapter IV.

(1) Supplying the same or similar goods or services to the same consumers or customers;

(2) Receiving supply of the same

The term "private monopolization" as used in this Law shall mean such business activities by which an entrepreneur, individually, or by combination, conspiracy or any other manner, excludes or controls the business activities of other entrepreneurs, thereby causing, contrary to the public interest, a substantial restraint of competition in any particular field of trade.

The term "unreasonable restraint of trade" as used in this Law shall mean such business activities by which an entrepreneur, by contract, agreement, or any other manner, in conjunction with other entrepreneurs, mutually restricts or conducts their business activities, thereby causing, contrary to the public interest, a substantial restraint of competition in any particular field of trade.

The term "undue substantial disparities in bargaining power" as used in this Law shall mean such substantial disparities in bargaining power which, when they exist between an entrepreneur and his competitors, is not justified on technological grounds, and whereby the said substantial disparities in bargaining power are of such extent as to render private monopolization possible for any one of the following reasons:

(1) because an entrepreneur controls the business in such particular field of trade or controls the materials used therein to such extent as to render it extremely difficult for another entrepreneur to start a new enterprise;

(2) because an entrepreneur controls production in a particular field of trade to such extent as to render it extremely difficult for another entrepreneur actually to compete;

(3) because an entrepreneur restrains or restricts free competition to

or similar goods or services from the same supplier.

5. The term "private monopolization" as used in this Law shall mean such business activities, by which any entrepreneur, individually, or by combination, conspiracy, or any other manner with other entrepreneurs, excludes or controls the business activities of other entrepreneurs, thereby causing, contrary to the public interest, a substantial restraint of competition in any particular field of trade.

6. The term "unreasonable restraint of trade" as used in this Law shall mean such business activities, by which any entrepreneur, by contract, agreement, or any other form, in conjunction with other entrepreneurs, mutually restricts their business activities to fix, maintain, or enhance prices, or to limit production, technology, products, facilities, or another party of trade, etc., or executes such activities, thereby causing, contrary to the public interest, a substantial restraint of competition in any particular field of trade.

[Deleted.]

such extent as to render private monopolization possible.

The term "unfair methods of competition," as used in this Law, shall mean such methods of competition which come under any one of the following items:

(1) unwarranted refusal to receive from or to supply to other entrepreneurs commodities, funds and other economic benefits.

(2) supplying of commodities, funds and other economic benefits at unduly discriminative prices;

(3) supplying of commodities, funds and other economic benefits at unduly low prices;

(4) inducing or coercing unreasonably customers of a competitor to deal with oneself by means of offering benefits or that of threatening disadvantages;

(5) trading with another party on condition that said party shall, without good cause, refuse acceptance of supply of commodities, funds and other economic benefits from a competitor of oneself;

(6) supplying of commodities, funds and other economic benefits to another party on such conditions that shall unduly restrain transactions between said party and his suppliers of commodities, funds and other economic benefits or customers or that shall unduly restrain relations between said party and his competitors, or on condition that the appointment of officers (hereinafter referring to directors, unlimited partners who are executive, auditors or persons similar thereto, manager or chief of the main or branch office) of the company of said party shall be subject to prior approval on part of oneself;

(7) methods of competition other than those stipulated by the preceding items which are contrary to the public interest and which are designated by the Fair Trade Commission in accordance with such procedure as provided for By Article 71 and Article 72.

7. The term "unfair business practices" as used in this Law shall mean such business practices as designated by the Fair Trade Commission out of those endangering fair competition and coming under any one (1) of the following items:

(1) To unjustly discriminate the other entrepreneurs;

(2) To deal with undue prices;

(3) To unreasonably induce or coerce customers of a competitor to deal with oneself;

(4) To undertake transaction with another party, the condition of which is to unjustly restrict the business activities of the said party;

(5) To trade with another party by unjustly making use of one's position in the transaction;

(6) To unjustly interfere with the transaction between the other entrepreneurs who compete in Japan with himself or with the company in which he is a stockholder or an officer of a company.

CHAPTER II. PRIVATE MONOPOLIZATION AND UNREASONABLE RESTRAINT OF TRADE

Article 3. No entrepreneur shall effect a private monopolization nor shall undertake any unreasonable restraint of trade.

Article 4. No entrepreneur shall participate in any one of the following types of concerted activities;

(1) establishment, stabilization or enhancement of prices;

(2) restriction on volume of production or that of sales;

(3) restrictions on technology, products, markets or customers;

(4) restrictions on construction or expansion of facilities or on adoption of new technology or methods of production.

The provisions of the preceding paragraph shall not apply in case the effects of such concerted activities on competition within a particular field of trade are negligible.

Article 5. No entrepreneur shall establish, organize or become a party to or a member of a juridical person or any other organization which controls distribution of all or a part of materials or products by methods of exclusive purchase or sale or which undertakes the allocation of all or a part of materials or products.

Article 6. No entrepreneur shall participate in an international agreement or an international contract with a foreign entrepreneur or participate in an agreement or contract on foreign trade with a domestic entrepreneur with regard to any one of the following items:

(1) any matter which comes under one of the items of Article 4 paragraph 1;

(2) an agreement or a contract relating to restrictions on exchange of scientific or technological knowledge or information necessary for business activities.

The provisions of the preceding

CHAPTER II. PRIVATE MONOPOLIZATION AND UNREASONABLE RESTRAINT OF TRADE

Article 3. No entrepreneur shall effect private monopolization or shall undertake any unreasonable restraint of trade.

[*Article 4.* Deleted.]

[*Article 5.* Deleted.]

Article 6. No entrepreneur shall enter an international agreement or an international contract which contains therein such matters as coming under the purview of unreasonable restraint of trade, or unfair business practices.

2. In the event that an international agreement or an international contract is concluded, every entrepreneur shall file a report of the said effect, together with a copy of the said agreement or contract (in the case of a verbal agreement or contract, a statement demonstrating the contents thereof), with the Fair Trade Commission within thirty (30) days as from the day of its conclusion pursuant to the provisions of its Regulations.

3. The provisions of the preceding

paragraph shall not apply in case the effects of such agreement or contract on competition in any particular field of international or domestic trade are negligible.

Any entrepreneur, when contemplating participation in an international agreement or an international contract with a foreign enterepreneur, or in an agreement or contract on foreign trade with a domestic entrepreneur, which agreement or contract shall continue for a considerable period of time (excluding such where delivery of the object due to one (1) transaction takes place over a considerable period of time), shall file an application with the Fair Trade Commission and receive its permission.

In such a case as provided for by the preceding paragraph, an entrepreneur shall not participate in said agreement or contract for a period of thirty (30) days from the day of filing said application.

Article 7. In case there exists any act which comprises a private monopolization or an unreasonable restraint of trade, the Fair Trade Commission may order the entrepreneur concerned in accordance with the procedures as provided for in Section 2 of Chapter 8, to cease such acts, to transfer a part of his business, or take any other necessary measures for eliminating private monopolization or unreasonable restraint of trade.

CHAPTER III. UNDUE SUBSTANTIAL DISPARITIES IN BARGAINING POWER

Article 8. When undue substantial disparities in bargaining power exist, the Fair Trade Commission may order the entrepreneur concerned in accordance with the procedures as provided for in Section 2 of Chapter 8, to transfer a part of his business facilities, or to take any other necessary measures for eliminating said substantial disparities in bargaining power.

In issuing an order prescribed in the preceding paragraph, the Fair

paragraph shall not apply to an agreement or contract regarding a single transaction (excluding such transactions as the delivery period of the object thereof exceeding one (1) year), or to an agreement or contract merely granting power of attorney on matters as is commerce and trade (excluding agreement or contract containing conditions that restrict the business activities of the other party or parties).

Article 7. The Fair Trade Commission may, in case there exists any act which violates the provisions of Article 3, or paragraph 1 or paragraph 2 of the preceding Article, order the entrepreneur concerned, in accordance with the proceedings as provided for in Section 2, Chapter VIII, to file reports, or to cease and desist such acts, to transfer a part of his business or to take any other necessary measure to eliminate such acts in violation of said provisions.

[Deleted.]

CHAPTER III. TRADE ASSOCIATION

Article 8. No trade association shall engage in any one (1) of the following items:

(1) To substantially restrict competition in any particular field of trade;

(2) To enter into an international agreement or an international contract as prescribed in Article 6 paragraph 1;

(3) To limit the present or future

Trade Commission shall give special consideration to the following items with respect to the entrepreneur concerned:

(1) capital, reserves, and other aspects of the assets;

(2) income and expenditures, and other aspects of operation;

(3) composition of officers and directors;

(4) location of factories, work yards and offices and other locational conditions;

(5) aspects of business facilities and equipment;

(6) existence or non-existence of patents, and other details thereof as well as other technological features;

(7) capacity for and aspects of production and sales, etc.;

(8) capacity for and aspects of obtaining funds and materials, etc.;

(9) relations with other entrepreneurs through investments and other means;

(10) comparison with competitors on all points enumerated in the above items.

number of entrepreneurs in any particular field;

(4) To unduly restrict the functions or activities of the constituent entrepreneurs (the constituent entrepreneurs shall mean entrepreneur being a member of the trade association);

(5) To cause entrepreneurs to commit such acts as falling under unfair business practices.

2. Every trade association shall file a report with the Fair Trade Commission within thirty (30) days as from the day of its formation in accordance with the provisions of its Regulations.

3. In the event that any change is made in the matters of the report as mentioned in the preceding paragraph, every trade association shall file a report to that effect with the Fair Trade Commission according to the provisions of its Regulations within two months as from the end of the business year in which such change took place.

4. Every trade association shall, when dissolved, file a report to that effect with the Fair Trade Commission within thirty (30) days as from the day of its dissolution in accordance with the provisions of its Regulations.

Article 8–2. The Fair Trade Commission may, when there exists any act in violation of the provisions of the preceding Article, order to file a report, or to cease and desist the said act, to dissolve the said association, and to take any other measure necessary to eliminate the said act pursuant to the proceedings as provided for in Section 2, Chapter VIII.

2. In the event that the Fair Trade Commission orders a trade association any of the measures set forth in the preceding paragraph, it may as well order its officer or administrator, or its constituent entrepreneurs (in case a

constituent entrepreneur is acting on behalf of another entrepreneur, such other entrepreneur is included) of the said association any necessary measure in order to ensure the measures as mentioned in the said paragraph when deemed particularly necessary

CHAPTER IV. STOCK HOLDINGS, MULTIPLE DIRECTORATES, MERGERS, AND TRANSFER OF WHOLE BUSINESS

Article 9. The establishment of holding company is hereby prohibited.

The term "holding company" as used in the preceding paragraph shall mean a company whose principal business is to control, by holding stock (including partnership shares; hereinafter the same) the business activities of another company.

Article 10. Any company whose business is other than financial (the definition of which shall be banking, trust, insurance, mutual financing or securities business; hereinafter the same) shall not acquire stocks (excluding those without voting rights; hereinafter the same) of another company.

The provisions of the preceding paragraph shall not apply to such a case where the Fair Trade Commission has concluded, when it receives application for acquisition of the whole stocks of a company which comes under all of the following conditions from a company (excluding one principally engaged in buying and selling of goods), that it does not constitute a substantial restraint of competition in any particular field of trade, and thereby is not contrary to the public interest and has granted permission:

(1) a company which stands in continuous close relation with regard to the supply of raw materials, semifinished products, accessory parts, by-

CHAPTER IV. STOCKHOLDING, INTERLOCKING DIRECTORATE, MERGER, AND TRANSFER OF BUSINESS

Article 9. The establishment of holding company shall be prohibited.

2. Any company (including a foreign company; hereinafter the same) shall neither become nor operate as a holding company in Japan.

3. The term "holding company" as used in the preceding two (2) paragraphs shall mean a company whose principal business is to control the business activities of a company or companies in Japan by means of stockholding (including partnership share; hereinafter the same).

Article 10. No company shall acquire or own stock of a company or companies in Japan in the event that the effect on such acquisition or owning of stock may be substantially to restrain competition in any particular field of trade, or that such acquisition or owning of stock is made through unfair business practices.

2. Every company in Japan whose business is other than financial (banking, mutual banking, trust, insurance, mutual financing or securities business; hereinafter the same) and whose total assets (total amount of the assets appearing in the latest balance sheet; hereinafter the same) exceed one hundred million (100,000,000) yen, or every foreign company whose business is other than financial, shall, in case it owns stock of another company or companies in Japan (including such cases wherein the trustor is the beneficiary and exercises the voting right in the security trust), submit a report on such

products, waste material or goods or other economic benefits necessary for its business activities, or a company which stands in relation of utilization of patent invention or model utility;

(2) a company which does not own stock in another company.

In addition to such a case as prescribed in the preceding paragraph, in case a company (in case of acquisition of stock of an existing company, the company which desires to acquire stock and the company issuing the stock) desiring to acquire stock has explained the fact that such acquisition of stock complies with the conditions contained in each of the following items, the provisions of the preceding paragraph shall apply if it complies with other conditions prescribed in said paragraph although it will not own the whole stock of said company;

(1) acquisition of stock issued to raise necessary funds;

(2) acquisition of stock issued because acquisition of capital by means other than issue of stock was practically difficult;

(3) acquisition of stock is not due to unfair methods of competition;

(4) acquisition of stock of a company whose stock is now owned by a company standing in competition with the company which desires to acquire the stock; provided, that with regard to acquisition of stock of a company whose principal business is the purchase and sale of commodities, the foregoing shall apply only in case a company other than the company which desires to acquire stock does not own such stocks.

Article 11. Any company whose business is financial shall not own stocks in a company with which it is competing and which operates in the same field of financial business.

No company whose business is financial and whose total assets (excluding unpaid-up capital stock, unpaid-up partnership share or claim rights) exceed five million (5,000,000)

stock owned or entrusted by it as of the end of every business year to the Fair Trade Commission within two months therefrom in accordance with the provisions of its Regulations.

Article 11. No company engaged in financial business shall acquire or own stock of another company or companies in Japan in the event that it may be to own stock of the said company or companies exceeding ten per cent (10%) of the total outstanding stock thereof; Provided, That the foregoing shall not apply to such cases as the approval of the Fair Trade Commission is

yen shall acquire stock of another company in case by so doing it holds in excess of five per cent (5%) of the total issued stock of said company.

The provisions of the preceding two paragraphs shall not apply to such a case coming under any one of the following items:

(1) in case of ownership of stocks by a company engaged in the securities business in the normal course of its business;

(2) in case of ownership of stocks by a company other than one engaged in the securities business and whose business is financial by underwriting for the purpose of public sale;

(3) in case of ownership of stocks by acceptance of security trust wherein the trustor is the beneficiary; provided, that the foregoing shall apply only when the trustor exercises the voting right;

In case of ownership of such stocks as coming under item 1 or item 2 of the preceding paragraph, said ownership of stocks for a period in excess of one (1) year from the date of acquisition of said stocks shall be limited to such a case where previous permission of the Fair Trade Commission has been obtained.

Article 12. No company shall own debentures (excluding bank financing debentures) of another company in case by so doing it holds in excess of an amount equivalent to twenty-five per cent (25%) of the capital (the definition of which shall be total capital stock, total amount of partnership shares, aggregate amount of total cap-

beforehand obtained pursuant to the provisions of its Regulations, or as the acquisition or owning thereof comes under any one (1) of the following items.

(1) In case the acquisition or owning of stock is made as the result of the enforcement of *bona fide* liens, or of the receipt of payment in kind;

(2) In case the acquisition or owning of stock is made by a securities company in the course of its business;

(3) In case the acquisition or owning of stock is made by acceptance of security trust wherein the trustor is the beneficiary. However, it shall apply only in case the trustor exercises the voting right.

2. Any company whose business is financial intending to own stock of another company or companies in Japan over the period of one (1) year as from the date of such acquisition of stock and in excess of ten per cent (10%) of the total outstanding stock in the case of items (1) and (2) of the preceding paragraph shall obtain the prior approval from the Fair Trade Commission pursuant to the provisions of its Regulations. In such case, the approval of the Fair Trade Commission shall be made by providing therein that the company engaged in financial business shall promptly dispose of the said stock.

3. The Fair Trade Commission shall, when intending to grant the approval as prescribed in the preceding two paragraphs, beforehand consult with the Minister of finance.

[*Article 12.* Deleted.]

ital stock and total amount of partnership shares, or total fixed funds) of
said company.

The provisions of paragraph 3 and
paragraph 4 of the preceding Article
shall apply *mutatis mutandis* to such a
case as provided for by the preceding
paragraph. In this case "stocks" shall
read "debentures."

Article 13. No officer or an employee (the definition of which shall
be a person other than an officer in
regular employment of a company in
business) of a company shall hold concurrently a position as an officer in
another company in any one of the
following cases:

(1) in case both of the companies
are in competition with one another;

(2) in case one fourth (¼) or
more of the officers of either of the
two (2) companies are holding concurrently positions as officers in a third
company.

No officer of a company shall in
any case hold a position of officer in a
company in four (4) or more companies.

Article 13. No officer or employee
(referring to a person continuously engaging in the business of a company
but being other than an officer; hereinafter the same in this Article) of a company shall hold at the same time a
position as an officer in another company or companies in Japan in the event
that the effect on such interlocking
directorate may be substantially to restrain competition in any particular
field of trade.

2. No company shall coerce another
company or companies in Japan in
competition with it through unfair
business practices to have its officer
hold at the same time a position as an
officer or an employee in another company or companies or to have its employee hold at the same time a position
as an officer in another company or
companies.

3. Every officer or employee of a
company shall, in case he holds at the
same time a position as an officer in
another company or companies in Japan in competition with it and whose
total assets of any one (1) of such companies exceed one hundred million
(100,000,000) yen, file a report to that
effect with the Fair Trade Commission
within thirty (30) days as from the day
of such interlocking directorate pursuant to the provisions of its Regulations.

Article 14. No person shall acquire
stock in two (2) or more companies
in competition with one another when
the effect of such ownership will substantially restrain competition in any
particular field of trade and thereby is
contrary to the public interest.

Any person whose ownership of
stocks of two (2) or more companies
in competition with one another will

Article 14. No natural, non-juridical, or juridical person other than a
company shall acquire or own stock of
another company or companies in Japan in the event that the effect of such
acquisition or owning of stock may be
substantially to restrain in any particular field of trade or that such acquisition or owning of stock is made by unfair business practices.

be in excess of ten per cent (10%) of the issued stock of said companies shall receive the permission of the Fair Trade Commission with regard to acquisition of said stocks.

No officer of a company shall acquire stock of another engaged in competition with said company.

In case an officer of a company, when assuming his position as an officer in said company, owns stock of another company in competition with said company, he shall file a report of said fact with the Fair Trade Commission.

The Fair Trade Commission may, in case it receives such a report as provided for in the preceding paragraph, and when it deems that such ownership of stock may substantially restrain competition in any particular field of trade and thereby be contrary to the public interest, order the disposal of the whole or a part of said stocks or to take any other necessary measures.

Article 15. No company shall effect a merger without the permission of the Fair Trade Commission.

The Fair Trade Commission, in case it receives an application for permission as provided for by the preceding paragraph, shall not grant permission when the said merger falls under any one of the following items and thereby is deemed to be contrary to the public interest.

(1) in case the merger does not contribute to the rationalization of production, supply or management;

(2) in case substantial disparities in bargaining power will arise due to the merger;

(3) in case the merger may cause a substantial restraint of competition in any particular field of trade;

(4) in case the merger has been coerced by unfair methods of trade.

2. Every natural, non-juridical, or juridical person other than a company shall, in case he may be to own stock of two (2) or more companies mutually competing in Japan in excess of ten per cent (10%) of the total outstanding stock of the respective company, submit a report on such stock to the Fair Trade Commission within thirty (30) days as from the day of such owning of stock in accordance with the provisions of its Regulations.

Article 15. No company in Japan shall effect a merger in any one (1) of the following cases:

(1) In case a substantial restraint of competition in any particular field of trade may be caused by the merger;

(2) In case unfair business practices have been employed in the course of merger.

2. Every company in Japan shall, when contemplating becoming a party to a merger, file a prior report with the Fair Trade Commission in accordance with its Regulations.

3. No company in Japan shall, in such cases as coming under the preceding paragraph, effect a merger for a period of thirty (30) days from the day of issuance of the receipt of the said report; Provided, That the Fair Trade Commission may, when deems necessary, shorten the said period, or extend it with the consent of the said companies for an additional period of time not exceeding sixty (60) days.

4. The Fair Trade Commission shall, in case it issues a complaint, or makes a recommendation for the pur-

pose of ordering to take necessary measures against the merger in question pursuant to the provisions of Article 17–2, make it within thirty (30) days as provided for in the preceding paragraph, or within the shortened or extended period of time as mentioned in the proviso to the said paragraph: Provided, however, That the foregoing provisions shall not apply in cases where there has been a false statement with respect to important matters in such report as stipulated in paragraph 2.

Article 16. No company shall, without receiving permission of the Fair Trade Commission, receive transfer of the whole or a part of the business of another company, lease the whole of the business of another company, receive entrustment of the management of another company, or enter into a contract which provided for a joint profit and loss account with another company.

The provisions of paragraph 2 of the preceding Article shall apply *mutatis mutandis* to such a case as provided for in the preceding paragraph; provided, that "said merger" shall read "said act."

Article 16. The provisions of the preceding Article shall apply *mutatis mutandis* in the event that any company intends to do such acts as coming under any one (1) of the following items:

(1) To absorb the whole or substantial part of the business in Japan of another company;

(2) To absorb the whole or substantial part of the fixed business assets in Japan of another company;

(3) To take on lease of the whole or substantial part of the business in Japan of another company;

(4) To receive the entrustment of management of the whole or substantial part of the business in Japan of another company;

(5) To enter into a contract which provides for a joint profit and loss account for business in Japan with another company.

Article 17. No act, in whatever form or manner, shall be committed to evade such prohibitions or restrictions as provided for in Article 9 to the preceding Article inclusive.

Article 17. No act in whatever form or manner shall be committed to evade such prohibitions or restrictions as prescribed in Article 9 to the preceding Article inclusive.

Article 17–2. In the event that there exists any act in violation of the provisions of Article 10, Article 11 paragraph 1, Article 15 paragraph 1 (including such cases where the said provisions shall apply *mutatis mutandis* in Article 16), or the preceding Article, the Fair Trade Commission may, in accordance with the proceedings as stipulated in Section 2, Chapter VIII, order the entrepreneur concerned to file a report, or to dispose of the whole or a part of his stock, to transfer a part of his business, or to take any other measure necessary for eliminating such acts in violation thereof.

2. In the event that there exists any act in violation of the provisions of Article 9 paragraph 1 or paragraph 2, Article 13, Article 14, or the preceding Article, the Fair Trade Commission may, in accordance with the proceedings as provided for in Section 2, Chapter VIII, order the said person violating such provisions to submit or file a report, or to dispose of the whole of a part of his stock, to resign from his position as an officer in a company, or to take any other measure necessary for eliminating such acts in violation thereof.

Article 18. The Fair Trade Commission may, when a company is established in violation of the provisions of paragraph 1 of Article 9, or when companies have merged in violation of the provisions of paragraph 1 of Article 15, institute a suit to have said establishment or merger be declared null and void.

Article 18. The Fair Trade Commission may, in case where any company has been established in violation of the provisions of Article 9 paragraph 1, or has merged in violation of the provisions of Article 15 paragraphs 2 and 3, institute a suit to have the said establishment or merger declared null and void.

CHAPTER V. UNFAIR METHODS OF COMPETITION

Article 19. No entrepreneur shall employ unfair methods of competition.

Article 20. In case there exists an act in violation of the preceding Article, the Fair Trade Commission may order the cessation of said act in accordance with the procedure provided for by Section 2 of Chapter 8.

CHAPTER V. UNFAIR BUSINESS PRACTICES

Article 19. No entrepreneur shall employ unfair business practices.

Article 20. The Fair Trade Commission may, when there exists any act in violation of the preceding Article, order to cease and desist the said act in accordance with the proceedings as stipulated in Section 2, Chapter VIII.

CHAPTER VI. EXEMPTIONS

Article 21. The provisions of this Law shall not apply to such business activities relating to production, sales or supply of persons or parties operating railroad, electricity, gas, and other enterprises whose business constitutes, by the very nature of said business, a monopoly.

Article 22. The provisions of this Law, in case a special law exists for a

CHAPTER VI. EXCEPTION AND EXEMPTION

Article 21. The provisions of this Law shall not apply to such act relating to the production, sale, or supply of a person engaging in railways, electric, gas, or any other enterprise being a monopoly by the very nature of said business itself.

Article 22. The provisions of this Law shall not apply to such legitimate

certain enterprise, shall not apply to
such legitimate acts of an entrepreneur
as are executed in accordance with the
provisions of said law or order under
said law.

Such special law as mentioned in
the preceding paragraph shall be stipulated by separate law.

Article 23. The provisions of this
Law shall not apply to such an act as
recognized to be within the execution
of rights under the Copyright Law,
the Patent Law, the Model Utility
Law, the Design Law and the Trade-
mark Law.

Article 24. The provisions of this
Law shall not apply to an association
(including federation of associations)
which conforms with each of the following qualifications and which, moreover, has been established in accordance with the provisions of separate
law; provided, that the foregoing shall
not apply to such a case where there
is employment of unfair methods of
competition or a restraint of competition in any particular field of trade
resulting in an undue enhancement of
price;

(1) the purpose shall be mutual-
aid among small-scale entrepreneurs or
consumers;

(2) establishment shall be voluntary, and participation in and withdrawal from membership shall be at
will;

(3) each member shall possess
equal voting rights;

(4) in case distribution of profits
among members is executed, limits for
distribution shall be fixed by law or
order, or under the articles of association.

act of an entrepreneur or a trade association conducted under the provisions
of a special law or an order to be issued
thereunder in the event that such special law has been established for the
specific enterprise.

2. Such special law as mentioned in
the preceding paragraph shall otherwise
be designated by the law.

Article 23. The provisions of this
Law shall not apply to such act as
recognized to be within the execution
of rights under the Copyright Law,
Patent Law, Model Utility Law, Design
Law and Trade-mark Law.

Article 24. The provisions of this
Law shall not apply to such act of an
association (including a federation of
associations) conforming to the following requirements and established in accordance with the provisions of the law;
Provided, That nothing herein contained shall apply to such cases where
unfair business practices are employed,
or a substantial restraint of competition
in any particular field of trade may tend
to create undue enhancement of prices;

(1) Its purpose is the mutual aid
among small-scale entrepreneurs or consumers;

(2) It is voluntary established, and
the participation in and withdrawal
from the association are at will;

(3) Its member possesses equal voting rights;

(4) The limitation for the profit
distribution among members is stipulated in a law or an order, or in the
articles of association, if such distribution is carried out.

Article 24-2. The provisions of this
Law shall not apply to justifiable acts
to be undertaken by an entrepreneur,
who produces or sells a commodity
which is designated by the Fair Trade
Commission and the identical quality
of which can be easily recognized, for
the purpose of fixing and maintaining
with the entrepreneur of the other
party selling the said commodity the
resale price thereof (such shall mean

price of the commodity to be sold by the entrepreneur of the other party, or to be sold by an entrepreneur who purchased it from the entrepreneur of the other party offering to sell; hereinafter the same); Provided, further, That nothing herein contained shall be lawful in the event that the said act may unduly injure the interest of the general consumer, or may be contrary to the will of the entrepreneur producing the commodity in the case of the entrepreneur offering to sell.

2. The Fair Trade Commission shall not make such designation of a commodity as stipulated in the preceding paragraph unless it comes under any one (1) of the following items:

(1) The said commodity is daily used by the general consumer;

(2) The said commodity is in free competition.

3. The designation of a commodity as mentioned in paragraph 1 is to be made by the notification.

4. Paragraph 1 shall apply *mutatis mutandis* to justifiable acts to be undertaken by an entrepreneur, who published the copyright objects or sells such published or reproduced objects, for the purpose of fixing and maintaining with the entrepreneur of the other party selling the said objects the resale price thereof.

5. The organizations established in accordance with the provisions of the following laws shall not be included in the purview of the entrepreneur of the other party as mentioned in paragraph 1 or the preceding paragraph; Provided, That the foregoing provisions shall, in the case of the organizations established under the provisions of the law as mentioned in items (8) and (8)–2, only apply in the event that the business cooperative association, business cooperative small association, federation of cooperative associations, commercial and industrial association or federation of commercial and industrial associations purchase such commodity as provided for in paragraph 1 or such objects as prescribed in paragraph 4, for the

consumption of persons directly or indirectly constituting the said business
cooperative association, federation of
cooperative associations, commercial
and industrial association or federation
of commercial and industrial associations.

(1) The National Public Service
Law;

(2) Agricultural Cooperative Association Law;

(3) The National Public Service
Mutual Aid Association Law;

(4) Consumptive Life Cooperative
Association Law;

(5) Fisheries Cooperative Association Law;

(6) Public Corporation Labor Relations Law;

(7) Labor Union Law;

(8) Medium and Small Enterprise,
etc. Cooperative Association Law.

(8)-2 Medium and Small Enterprise Organization Law;

(9) Local Public Service Law;

(10) Forest Law;

(11) Local Public Enterprise Labor
Relations Law.

6. When any entrepreneur as stipulated in paragraph 1 fixes the resale
price as prescribed in the said paragraph and has entered into a contract
for the purpose of maintaining it, he
shall file a report to that effect with the
Fair Trade Commission within thirty
(30) days as from the day of the conclusion thereof in accordance with the
provisions of its Regulations; Provided,
That the foregoing shall not apply in
case the Fair Trade Commission so
stipulates in its Regulations.

Article 24-3. The provisions of
this Law shall, in the event that circumstances falling under the following,
each item having risen because of
greatly unbalanced demand and supply
of the specific commodity, not apply
to such concerted activity (including
activity of a trade association to have
its constituent members undertake concerted activity; hereinafter the same)
as approved in accordance with the fol-

lowing paragraph or paragraph 3, of entrepreneurs producing such commodity, or of a trade association constituted by such entrepreneurs as its members (hereinafter referred to as "producers, etc."): Provided, however, That nothing herein contained shall be lawful in the event that unfair business practices are used, or entrepreneurs are compelled to undertake activity coming under unfair business practices.

(1) Prices of the said commodity are lower than the average production cost thereof, and there exists the possibility of endangering the continuation of enterprise on the part of the majority of the said entrepreneurs;

(2) It is difficult that such circumstances as mentioned in the preceding item can be overcome by the enterprise rationalization.

2. Producers, etc., desirous of carrying out concerted activity (excluding that of prevention of renewal or improvement of facilities) regarding the limitation on volume of production and sale, or on facilities in order to overcome such circumstances as prescribed in the preceding paragraph, may beforehand obtain the approval from the Fair Trade Commission according to its Regulations.

3. Producers, etc., intending to undertake concerted activity to fix price in such case as provided for in paragraph 1, and as deemed extremely difficult to limit the volume of production of a commodity in the said enterprise due to the technical reasons, may beforehand obtain the approval from the Fair Trade Commission in accordance with its Regulations. After concerted activity has been undertaken by the approval as provided for in the preceding paragraph, producers, etc., desirous of simultaneously undertaking concerted activity to fix price together with concerted activity as stipulated in the preceding paragraph in the event that it is extremely difficult to overcome such circumstances as mentioned in paragraph 1 only by such concerted activity

as provided for in the said paragraph, may, also, obtain the approval in the same manner as stipulated therein.

4. The Fair Trade Commission shall not give approval as indicated in the preceding two paragraphs unless concerted activity under application conforms to such requirements as prescribed in the preceding two paragraphs, and falls under any one (1) of the following items:

(1) It is within and not beyond the limit necessary for overcoming such circumstances as prescribed in paragraph 1;

(2) It does not endanger unduly the interest of general consumer and of the related entrepreneurs;

(3) It is not unjustly discriminative;

(4) It does not restrict unreasonably the participation in or withdrawal therefrom.

5. In the event that when an application for approval as mentioned in paragraph 2 or paragraph 3 has been submitted, the Fair Trade Commission approves or turns down the said application or makes disposition pursuant to the provisions of Article 66 paragraph 1 with regard to the approval as indicated in paragraph 2 or paragraph 3, it shall without delay make public that effect showing the reasons for the said disposition.

6. In the event that producers, etc., carrying out concerted activity with the approval obtained pursuant to the provisions of paragraph 2 or paragraph 3, discontinued the said concerted activity, they shall without delay file a report of that effect with the Fair Trade Commission.

7. Any interested person aggrieved by the approval as indicated in paragraph 2 or paragraph 3, may appeal to the Fair Trade Commission within thirty (30) days as from the day of the approval by filing a petition in writing stating the substance of his grievance.

8. The Fair Trade Commission upon the receipt of such petition for appeal as mentioned in the preceding paragraph, shall render its ruling after

an open hearing pursuant to the provisions of its Regulations, and shall in-
form the petitioner of it in writing.

9. The Fair Trade Commission
shall, when intending to give such approval as stipulated in paragraph 2 or
paragraph 3 or to turn down the application therefor, consult beforehand
with the competent minister of the said
enterprise. The same shall apply in the
event that the Fair Trade Commission
intends to make the disposition as prescribed in Article 66 paragraph 1 with
respect to such approval as mentioned
in paragraph 2 or paragraph 3.

Article 24–4. The provisions of this
Law shall not apply to such concerted
activity of producers, etc., as approved
in accordance with the following paragraph in the event that it is particularly
necessary for effecting technical promotion, quality improvement, cost reduction, efficiency increase and any other
enterprise rationalization.

2. Producers, etc., desirous of undertaking concerted activity regarding
the limitation on technology or kinds
of products, utilization or purchase of
by-products, refuse, or waste in the
case of the preceding paragraph, may
beforehand obtain approval from the
Fair Trade Commission in accordance
with its Regulations.

3. The Fair Trade Commission
shall not give approval as indicated in
the preceding paragraph unless concerted activity under application conforms to such requirements as prescribed in the preceding paragraph, and
falls under any one (1) of the following
items:

(1) It does not endanger the interest of customer;

(2) There is no fear of unduly destroying the interest of the general consumer and of related entrepreneurs (excluding customer);

(3) It is not unjustly discriminative;

(4) It does not restrict unreasonably
the participation in or withdrawal
therefrom;

(5) It does not concentrate unduly
the production of specific kinds of

products to a particular entrepreneur
in the event that the substance of limitation on kinds of products is different
between persons participating in concerted activity.

4. The provisions of the proviso to
paragraph 1 of the preceding Article
and of paragraphs 5 to 9 inclusive of
the said Article shall apply *mutatis
mutandis* to such concerted activity as
mentioned in paragraph 2.

BIBLIOGRAPHY

SOURCES IN ENGLISH

Adelman, M. "The Measures of Industrial Concentration," *Review of Economics and Statistics*, XXXIII (November 1951).

Allen, G. C. *A Short Economic History of Modern Japan, 1867–1937*. London, 1946.

————. *Japanese Industry: Its Recent Development and Present Condition*. Institute of Pacific Relations, 1940.

————. "The Concentration of Economic Control in Japan,'" *Economic Journal* (June 1937).

Baumol, W. *Business Behavior, Value and Growth*. New York: The Macmillan Co., 1959.

Bisson, T. A. *Zaibatsu Dissolution in Japan*. Berkeley and Los Angeles: University of California Press, 1954.

Bronfenbrenner, M. and K. Kogiku. "The Aftermath of the Shoup Tax Reform," *National Tax Journal*, X (December 1957).

Cohen, J. B. *Japan's Economy in War and Reconstruction*. New York, 1949.

————. *Japan's Postwar Economy*. Bloomington: Indiana University Press, 1958.

————. "Japan's Economy on the Road Back," *Pacific Affairs* (September 1948).

Council of Economic Advisers. *Economic Report of the President*. Washington, January 1965.

Davidson, S. and Y. Yasuba. "Asset Reevaluation and Income Tax in Japan," *National Tax Journal*, XIII (March 1960), 45–48.

Domar, E. *Essay on the Theory of Economic Growth*. New York: Harper, 1957.

Dore, R. P. *Land Reform in Japan*. New York: Oxford University Press, 1959.

Economic Planning Agency, Japanese government. *New Economic Plan of Japan (1961–1970)—Double National Income Plan*. Tokyo: Japan Times, 1961.

Edwards, C. D. "The Dissolution of Zaibatsu Combines," *Pacific Affairs*, XIX (September 1946).

Fair Trade Commission. *Fair Trade*. Tokyo, 1956–1958, Vol. 1–3.

Fearey, R. A. *The Occupation of Japan*. New York: The Macmillan Co., 1950.

Fellner, W. "The Influence of Market Structure on Technological Change," *The Quarterly Journal of Economics*, LXV (1951).

Florence, S. P. *Ownership, Control, and Success of Large Companies: An Analysis of English Industrial Structure and Policy, 1936–1951*. London: Sweet and Maxwell, 1961.

Harrod, R. F. *Toward a Dynamic Economics*. London, 1956.

Hayashi, H. "Capital Accumulation and Taxation in Japan," *National Tax Journal*, XVI (June 1963), 174–192.

Heflebower, R. B. "The Firm in Oligopoly Analysis," *Weltwirtschaftliches Archiv*, Band 84, 1960.

————. "Toward a Theory of Industrial Markets and Prices," *Readings in Industrial Organization*, American Economic Association, eds. G. W. Stocking and R. B. Heflebower, Irwin, 1958.

Ito, H. *Essays in Public Finance*, The Science Council of Japan, English Series, No. 3, Tokyo, 1954.
Ito, T. "Structural Peculiarities and Labor Problems of Small Business in Japan," *Small Business in Japan*, ed. T. Yamanaka, Tokyo: Japan Times Co., 1960.
————. *The High Growth of the Japanese Economy and the Problem of Small Enterprises*, Management and Labor Studies Series, No. 9, Keiō University English Monographs, 1964.
Japan Economic Planning Agency. *Economic Survey of Japan*. Tokyo: Japan Times Co., Ltd., 1964.
Klein, L. "A Model of Japanese Economic Growth, 1878–1937," *Econometrica* (July 1961).
Komiya, R., ed. *Postwar Economic Growth in Japan*. Berkeley and Los Angeles: University of California Press, 1966.
Levine, S. *Industrial Relations in Postwar Japan*. Urbana: University of Illinois Press, 1958.
Lewis, W. A. "Economic Development with Unlimited Supplies of Labor," *The Manchester School of Economics and Social Studies*, Vol. 22, No. 2 (May 1954).
Lockwood, W. W. *The Economic Development of Japan*. Princeton: Princeton University Press, 1954.
————. *The State and Economic Enterprise in Japan*. Princeton: Princeton University Press, 1965.
Mansfield, E. "Size of Firm, Market Structure, and Innovation," *Journal of Political Economy*, LXXI (December 1963).
Martin, E. N. *The Allied Occupation of Japan*. New York: American Institute of Pacific Relations, 1948.
Miyazawa, K. "The Dual Structure of the Japanese Economy," *The Developing Economies*, II (June 1964).
Ōkochi, K. *Labor in Modern Japan*. Science Council of Japan Series, No. 18, Tokyo, 1958.
The Oriental Economist (September 25, 1948, and October 30, 1948).
Patrick, H. *Monetary Policy and Central Banking in Contemporary Japan*. Bombay: University of Bombay Press, 1962.
Pauley, E. W. *Reports on Japanese Reparations to the President of the United States*. Washington, D.C. (November 1945).
Ranis, G. "The Financing of Japanese Economic Development," *Economic History Review*, Vol. XI, No. 3 (April 1959).
Ranis, G. and J. C. Fei. *Development of Labor Surplus Economy: Theory and Policy*. Irwin, 1964.
————. "Innovation, Capital Accumulation, and Economic Development," *American Economic Review*, LIII (June 1963).
Rosovsky, H. "Japanese Capital Formation: The Role of the Public Sector," *The Journal of Economic History*, No. 3, 1959.
Russel, Oland D. *The House of Mitsui*. Boston, 1939.
Sakurai, K. "Financial Aspects of Economic Development of Japan from 1868 to Present." Unpubl. Ph.D. thesis, Syracuse University, 1960.
Schumpeter, E. B. "Japanese Economic Policy and the Standard of Living," *Far Eastern Survey* (January 1938).
Shavell, H. "Postwar Taxation in Japan," *Journal of Political Economy*, LVI (1948).
————. "Taxation Reform in Occupied Japan," *National Tax Journal*, I (1948).
Shinohara, M. *Growth and Cycles in the Japanese Economy*. Tokyo: Kinokuniya, 1962.
————. "Some Causes and Consequences of Economic Growth in Japan," *The Malayan Economic Journal* (April 1961).
Shone, Sir Robert. "Problems of Planning for Economic Growth in a Mixed Economy," *Economic Journal*, LXXV (March 1965).

Stocking, George W. *Workable Competition and Antitrust Policy*. Nashville: Vanderbilt University Press, 1961.

Supreme Commander for the Allied Powers. *Missions and Accomplishments of the Supreme Commander for the Allied Powers in the Economic and Scientific Fields*. Tokyo, 1952.

Sylos-Labini, Paolo. *Oligopoly and Technological Progress*. Trans. E. Henderson. Cambridge: Harvard University Press, 1962.

Tsuru, Shigeto. "Toward Economic Stability in Japan," *Pacific Affairs* (December 1949).

————. *Essays on Japanese Economy*. Tokyo, 1958.

————. "Formal Planning Divorced from Action: Japan," *Planning Economic Development*, ed. E. E. Hagen, Irwin, 1963.

United States Department of State. *Reports on the Economic Position and Prospects of Japan and Korea and the Measures Required to Improve Them*. Washington, D.C. (April 26, 1948).

————. *Occupation of Japan, Policy and Progress*. Publication 261, Far Eastern Series 17, n.d.

Yamamura, K. "Monopolies and Competition in Postwar Japan." Unpubl. Ph.D. thesis, Northwestern University, 1964.

Yamanaka, T., ed. *Small Business in Japan*. Tokyo: Japan Times Co., 1960.

Yamane, T. "Postwar Inflation in Japan," unpubl. doctoral diss. (University of Wisconsin, 1955).

SOURCES IN JAPANESE

Aihara, S. *Nippon no Dokusen Shihon: Sengo ni okeru sono Kōzō to Kinō* (Monopolistic Capital of Japan: Its Postwar Functions and Structure). Tokyo, 1959, pp. 33–57.

Arisawa, H. *Nippon Kōgyō Tōseiron* (The Theory of Industry Control in Japan). Tokyo, 1937.

Asano, H. "Dokusen Kinshi-Hō wa dokoni ikuka?" (Where Does the Anti-Monopoly Act Go?), *Kōsei Torihiki* (September 1952).

Bank of Japan. *Hompō Keizai Tōkei* (Economic Statistics of Japan). Tokyo, 1957.

Chigusa, T., ed. *Sangyō Taikei no Sai-hensei* (A Reorganization of Industrial Structure). Tokyo: Shunjyū Publishing Co., 1963.

Echigo, K. *Gendai Nippon Kōgyōron* (A Treatise on the Current Japanese Industries). Tokyo, 1959.

The Economic Planning Agency. *Sengo Nippon no Shihon Chikuseki to Kigyō Keiei* (Capital Accumulation and Business Management in Postwar Japan). Tokyo, 1957.

————. *Kokumin Shotoku Baizō Keikaku* (Doubling the National Income Plan). Tokyo: Ministry of Finance Press, 1961.

————. *Shihon Kōzō to Kigyō-kan Kakusa* (Structure of Capital and Size Differential Among Firms). Tokyo, 1960.

Fair Trade Association (a private group). *Jidōsha Kōgyō no Keizairyoku Shūchū no Jittai* (The Reality of Concentration of Economic Power in the Automobile Industry). Tokyo, March 1959.

Fair Trade Commission. *Nippon Sangyō Shūchū no Jittai* (The Reality of Industrial Structure). Tokyo, 1957.

————. *Shuyō Sangyō ni okeru Seisan Shūchū-do* (Degree of Concentration of Output in Major Industries). Tokyo, 1960.

————. *Shuyō Sangyō ni okeru Shūchū-do* (Degree of Concentration in Major Industries). Tokyo, 1964.

————. *Kōsei Torihiki Iinkai Shinketsu-Shū* (The Annual Report of Adjudged Cases). Tokyo, 1953.

Funahashi, N. and M. Shinohara, eds. *Nippon-gata Chingin-Kōzō no Kenkyū* (A Study of the Japanese Wage Structure). Tokyo, 1961.

Giga, S. *Gendai Nippon no Dokusen Kigyō* (Monopolistic Enterprise of Contemporary Japan). Tokyo, 1962.

Giga, S. "Wagakuni okeru Saikin no Sangyō Shūchū" (Recent Industrial Concentration), *Kōsei Torihiki* (February 1964).

Hayashi, Y. *Sengo Nippon no Sozei Kōzō* (The Tax Structure of Postwar Japan). Tokyo, 1958.

Higuchi, Hiroshi. *Zaibatsu no Fukkatsu* (The Revival of Zaibatsu). Tokyo, 1953.

Holding Company Liquidation Committee. *Nippon Zaibatsu to sono Kaitai* (The Japanese Zaibatsu and Their Dissolution). Tokyo, 1950.

Imai, N., ed. *Gendai Nippon no Dokusen Shihon* (Monopoly Capital of Contemporary Japan). Vol. I, Tokyo, 1965.

Imura, Kyōkō. "Kigyō Kakusa ni yoru Chingin Kausa ni tsuite no Kōsatsu" (Several Considerations on the Theory of Wage Differential by Firm Size), *Mita Gakkai Zassi*, Keiō University (June–July 1963).

Institute of Economic Statistics, Japan. *Keizai Shihyō* (Economic Indicators). Tokyo, 1964.

Ishizaki, T. "Nijyū Kōzō to Shotoku Bumpai" (Dual Structure and Income Distribution), *Nijyu Kōzō no Bunseki* (Analyses of the Dual Structure), eds. Y. Tamanoi and T. Uchida. Tōyō Keizai, 1964.

Japan Productivity Center. *Kigyō no Kibo ni kansuru Kenkyū Chōsa* (Reports on the Scale of Enterprise). Tokyo, 1956.

Japan Tax Research Association. *Zeisei Kenkyū Sankō Shiryō-shū* (Collected Data for Research in Taxation). Tokyo, 1965.

Kaneko, Seiji. *Nippon Keizai no Seicho to Kōzō* (Japan's Economic Growth and Structure). Tokyo, 1965.

Katō, T. *Nippon Ginkō-shi Ron* (The History of Japanese Banks). Tokyo, 1957.

Kitajima, T. "Iinchō ni Shūnin shite" (Upon Assuming the Commissionership), *Kōsei Torihiki* (September 1965).

Kobayashi, Takehiko. "Tosan no Tokei wa Nani o kataru" (What Statistics of Bankruptcies Tell), *Kinyū Journal*, Tokyo, Vol. V, No. 10 (October 1964).

———. "Tōsan, sono Genjō to Mondai" (Bankruptcies, Their Patterns and Problems), *Kinyū Journal*, V (August 1964).

Koga, H. *Nippon Kinyū Shihon Ron* (The Theory of Japanese Financial Capital). Tokyo, 1957.

Komiya, R., ed. *Sengo Nippon no Keizai Seichō* (Postwar Economic Growth in Japan). Tokyo, 1963.

Kōsei Torihiki Kyōkai. "Tokushin-hō to Dokkin-hō no Shōrai" (The Special Industry Promotion Bill and the Future of the Anti-Monopoly Act), *Kōsei Torihiki* (May 1963).

Maruyama, M. "Shōkenhoji Seigen no Kaisei" (The Amendment of Limitation on Stockholding), *Kōsei Torihiki* (November 1949).

Matsukuma, H., ed. *Sengo Nippon no Zeisei* (The Tax Systems of Postwar Japan). Tōyōkeizai Shimpo-sha, 1959.

Ministry of International Trade and Industry. *Nippon Sangyō no Genjyō* (The Reality of Japanese Industries). Tokyo, 1958.

———. *Sangyō Kōzō Chōsakai, Sangyō-Taisei-Bukai Hōkokusho* (Commission on Industrial Structure, Report of Industry Structure Committee) ("The Arisawa Commission Report"). Tokyo, September 1963.

———. *Shuyō Sangyō no Setsubi Tōshi Keikaku* (The Plans for Capacity Investment in Major Industries). Tokyo, 1961.

———. *Kogyō Tōkeihyō Sangyōhen* (Industrial Statistics, Manufacturing Volume). Tokyo, annual issue.

———. *Sangyō Gōrika Hakusho* (Industry Rationalization White Paper). Tokyo, 1957.

———. *Tsusan Tōkei Geppō* (Monthly Statistics of International Trade and Industry). Tokyo, monthly issue.

Ministry of Labor. *Chiikibetsu Sangyōbetsu Koyō Keikaku Shian* (A Plan for Employment for Respective Regions and Industries). Tokyo, 1961.

Ministry of Labor. *Mai-getsu Chingin Tōkei Sōgō Hōkoku-shū* (Aggregate Report of Monthly Wages). Tokyo, 1963.
——. *Keizai Seichōka no Rōdō Seisansei* (Labor Productivity in the Growing Economy). Tokyo, 1961.
——. *Maigetsu Kinrō Tōkei Chōsa Sōgō Hōkokusho* (Monthly Labor Statistics Study, An Aggregate Report). Tokyo, 1961.
——. *Maigetsu Kinrō Yōran* (Monthly Labor Statistics Report). Tokyo, 1964.
Ministry of Welfare. *Kokumin Sēkatsu Jittai Chōsa* (Examinations of the Reality of the National Living Standard). Tokyo, 1963.
Minobe, R. *Sengo Keizai no Saihensei* (Reorganization of Postwar Economy). Tokyo, 1953.
Misonou, H. *Nippon no Dokusen* (Monopolies in Japan). Tokyo, 1960.
——. *Kigyō Gōdō* (Enterprise Mergers). Tokyo, 1964.
——. "Sengo Dokusen Taikei no Tokushitsu" (Characteristics of the Postwar Monopolistic Organization), *Keizai Hyoron* (Tokyo, 1962).
Miyashita, T. "Zaibatsu no Saihensei" (Reconstruction of Zaibatsu), *Nippon Shihon Shugi Taikei* (The System of Japanese Capitalism) (Tokyo, 1957).
Nagasu, Kazusi. *Nippon Keizai Nyūmon* (Introduction to the Japanese Economy). Tokyo, 1959.
Nomoto, T. "Saikin no Gappei no Dōkō" (The Recent Trend of Mergers), *Kōzei Torihiki* (May 1964).
Ouchi, H. *et al. Nippon Keizai Zusetsu* (The Japanese Economy in Graphs). Tokyo, 1963.
Prime Minister's Office. *Kakei-Chōsa Hōkoku* (The Family Budget Study Report). Tokyo, January 1953–December 1962.
Shimazaki, T. *Nippon no Ginkō* (Banks in Japan). Tokyo, 1961.
Suzuki, K. "Sengo Nippon no Dokusen Keikō ni Kanshite" (On the Monopolistic Tendencies of Postwar Japan), *Riron Keizaigaku*, Vol. XIII, No. 2 (February 1962).
Suzuki, M. *Nippon Dokusen Shihon no Kaibō* (Anatomy of the Japanese Monopolistic Capital). Tokyo, 1935.
Taniyama, H. *Zeikin ni Mesu o ireru* (Dissection of the Tax System). Tokyo, 1964.
Tax System Investigation Commission. *Showa 35-nen Zeisei Iinkai Hōkoku* (Tax Commission Report of 1960). Tokyo, 1960.
Tokyo Security Exchange. *Showa 34-nen Toshō Tōkei Geppō* (Tokyo Stock Exchange Annual Statistics, 1959). Tokyo, 1959.
——. *Tokyo Shōkenjo Tōkei Nempō* (Tokyo Security Exchange Annual Report). Tokyo, 1960.
Tōyōkeizai Shimpō-sha. *Keizai Tōkei Nenkan* (Year Book of Economic Statistics). Tokyo, 1962.
Tsuchihara, H. "Mitsubishi no Gappei ni tsuite" (Views on the Mitsubishi Merger), *Kōsei Torihiki* (February 1965).
Umemura, Mataji. *Sengo Nippon no Rōdō-Ryoku* (The Labor Force in Postwar Japan). Hitotsubashi University Economic Research Paper, No. 13, Tokyo, 1964.
Usami, S. *Nippon no Dokusen Shihon* (Monopolistic Capital of Japan). Tokyo, 1953.
Yamamura, K. "Nihon no Dokkin Seisaku ni tsuite" (A Few Observations on the Japanese Anti-Monopoly Act), *Kōsei Torihiki* (June 1962).
Yonemura, H. "Seijyōka Katei ni okeru Keiretsuyūshi no Kentō" (An Examination of Financial Connection in the Stage of Normalization), *Kōsei Torihiki* (May 1956).
Yoshida, H. "Shakai Fukushi no Genjō to Seisaku" (Conditions and the Policy of Social Welfare), *Ekonomisuto* (March 16, 1963).

Accessions tax, 130

Act Concerning Promotion of Export Marine Product Industry, 61

Act Concerning the Preservation of Liquor Tax and Liquor Business Association, 61

Adelman, M., 117n.

Aihara, S., 110n.

Ammonium Export Adjustment Temporary Measure Act, 61

Ammonium Sulphate Industry Rationalization Act, 61

Anti-Monopoly Act: enactment of, 9; main clauses of, 10–11; Amendment in 1949, 30–31; Amendment in 1953, 56–58; laws enacted to circumvent, 61; 1958 attempt to amend, 71–72; consumers' view of, 73; industry favors large scale amendment of, 81; Marxist view of, 175

Arisawa Commission: recommendation by, 82–83; composition of, 91; findings of, 183

Asano, H., 46

Bankruptcy: increasing rate of, 105; of smaller firms, 164

Barckley, R., 87n.

Belassa, B., 155n.

Bill to Promote International Competitive Ability of Specified Industries, 78–79, 82–83

Bisson, T. A., 22n., 115n.

Bronfenbrenner, M., 149, 149n.

Capital gains tax, 129–130

Capital levy, 9, 19

Cartels: for recession and rationalization, 56; legal conditions for, 57; authorized for industries, 60–61; for international trade, 61n.;

in cement industry, 63; M.I.T.I. view of, 73; 1958 Recommendation on, 75; functions in rationalization, 93–94; anti-concentrationists' view of, 177. See also *So-tan*

Chemical Industry Promotion Act, 70, 72

Coal Industry Rationalization Temporary Measure Act, 62

Cohen, J. B., 9n., 29n., 32n.

Communist party, 22–23

Consumer League: objects to Anti-Monopoly Act relaxation, 44; objects to *so-tan*, 73

Corporate income tax: 1947–1948 laws, 19; revaluation allowed, 42; special depreciation authorized by, 50; raised after Korean War, 51; special reductions authorized in, 135

Davidson, S., 145n.

Designated companies, 4

"Distribution revolution," 100, 168n.

Dodge, Joseph M., 29n.

Dodge Line, 29, 31, 32

Domar, Evsey, 85n.

Dore, R. P., 17n.

Doubling the National Income in Ten Years Plan, 76

"Economic Deconcentration": initial intent of, 1–2; recreaction of political groups on, 3; impact on Zaibatsu families, 11; policy questioned, 21–22; policy vacillates, 24–25; policy reviewed, 32–38

Economic Stabilization Committee, 14

Edwards, Corwin, 2–3, 111n.

Elimination of Excessive Concen-